THE OFFENSIVE INTERNET

The Offensive Internet

Speech, Privacy, and Reputation

Edited by
Saul Levmore and Martha C. Nussbaum

HARVARD UNIVERSITY PRESS
Cambridge, Massachusetts, and London, England   2010

Copyright © 2010 by the President and Fellows of Harvard College
All rights reserved
Printed in the United States of America

Library of Congress Cataloging-in-Publication Data

The offensive Internet : speech, privacy, and reputation / edited by Saul Levmore
and Martha C. Nussbaum.
     p. cm.
  Includes bibliographical references and index.
  ISBN 978-0-674-05089-1 (alk. paper)
  1. Internet—Law and legislation—United States. 2. Libel and slander—United States.
3. Privacy, Right of—United States. 4. Reputation (Law)—United States. 5. Privacy,
Right of—United States. I. Levmore, Saul X. II. Nussbaum, Martha Craven, 1947–
  KF390.5.C6O344 2010
  343.7309'944—dc22

2010022409

Contents

III   Speech

IV   Privacy

THE OFFENSIVE INTERNET

Introduction

SAUL LEVMORE AND MARTHA C. NUSSBAUM

In many ways the Internet has succeeded in remaking us as inhabitants of a small village. No one is a stranger either in the village or on the Internet; in both settings the savvy citizen knows how to process information. The Internet may be offensive to some, as the title of this book warns, but it benefits far more than it offends the well-informed. If we know something of American history, and now wish to know whether Betsy Ross really made that first flag, the Internet allows us to work our way through noisy websites to the few that seem ably written and reliable. Similarly, we can, as never before, find a hotel on some vacation island that serves our preferences, even as many competitor hotels exaggerate their own qualities, and even as amateur reviewers carry on about the manner in which they were wronged at the reception desk. But no medium, and certainly not one with such low entry barriers, can protect the ignorant except perhaps with extraordinary regulation and consumer protection. If we wish to learn how to pronounce names in Korean, we can visit what seems like a terrific website, but must hope that the site does not mislead, for most of us cannot there distinguish fidelity from fraud. In the case of pronunciation, as opposed to hotel quality, it is unlikely that someone profits by misleading those who search for information, so we tend to trust the website. In all these things, the Internet is a valuable medium for a far-flung world. In the days when one's reach could extend no farther than one's own village, gossip and experience protected, or at least covered, the terrain. Social norms and some legal rules worked to create an atmosphere, or market of sorts, in which one could operate reasonably well. In a more cosmopolitan world, the Internet helps re-create the world of the village, where one learned to trust here and to avoid there. If one needed shoes to be repaired, there was good information about the village shoemakers; if one needs a

1

camera today, there is excellent information on the Internet. In both places, self-promotion and misleading information can be overcome. The key tool in the village was personal experience, or what we might now call repeat play, while on the Internet it is the fact of numerous, communicative players.

In the absence of personal experience, it is especially difficult to become well-informed about people. In the village and on the Internet one can ask about a shoemaker or a camera, and in both cases a great deal of information will be forthcoming from people who have experienced those services or that item. But information about the shoemaker's character is somewhat more difficult to obtain because reputations are often deservedly—or undeservedly—made or broken by one or two important events. If one defrauds another or heroically rescues someone from a fire, life in the village will be far worse or much better, as this episode comes to be known. If honor is claimed where it is undeserved, or honesty is misreported as fraud by a competitor, our hero must hope that the truth will win out because of repeat or multiple play. If one does evil, one must try to recover by doing good, and eventually reputations can be redeemed. But the tendency of some humans to harass others, and even to inflict emotional harm, casts some doubt on the reliability of reputations. If one tries to escape the past by moving to another village, it is likely that the newcomer will be mistrusted. In the village, every longtime resident knows whom to ask about a third party, but in the cosmopolitan world it is rare to find but one degree of separation between an employer and an applicant, or a landlord and prospective tenant. "Googling" a target is therefore the best one can do, though that is more like asking a randomly chosen person for a reference. In contrast, a village elder or other known source likely has personal knowledge of the target and also some reputation of his or her own.

Googling, like other Internet searching strategies, is fraught with peril. In the first place, it is cheap to slur someone on the Internet, for it can be done with a few keystrokes, with complete anonymity, and—as we will see repeatedly in this book—with no fear that the Internet forum provider on whose website the slur is found will somehow be held responsible for incorrect, mean-spirited, or defamatory statements. And yet someone who searches a name and finds a slur might rationally decline to hire or trust that named person because there is no reason to take a risk when there are so many other, untainted applicants or contacts. In the village, one might make further inquiries, and one might discover that the source of the slur is the problem. On the Internet it is very difficult to do so. Inasmuch as positive information on the Internet is often a product of self-presentation, such positive information is unlikely to offset even a single negative revelation or fabrication in the mind of the inquirer. Moreover, as Cass Sunstein explores in the essay "Believing False Rumors," certain kinds of false rumors spread especially well on the Internet because of social cascades and group polarization.

The speed with which reputations can be made and altered is just one way in which the Internet has changed everything. It is surely the case that most of the changes are for the better but, sadly, the Internet is a curse when one is the subject of negative information, whether self-presented, and then indelible, or communicated by others. And yet the Internet has changed nothing, which is to say it has returned us to the world of the village. In both settings, we wonder what can be done about irrepressible information that is not to our liking. We are drawn to horror stories of bullying, harassment, and sordid pasts, real or not. It is this question that dominates the present volume. The Internet can be offensive to many of its users and an absolute nightmare for those who cannot escape harassment on it.

One reaction to false information is to regulate the providers of information. In the village, an unfavorable credit report disciplined borrowers, but an unfair credit report presented a serious flaw in the social and economic fabric. It could be overcome by experience, as others vouched for the unfairly maligned debtor. Eventually, perhaps because information traveled far beyond the village, fair credit reporting became a part of law, and law sought to protect individuals from false disclosures and even from mere errors in their records. This is the analogy that Frank Pasquale suggests to us in his essay "Reputation Regulation: Disclosure and the Challenge of Clandestinely Commensurating Computing." Pasquale encourages us to develop a "Fair Reputation Reporting Act." He takes aim at employers, and others who use information: asking them to explain the nature and source of information they use is like asking banks to disclose their lending decisions. In the world of credit it has been important to provide consumers with access to the intermediaries who collect information and sell it to lenders. It is possible that the analogy demands that we think of forcing Internet forum providers to disclose their sources and to give those who have unfavorable reputations the chance to correct misinformation. If so, we would have a very different cyberspace, because anonymity is at present a common feature in that domain.

Providers of false information on the Internet can also be regulated with rules drawn from tort law, much as defamation and other law came to the village. Anupam Chander, in "Youthful Indiscretion in an Internet Age," would regulate the Internet, like the village, with a narrowly drawn tort meant to deter the public disclosure of information plainly meant to be private. Danielle Citron's "Civil Rights in Our Information Age" shares Chander's sense that hurtful (and "low-value") speech on the Internet disproportionately affects women, and she advances the idea of cyberspace civil rights law. Martha Nussbaum's essay "Objectification and Internet Misogyny" also focuses on suits brought by injured victims. Her inquiry into the source of the attacks on victims leads to a call for the success of suits by women who are assaulted, but it suggests that the problems reflected in these Internet episodes will not truly be solved without large-scale social change. All three of these authors presumably favor the presence of similar legal tools in the village, where assaults may be met with social sanctions but where they can, in modern times, be treated with legal remedies as well.

Regulation can take the form of advance instructions, or structural change, rather than the availability of punitive or compensatory remedies following a harm. One possibility is to rely on private institutions more than law itself. Just as employers can create safe work environments, whether encouraged to do so by law or not, other institutions can play a role in controlling harassment and other ills. Karen Bradshaw and Souvik Saha, in "Academic Administrators and the Challenge of Social Networking Websites," concentrate on what schools might do to influence behavior on social-networking sites. Educational and other institutions are often able to exert extraordinary and extralegal influence over their constituents, though it must be said that the "offensive Internet" reaches well beyond where schools, churches, and employers may choose to go.

More of our authors look not to educators but to Internet forum providers as the means of combating the offensive Internet. They may well be the best problem solvers, or least cost avoiders, because their reach is coextensive with the Internet. Brian Leiter, in "Cleaning Cyber-Cesspools: Google and Free Speech," makes progress with the observation that search engines, like that managed by Google, influence the construction of cyberspace cesspools by the means with which they array sites in response to a search request. Daniel Solove's essay "Speech, Privacy, and Reputation on the Internet" is more anxious about invasions of privacy than the facts of harassment, but he too is inclined to lessen the problem not with a tort but with instructions to forum providers. He recommends, as do other authors in this volume, a notice-and-takedown policy, of the kind found in copyright law. A provider would be informed that something offensive was in the air, and the provider could or should then remove the offensive communication—though there would be sanctions against those who abused the notice-and-takedown policy. Saul Levmore takes a similar tack in "The Internet's Anonymity Problem," but is more inclined to think the problem can be solved by eliminating much of the anonymity that reigns on the Internet. With the exception of Solove, we might say that these authors seek to reform the Internet so that it is yet more like the village. Old solutions are sometimes appropriate for new problems.

Old solutions will probably not do if the Internet's problem is truly new and different. Ruben Rodrigues's "Privacy on Social Networks: Norms, Markets, and Natural Monopoly" argues that social-networking sites have such substantial natural monopolies—because users want to be where everyone else is also located—that the normal remedy of exit, from where one finds one's privacy invaded for instance, is too costly. If this is so, it is important to emphasize that much of the offense on the Internet takes place on blogs or on other sites that do not have this natural monopoly feature. The larger question is, of course, whether understanding the novelty of the Internet is the key to combating its offenses.

Speech

Thus far, we have thought about the offensive Internet from the perspective of defending one's reputation, or discouraging harassing attacks on it. The promise of our title, however, is that the importance and value of speech should also be taken into account. The balance between valuable speech and offensive speech is hardly a novel one, peculiar to the Internet. Our authors refer to speech that harasses, bullies, threatens, defames, invades privacy, and inflicts reputational damage as well as emotional distress. But non-Internet speech also does these things. When we consider how to prevent such damages, or to remedy them once they have occurred, we immediately have to consider the possibility that our proposals will place unjustifiable limits on free speech. But what is freedom of speech? Why is it valuable? And what types of harm might be sufficient to justify its regulation? These are general human questions but if our purpose is to think about directions for legal regulation, we ought to think in the context of the First Amendment, which constrains limitations on speech.

According to a popular misconception, freedom of speech is an absolute, and the First Amendment protects all speech from any type of government regulation. We often hear any proposal to limit or regulate speech described, without further argument, as censorship or as "a violation of the First Amendment." But the absolutist view of the First Amendment is implausible, and it has never prevailed. Regulation of speech is uncontroversially constitutional with respect to threats, bribery, defamatory statements, fighting words, fraud, copyright, plagiarism, and more. What courts have said is that the First Amendment, properly understood, does not protect these forms of speech. Moreover, few people would defend the position that the "marketplace of ideas" should be trusted to sort out the problems posed by fraud, bribery, and their cousins.

One question, then, is whether offensive speech on the Internet deserves First Amendment protection. The answer is far from obvious, and cannot be arrived at by treating the First Amendment as self-explanatory. It calls for patient work with both legal doctrine and more general theories of speech. A good starting place is Geoffrey Stone's essay "Privacy, the First Amendment, and the Internet," which presents a broader normative account of First Amendment protections than do our other essays. But before getting to details, it is useful to step back and ask whether disparate approaches—as collected in this volume—can connect on the question of Internet offense. Why might abstract philosophical analysis as well as law-and-economics approaches illuminate difficult legal issues about speech?

The First Amendment is concise and abstract: "Congress shall make no law abridging the freedom of speech." But what is "abridging," and what sort of "freedom" is protected for what sorts of "speech"? The difficulty and indeterminacy of these questions can be appreciated from the evident fact that our understanding of what the First Amendment protects has changed over the years. For much of our history, for example, it was generally agreed that the First Amendment did not protect the political speech of dissidents during wartime. Today that sort of speech would seem to most interpreters (and to the public) to lie right at the heart of the First Amendment's protections. When judges or legal thinkers grapple with the difficult issues posed by the constitutional text, it is natural for them to look for help in other theoretical understandings of free speech that offer more in the way of analysis and rationale.

If the interpreter is an "originalist," who believes that the Constitution should best be interpreted in keeping with the public meaning of its text at the time of the Founding, he or she might look at philosophical theories to determine what the public culture of that time thought about speech. Temporally, such an inquiry might not be strictly limited to the time of the Founding, because the First Amendment was not incorporated—that is, applied to those other (nonfederal) acts—until after the Civil War. For the meaning of the Bill of Rights at the time of incorporation, we might therefore look at mid-nineteenth–century ideas. Later philosophical theories might also be considered, insofar as they render explicit ideas that were already part of the public culture at an earlier time. Thomas Scanlon's theory of free speech—based, as it is, on Kantian ideas of autonomy and respect that were highly influential by the late eighteenth century—and Alexander Meiklejohn's theory, which conceives of protected speech as that which contributes to democratic deliberation—and which almost certainly has strong historical antecedents—would probably both pass this test.

The non-originalist is even more interested in philosophical theories. An interpreter of a disputed text might simply try to arrive at a deeper understanding of goals and purposes that animate the text. But philosophical theory is unlikely to be conclusive. These theories are ahistorical and transnational, while drafters and judges inhabit a particular legal tradition and must consider relevant precedents and conventions. They cannot simply ask what is best, but rather ask what is best justified in light of the available text, precedents, and history. Theories are sometimes most useful where these materials leave room for fine distinctions.

One difficult area of our First Amendment doctrine concerns the category of "low-value speech." As Geoffrey Stone points out, our tradition has recognized that some speech is of "high value" and deserves very strong protection. That sort of speech can be regulated only in very narrow circumstances, where it is "likely to produce a clear and present danger of a serious substantive evil." Terminiello v. Chicago, 337 U.S. 1, 3 (1949). But the Supreme Court regards other forms of speech as of "low value," less deserving of protection. If the low-value speech inflicts harm, regulation is often permitted. Unfortunately, the line between these categories has not been well drawn. Theories of the First Amendment here come into play. John Deigh, Brian Leiter, and Danielle Citron agree on the theories of free speech that are particularly useful for constitutional interpreters to ponder, along with the materials already noted. Each of these theories focuses on a different core value: truth, autonomy, and democratic deliberation. A short introduction to these theories is useful for readers embarking on this volume.

For John Stuart Mill, the main point of free speech protections is to help society arrive at the truth. When speech is restricted, people may fail to discover the errors embedded in their current ways of thinking. Even if their opinions are true, they may be incomplete, and suppressed material may help citizens reach a more comprehensive understanding. And even if the suppressed opinions are false, they may help people by sharpening their understanding of the true views and preventing lazy or complacent endorsement. On Mill's view of speech, speech that is not part of an argument aimed at truth—purely emotive speech, bullying speech, and speech that does not make truth-claims at all—deserves no particular protection.

The second prominent theory of speech focuses on autonomy; we owe people access to a wide range of opinions because we respect them as free beings who are entitled to make their own choices. Restriction of speech stifles awareness of options and in this way threatens autonomy. Within this view, speech that itself diminishes autonomy by insulting, denigrating, or intimidating others is ripe for regulation rather than protection.

Finally, there is again Alexander Meiklejohn's influential account of the First Amendment, which holds that the key purpose underlying a system of free speech is the preservation of the sort of open debate that is a necessary part of democracy. Meiklejohn's view, which has had great influence on legal doctrine, is that political speech, whether in public settings or simply on matters of political interest, is at the core of the First Amendment. Other forms of speech—including commercial speech and perhaps artistic expression—are less important for the First Amendment, and can be more readily regulated.

These three theories are binary in that they identify a category of high-value speech worthy of serious protection, and thus also identify, if only by elimination, all other speech as low value. In reality, things are not so convenient, and theories of free speech sometimes recognize additional categories. For example, artistic speech will often be regarded as more important than threatening speech or bribery, but not nearly as important as recognizable political speech. Most of the authors in this volume are content to proceed with the understanding that offensive speech on the Internet is, for the most part, not of the high-value sort. Deigh and Leiter demonstrate that none of the major philosophical theories gives us reason to think that repeated slurs, or cyber bullying, are high-value speech. And, as a matter of law, harmful non-newsworthy speech about private figures (for most of the cyber bullying is of classmates and neighbors rather than celebrities) has not been held to deserve First Amendment protection. There is, to be sure, room to argue about what is newsworthy, or relevant to political discourse, and Geoffrey Stone, for one, fears that we risk endangering free speech if we understand low-value speech to include most of the communications discussed in this volume, simply because it invades privacy or inflicts emotional distress. Under that last view, the low-value category should be restricted to threats, bribery, and only a very few other, narrowly constructed subcategories. Citron and Solove disagree. Citron points out that the Court has upheld enhanced penalties for crimes expressing hatred, denying that the expressive aspect of that activity is protected by the First Amendment, so long as the law is framed broadly and does not involve discrimination on the basis of the ideas expressed. Both point out that bullying, harassment, and hate speech deter or suppress valuable speech, so the net result of intelligent government regulation may well be *more* valuable speech. This is certainly the majority position of our authors. All of our authors think that speech on the Internet may be regulated at least as much as speech in other venues and media, and many take particular aim at one section of the Communications Decency Act, which has been interpreted to immunize the operators of websites and blogs against liability for comments posted by others. A withdrawal of that immunity could, without constitutional difficulty, restore the symmetry between website operators and publishers of newspapers, who can of course be sued for damages if they publish defamatory material.

Privacy

If a focus on reputation and then on the First Amendment reminds us that the Internet presents old problems in new clothing, then a spotlight on privacy clarifies the novelty of the Internet. A bit of information once thought confidential may now blanket the globe with the help of the Internet; a false and defamatory accusation about a person may become a constituent part of that person's Internet identity, where it affects relationships and employment opportunities for all time. A romantic breakup can lead to retaliation on the Internet, where details of a sexual relationship can injure one of the party's reputations and mental equanimity. How should law respond to these new, or at least more intense, threats to privacy, and are these responses consistent with free speech requirements?

Privacy can refer to a number of distinct ideas, or interests. There is the value of *seclusion*, which is the right to be beyond the gaze of others. There is *intimacy*, in which one chooses with whom to share certain information and experiences. There is also the interest in *secrecy*, which is to information as seclusion is to the physical person. And then there is *autonomy*, which is the set of private choices each person makes. These ideas are not unconnected. Thus, sexual relationships—a constant topic of offensive communications on the Internet—are often kept from prying eyes in ways that reflect all four of these interests. In the realm of sex, autonomy is probably the most controversial, but we can at least surmise that those who insist on a right of autonomy in this sphere often do so because they think that sexual choices are particularly intimate and self-defining.

The four privacy interests, or meanings, can also diverge. A married couple might value intimacy and seclusion, but not resist the inference that they are engaging in sexual activity with one another. The lack of secrecy does not mean they welcome others into their bedrooms or intimate conversations. And then a secret and secluded relationship may have no intimacy, as might be the case between a client and a commercial sex worker. There is even more divergence when we add to seclusion the special zone that we call home, though this is not a well-articulated idea in law. Even in the home the government is likely to have every right to police such things as domestic violence and child abuse. In any event, if the privacy interest, and perhaps the special treatment of the home, is understood to involve an element of autonomy, then there may be room for its expansion to other zones, including the Internet.

All four of these notions of privacy make appearances in these essays, though it is not always clear which privacy interest an author holds most dear. The confusion is found in constitutional law itself, and may simply derive from the fact that we use the word "privacy" to mean so many things. When we say that medical information and financial records are private, we refer to autonomy or a version of secrecy, because the information is obviously known to some strangers, is maintained in a non-secluded place, and is not normally an important ingredient of intimacy. Solove argues that we have overindulged the secrecy aspect of privacy, and have therefore been deficient in protecting information that people have communicated to a small circle of intimates. He observes a generational shift, such that a new generation that has not known seclusion is more concerned with the ability to control the access others have to information about them. A more nuanced understanding of privacy could generate doctrines that would protect information even if it has been previously divulged. Pasquale also looks to new constructions in order to restore to individuals the control that the Internet has weakened. Stone draws a very different conclusion about the Internet era. For him, the era of informational privacy is over, and we will just have to learn to live with it. "Once information is out of the bottle, once we share it with others, once others know it, we can no longer hope to put it back. If that era ever existed, it is now the past."

It is clear that new thinking is required if privacy is to flourish in the Information Age, and especially so where the intimacy and secrecy interests are concerned. The problem is not simply one of dissemination and selective control, but also one of choosing among competing interests. In "Collective Privacy," Lior Strahilevitz focuses attention on the fact that privacy disputes often emerge not when something entirely secret is made public, but rather when information shared carefully is then revealed more broadly by the first recipient. If the revelation concerns multiple individuals, then there will often be privacy collective action problems, because the individuals may have disparate views of the value of confidentiality or revelation. Strahilevitz suggests that law identify the party best able to resolve the privacy issue, and require that person's consent.

Privacy, speech, and reputation can be thought of as separate topics, but they come together rather often where the offensive Internet is concerned. Most of these essays explore connections among all three of these values, or subjects. If the Internet is truly different from the village, it is not just because one is global and the other local. In the village, privacy and reputation were important matters, and threats to these interests were often dealt with in kind or, perhaps, through exit. In the Internet era, the means we have of controlling threats to privacy and reputation all involve constraints on speech, so that there are three balls in the air rather than two. With so many ideas in play, and human relationships at stake, it is no wonder that these essays are both informative and provocative.

PART I

The Internet and Its Problems

CHAPTER 1

Speech, Privacy, and Reputation on the Internet

DANIEL J. SOLOVE

He has a name, but most people just know him as "the Star Wars Kid." In fact, he is known around the world by tens of millions of people. Unfortunately, his notoriety stems from one of the most embarrassing moments in his life.

In 2002, as a 15-year-old, the Star Wars Kid videotaped himself waving around a golf-ball retriever while pretending it was a light saber. Without the help of the professional choreographers working on the *Star Wars* movies, he stumbled around awkwardly in the video. The video was found by some of the boy's tormentors, who uploaded it to an Internet video site. It went viral with a multitude of fans. All across the blogosphere, people started mocking the boy, making fun of him for being pudgy, awkward, and nerdy.

Several remixed videos of the Star Wars Kid started popping up, adorned with special effects. People edited the video to make the golf-ball retriever glow like a light saber. They added *Star Wars* music to the video. Others mashed it up with other movies. Dozens of embellished versions were created. The Star Wars Kid appeared in a video game and on the television shows *Family Guy* and *South Park*. It is one thing to be teased by classmates in school, but imagine being ridiculed by masses the world over. The teenager dropped out of school and had to seek counseling. What happened to the Star Wars Kid can happen to anyone, and it can happen in an instant. Today, collecting personal information has become second nature. More and more people have cell phone cameras, digital audio recorders, web cameras, and other recording technologies that readily capture details about their lives. For the first time in history nearly anybody can disseminate information around the world. People do not need to be famous enough to be interviewed by the mainstream media. With the Internet, anybody can reach a global audience.

For centuries—perhaps since the dawn of human society—people have spread rumors, gossiped about each other, and engaged in shaming for social transgressions. These social practices are now moving over to the Internet, where they are taking on new dimensions. Gossip used to travel in local circles. It rarely spread widely and would be forgotten over time. On the Internet, however, gossip is no longer ephemeral. As with gossip, the Internet is having similar effects on the practice of shaming. Once localized and fleeting, shaming online creates a permanent record of people's past transgressions—a digital scarlet letter.

Although a common argument is that more information will be useful in judging each other, there are many reasons why less information can be preferable. Personal information taken out of context often does not foster a more accurate impression of other people. In fact, it can result in hasty and hypocritical judgments, as well as severe misunderstandings. There is a grave danger that people will enslave themselves and each other by making their past mistakes permanently and readily available for the rest of their lives. The long-standing value of giving people a second chance, of allowing people to reinvent themselves, might soon become a relic of a bygone era. This has profound effects on people's freedom to experiment, to grow, and to change.

We must protect privacy to ensure that the freedom of the Internet does not make us less free. But to do so, we must rethink our notions of privacy and recalibrate the way privacy is balanced against freedom of speech.

The Rise of Generation Google

Before the Internet, gossip would spread by word of mouth and remain within the boundaries of a social circle. Private details would be confined to a diary and kept locked in a desk drawer. Social networking spawned by the Internet allows communities worldwide to revert to the close-knit culture of preindustrial society, in which nearly every member of a tribe or a farming hamlet knew everything about the neighbors. Except that now the "villagers" span the globe.

In the village of yesteryear, people had to live under the ever-present judgmental eye of their fellow villagers. The small village mythos of bygone days—a sunny happy place, where everybody got along—is an idealized image. A brief dip into history and literature (such as Nathaniel Hawthorne's *The Scarlet Letter*) shows a world rife with oppressive norms, with nosy neighbors and communities ready to condemn, often unfairly. One example of the problematic nature of community nosiness was the common double standard imposed on women who committed extramarital sex—women were watched much more carefully and condemned much more readily than men. While social control can be good, not all is, and sometimes it can be downright unfair, stifling, misguided, and cruel.

One of the benefits of the modern world was that people could escape from the oppressiveness of the small village fishbowl. But no longer. We now live in a "global village," to use Marshall McLuhan's term. The return of the village fishbowl comes with a pernicious twist. In the small village, people knew each other well, and disreputable information would be judged within the context of a person's entire life. Now, people are judged out of context based on information fragments found online. The amount of these fragments is vastly increasing and the kind of information involved is becoming more personal and potentially discreditable.

College students have begun to share salacious details about their schoolmates. Until it was shut down in 2009, a website called JuicyCampus served as an electronic bulletin board where students nationwide posted anonymously and without verification a sordid array of tidbits about sex, drugs, and drunkenness. Another site, Don't Date Him Girl, invites women to post complaints about the men they have dated, along with real names and actual photographs. On a site called AutoAdmit, users spread gossip, lies, and invective about others, including two female students at Yale Law School. As Danielle Citron observes: "Thirty-nine posters targeted named students on the site's message board. The posters, writing under pseudonyms, generated hundreds of threatening, sexually-explicit, and allegedly defamatory comments about the victims."[1]

The number of young people using social-networking websites such as Facebook and MySpace is staggering. At most college campuses, more than 90 percent of students maintain their own sites. I call the people growing up today "Generation Google." For them, many fragments of personal information will reside on the Internet forever, accessible to this and future generations through a simple Google search.

The new openness on the Internet is both good and bad. People can now spread their ideas everywhere without reliance on publishers, broadcasters, or other traditional gatekeepers. This enhances free speech and individual expression and communication. But these changes also create profound threats to privacy and reputations. The *New York Times* is not likely to care about the latest gossip at Dubuque Senior High School or Oregon State University. Bloggers and others communicating online may care a great deal. For them, stories and rumors about friends, enemies, family members, bosses, coworkers, and others are all prime fodder for Internet postings.

Broad-based exposure of personal information diminishes the ability to protect reputation by shaping the image that is presented to others. Reputation plays an important role in society, and preserving private details of one's life is essential to it. We look to people's reputations to decide whether to make friends, go on a date, hire a new employee, or undertake a prospective business deal.

Some would argue that the decline of privacy might allow people to be less inhibited and more honest. But when everybody's transgressions are exposed, people may not judge one another less harshly. Having your personal information may fail to improve my judgment of you. It may, in fact, increase the likelihood that I will hastily condemn you. Moreover, the loss of privacy might inhibit freedom. Elevated visibility that comes with living in a transparent online world means you may never overcome past mistakes.

People want to have the option of "starting over," of reinventing themselves throughout their lives. As American philosopher John Dewey once said, a person is not "something complete, perfect, [or] finished," but is "something moving, changing, discrete, and above all initiating instead of final."[2] In the past, episodes of youthful experimentation and foolishness were eventually forgotten, giving us an opportunity to start anew, to change, and to grow. But with so much information online, it is harder to make these moments forgettable. People must now live with the digital baggage of their pasts.

This openness means that the opportunities for members of Generation Google might be limited because of something they did years ago as wild teenagers. Their intimate secrets may be revealed by other people they know. Or they might become the unwitting victim of a false rumor. Many people will face significant consequences from having their personal information online.

Employers and others increasingly look at applicants' social-networking website profile pages when making their hiring decisions. College admissions officers also use social-networking sites like Facebook and MySpace to make decisions on applicants. According to a survey of 500 colleges, 10 percent of admissions personnel stated that they examine social-networking websites when making decisions about applicants, and 38 percent found that the online information had a negative impact.[3] In some cases, the information they gleaned led them to turn down applicants.[4]

Most colleges lack policies with regard to when and how college admissions officers can use social-networking website profiles in making admissions decisions.[5] Moreover, many companies and college and graduate school admissions officers lack a policy or guidelines about the appropriate and inappropriate use of the information they find online about a candidate. Policies are sorely needed, as there are many issues that need to be thought about: Should information found online about an applicant be used? When? How heavily should it be relied upon? What kinds of things should negatively impact an applicant? Information about sex life? Drug use? Drinking? Bad behavior? What steps should be taken to make sure that the information is accurate? Should a distinction be made between information that people post about themselves and information that others have posted about them, perhaps invading their privacy without their consent? What steps should be taken to make sure that the information used in fact relates to the applicant and not to somebody else with the same name? Should people be notified that information online was used against them and given an opportunity to be heard to explain it?

In most contexts involving hiring or other important decisions affecting people's lives, not enough thought has been devoted to the issue of when and how that online data should be used in the decision-making process. Nor are parents and educators devoting enough attention to the issue. Therefore, it is not just Generation Google that is being careless about online gossip and rumors. Those who are using the data to make decisions about people also need to ponder the consequences of their own behavior.

Rethinking Privacy

There are a surprising number of torts, statutes, and other legal protections of privacy. The problem is that they are currently so weak they cannot serve as an adequate response to the burgeoning problems caused by the spread of online gossip. One of the primary problems with the law is that it is bogged down by antiquated conceptions of privacy.

Can we prevent a future in which so much information about people's private lives circulates beyond their control? Some technologists and legal scholars flatly say no. Privacy, they maintain, is just not compatible with a world in which information flows so freely. As Scott McNealy of Sun

Microsystems once famously declared: "You already have zero privacy. Get over it."[6] Countless books and articles have heralded the "end," "death" and "destruction" of privacy.[7]

Those proclamations are wrongheaded at best. It is still possible to protect privacy, but doing so requires that we rethink outdated understandings of the concept. A long-standing and antiquated conception of privacy is that it involves secrecy and is lost once information is disclosed. I call this the "secrecy paradigm." If any information is exposed to others, many courts, policy makers, and commentators conclude that it is not private since it is no longer hidden or concealed.

The secrecy paradigm leads to two very significant limits on privacy protection that cripple privacy law. First, the secrecy paradigm holds that when a person appears in a public place, she no longer has a reasonable expectation of privacy. The problem with this view is that so much of our lives occur in public places, and modern technology enables information to be captured so readily in cell phone cameras, video, and audio recording devices, and other surveillance technologies. We frequently have conversations in restaurants where we expect to be partially overheard by people near us, but we do not expect our entire conversations to be recorded and disclosed to the world. Likewise, we expect others in the drugstore to see what we are purchasing, but we expect that they do not know who we are or care about what we are buying. For all purposes, we are anonymous. If this anonymity disappears, we lose a lot of freedom that we currently enjoy in our daily lives.

Second, the secrecy paradigm views information exposed to others as no longer secret, and hence, no longer private. However, in today's Information Age, it is nearly impossible to expect much information to be completely secret. So many companies and other individuals hold pieces of information about our lives. But that should not mean that information is not private. Although we share secrets with others, the law should recognize that we have expectations of trust and confidentiality. In particular Professor Neil Richards and I propose expanding the breach of confidentiality tort, which provides a remedy when a duty of confidentiality is breached.[8] In the United States, the tort applies to professional relationships, such as doctor-patient and attorney-client. But in England, it applies to a broader array of relationships, such as those among family and friends. Expanding the American version of the tort could provide considerable protection against the spread of gossip online.

If the law abandoned the secrecy paradigm and recognized greater protections of privacy in public as well as confidentiality, this would go a long way in helping to protect against spurious rumors and gossip spreading online.

As the generation growing up today understands, privacy is not all-or-nothing as the secrecy paradigm holds. Members of this generation know that personal information is routinely shared with countless others, and that they leave a trail of data wherever they go. The more subtle understanding of privacy embraced by Generation Google recognizes that a person should retain some control over personal information that becomes publicly available. This generation wants a say in how private details of their lives are disseminated.

The issue of control over personal information came to the fore in 2006, when Facebook launched a feature called News Feeds, which sent a notice to people's friends registered with the service when their profile was changed or updated. To the surprise of those who run Facebook, many of its users reacted with outrage. Nearly 700,000 of them complained. At first blush, the outcry over News Feeds seems baffling. Many of the users who protested had profiles completely accessible to the public. So why did they think it was a privacy violation to alert their friends to changes in their profiles?

Instead of viewing privacy as secrets hidden away in a dark closet, they considered the issue a matter of accessibility. They figured most people would not scrutinize their profiles carefully enough to notice minor changes and updates. They could make changes inconspicuously. But Facebook's News Feeds made information more noticeable. The privacy objection was not about secrecy, but about accessibility.

In 2007 Facebook encountered another privacy outcry when it launched an advertising system with two parts, called Social Ads and Beacon. With Social Ads, whenever users wrote something positive about a product or a movie, Facebook would use their names, images, and words in advertisements sent to friends in the hope that an endorsement would induce other users to purchase a product more than a generic advertisement. With Beacon, Facebook made data-sharing deals with a variety of other commercial websites. If a Facebook user bought a movie ticket on Fandango or an item on another site, that information would pop up in the user's public profile.

Facebook rolled out these programs without adequately informing its users. People unwittingly found themselves shilling products on their friends' websites. And some people were shocked to see their private purchases on other websites suddenly displayed to the public as part of their profiles that appeared on the Facebook site.

The outcry and an ensuing online petition called for Facebook to reform its practices—a document that quickly attracted tens of thousands of signatures and ultimately led to several changes. As witnessed in these instances, privacy does not always involve sharing of secrets. Facebook users did not want their identities used to endorse products with Social Ads. It is one thing to write about how much one enjoys a movie or album; it is another to be used on a billboard to pitch products to others.

Protecting privacy extends beyond the mere keeping of secrets. It also involves providing greater rights to control how information is disseminated and used. There are some who contend that it is too late to protect privacy because so much information is already out there. David Brin argues that the *"djinn* cannot be crammed back into its bottle" and that "[l]ight *is* going to shine into every corner of our lives."[9] But even if information is already exposed in some contexts, this does not mean that protecting privacy with respect to that information is futile.

In some areas, U.S. law has a well-developed system of controlling information. Copyright recognizes strong rights for public information, protecting a wide range of works, from movies to software. Procuring copyright protection does not require locking a work of intellect behind closed doors. You can read a copyrighted magazine, make a duplicate for your own use, and lend it to others. But you cannot do whatever you want: for instance, photocopying it from cover to cover or selling bootleg copies in the street. Copyright law tries to achieve a balance between freedom and control, even though it still must wrestle with the ongoing controversies in a digital age.

The appropriation tort, one of the U.S. privacy torts, bears some similarities to copyright law. The tort prevents the use of someone else's name or likeness for financial benefit. Unfortunately, the law has developed in a way that is often ineffective against the type of privacy threats now cropping up. Copyright primarily functions as a form of property right, protecting works of self-expression, such as a song or painting.

To cope with increased threats to privacy, the scope of the appropriation tort should be expanded. The broadening might embody the original early twentieth-century interpretation of this principle of common law, which conceived of privacy as more than a means to protect property: "The right to withdraw from the public gaze at such times as a person may see fit . . . is embraced within the right of personal liberty," declared the Georgia Supreme

Court in 1905.[10] Today, however, the tort does not apply when a person's name or image appears in news, art, literature, or on social-networking sites. At the same time the appropriation tort protects against using someone's name or picture without consent to advertise products, it allows these representations to be used in a news story. This limitation is significant, since it means the tort would rarely apply to Internet-related postings.

Any expansion of the appropriation tort must be balanced against the competing need to allow legitimate news gathering and dissemination of public information. The tort should probably apply only when photographs and other personal information are used in ways that are not of public concern—a criterion that will inevitably be subject to ongoing judicial deliberation.

Appropriation is not the only common-law privacy tort that needs an overhaul to become more relevant in an era of networked digital communications. We already have many legal tools to protect privacy, but they are currently crippled by conceptions of privacy that prevent them from working effectively. A broader development of the law should take into account problematic uses of personal information illustrated by the Star Wars Kid or Facebook's Beacon service.

Ideally, most of these disputes should be resolved without recourse to the courts, but the broad reach of electronic networking will probably necessitate changes in common law. The threats to privacy are formidable, and people are starting to realize how strongly they regard privacy as a basic right. Toward this goal, society must develop a new and more nuanced conception of public and private life—one that acknowledges that more personal information is going to be available yet protects some choice over how that information is shared and distributed.

Reforming the CDA §230

In addition to failing to adequately protect privacy, the law is hampered because it overprotects free speech. In particular, the Communications Decency Act (CDA) §230 promotes a culture of irresponsibility when it comes to speech online. The CDA §230 states: "No provider or user of an interactive computer service shall be treated as the publisher or speaker of any information provided by another information content provider."[11] Most courts have interpreted §230 to immunize the operators of websites or blogs against liability for comments posted by others.[12]

This rule is generally sound, for the author of a blog should not be responsible for a comment posted by another. However, most courts have gone further—they have held that the immunity applies even when a blogger, ISP, or website operator fails to remove a comment despite having knowledge that it is defamatory or invasive of privacy.[13] This extension of §230 does nothing to prevent irresponsibility when it comes to privacy-invasive speech that harms others.

For example, in 2007, a website called JuicyCampus encouraged college students to post rumors and gossip about each other.[14] As a *Newsweek* article reported: "The posts have devolved from innocuous tales of secret crushes to racist tirades and lurid finger-pointing about drug use and sex, often with the alleged culprit identified by first and last name."[15] Some titles of posts included the "Best BlowJ" and "GUYS WITH STDS!" and the "Dumbest Duke Student."

JuicyCampus flaunted its §230 immunity. Since JuicyCampus did not supply the gossip and rumor itself, it could claim immunity for the comments others posted. According to JuicyCampus's FAQs:

> Is JuicyCampus liable for the content posted on the site?
>
> No. JuicyCampus is not the author of the posts on the site. Rather, JuicyCampus is the provider of an interactive computer service. Pursuant to Title 47 U.S.C. Section 230, JuicyCampus is immune from liability arising from content posted by users.[16]

The website deliberately tried to cloak gossip and rumormongers with anonymity. The FAQs stated:

> Is the site really anonymous?
>
> Yes. We don't ask for your name, email address, or other personally identifiable information in order for you to make a post. In fact, we prefer not to know who you are.[17]

Those who were the subject of gossip or rumor on JuicyCampus were helpless to do much about it. According to the website's FAQs:

> How do I remove a post that someone else made?
>
> You can't. Only we can remove posts made by others, and generally we don't. We do remove spam, but otherwise it's pretty rare.[18]

JuicyCampus shut down in 2009, a victim of the bad economy.[19] Although JuicyCampus is gone, the problems it raises persist, for there are countless other websites that encourage and spread rumor and gossip in irresponsible ways. Websites like JuicyCampus are a prime illustration of why §230 goes too far, promoting the dissemination of harmful gossip and rumor. This is why I recommend that §230 be modified to have a notice-and-takedown system rather than complete unmitigated immunity. Whenever bloggers or website operators know that a comment posted by another is tortious, the law should create an incentive for them to remove it. If a person promptly removes a tortious comment after being notified, then that person would be immune. If the person fails to remove the comment, only then would the person be subjected to potential liability.[20]

In a thoughtful response to this proposal, Amber Taylor argues that notice and takedown will open up a Pandora's box of problems. She points to the Digital Millennium Copyright Act (DMCA), which contains a notice-and-takedown procedure for information that violates copyright law.[21] A person will not be held liable for a copyright violation for improperly posting copyrighted material if, after receiving notice from the copyright holder, she "responds expeditiously to remove, or disable access to, the material that is claimed to be infringing or to be the subject of infringing activity."[22] Taylor contends that "[Solove] does not recognize that his own proposal would result in over-enforcement of privacy norms, since the threat of litigation is often enough for webmasters to take down protected speech."[23] Likewise, in a similar critique of my proposal, Professor Rebecca Tushnet argues:

> Given how easily notice and takedown can be abused, and how rarely posters challenge notices (which must seem very high-stakes indeed to nonlawyers), I am unenthusiastic about this idea unless the procedure was made very transparent and the penalties for ISPs were pretty limited.[24]

These criticisms are formidable, especially in light of how the DMCA notice-and-takedown system for copyright violations has been abused. The DMCA regime is fraught with problems, as zealous copyright owners are making overbroad takedown requests for material that is fair use. YouTube, for example, quickly removes any videos upon receiving a takedown request, even when there is a good argument for fair use. And for the blogger, it is difficult not to be shaking in one's boots when receiving a nasty takedown letter from a corporate lawyer threatening the apocalypse if one does not comply. Facing such a leviathan, with the muscular copyright law in its corner and armed with the threat of huge statutory damages, the wisest course of action is to back down and take down.

Would notice and takedown for defamatory or privacy-invasive speech run into similar problems? I do not believe it would for several reasons. First, abusing the notice-and-takedown system should be penalized.[25] Those who wrongly issue takedown threats for material that is not defamatory or invasive of privacy should be punished for making unjustified claims. Second, the entities enforcing copyright law are often very wealthy, powerful, and aggressive. Significant amounts of money are at stake. The DMCA takedown notices are part of a corporate campaign to stop music piracy and to push beyond for even greater control over content, often threatening fair use. In contrast, most privacy or defamation plaintiffs are ordinary individuals, without the ability to hire armies of lawyers or to pursue cases relentlessly to the four corners of the globe. Most individuals who request information be taken down to protect their personal reputations lack the litigating power of the music or movie industry, and the stakes are much lower.

The damages for defamation and invasion of privacy actions should be limited. This will prevent predatory lawsuits that aim to extort money. More importantly, mediation should be required before any lawsuit can proceed to trial. Most cases should not proceed to trial. The law should primarily function to incentivize parties to resolve their disputes. The measures I propose will push law into this function and prevent opportunistic litigation as well as help keep costs under control.

A related objection is that a notice-and-takedown regime will result in excessive takedown. Website operators will err on the side of takedown even when they believe that a comment is not tortious because they want to avoid the hassle of litigation and the risk that they might be incorrect. Although this is a valid objection, it should not deter us from lessening §230 immunity in the manner I propose. The risk of excessive takedown objection can be made against any potential liability for speech. Taken to its logical extreme, the excessive takedown objection suggests that if we truly want free speech uninhibited by any chilling effect from potential litigation, there should be absolute immunity for speech—immunity should be expanded to apply to all speech, whether online or offline, whether one is the speaker or not. Few would argue, however, in favor of such a broad immunity. Excessive takedown is always a concern, but the law already accounts for and deals with that risk. Lessening §230 immunity is unlikely to increase the existing risk of excessive takedown in a dramatic fashion.

Part of the analysis of how minor modifications to §230 immunity will impact speech depends upon empirical questions that remain unanswered: How often will people attempt to request to have information taken down? How frequently will such a notice-and-takedown system be abused? I do not think there will be rampant abuse. Nor do I predict a barrage of takedown requests. Indeed, even under our current system, where §230 immunizes bloggers for comments of others, there is no reason why a person should not at least ask for something to be taken down—at worst, the blogger says no. I am not aware of much evidence that takedown requests are currently out of control, and I doubt changing the system from voluntary takedown to a more mandatory takedown will result in a sudden tsunami of problems. But this is a guess. The only way to find out for certain is to experiment. The costs of leaving the law as it is are real and significant—people's lives are being ruined, their future opportunities are being limited, their freedom to grow, develop, and achieve their dreams is being hampered. Given these costs, something should be done to address the problem, even if there is some risk to free speech. The risk is likely to be small, but it is impossible to know for certain. If altering §230 immunity suddenly leads to widespread abuses and excessive chilling of non-tortious speech, then the law can always be restored.

The balance between privacy and free speech is currently out of kilter. My proposals might tip the balance too much in the privacy direction, but given the status quo of a balance tipped too far on the side of speech, I believe it is worth tinkering with the scale and taking the risk. In the unlikely event that the balance shifts too far toward privacy, adjustments can be made. The objections to my proposals certainly suggest caution, as there is indeed a risk of rampant abuses, but that is a risk, not a certainty, and we should not let it paralyze us from trying to fix an existing problematic imbalance.

The most effective solutions encourage norm change, and that occurs not just through the law but through increasing people's awareness of the consequences of their online speech. Currently, I see both in the law and in the discourse an exaltation of speech over privacy, a strong sentiment that people should be able to say whatever they want with impunity. Shaping these norms into a better balance between free speech and privacy is key if we are going to make any headway in addressing these problems.

Whom Should We Protect?

Some people, like the Star Wars Kid, are the unwitting victims of those who release their personal information online. Others willingly expose their own personal information online and may later want to remove or conceal it. Should these two instances be treated differently? Regarding the non-consensual victim of personal information disclosure, I believe that the law should provide strong protection. As for the person who self-exposes, that person is engaging in risky behavior and cedes some rights to privacy. But what if that person is a juvenile who lacks judgment? Suppose later on, as an adult, she regrets what she posted about herself online and wants it removed and others who disseminated it to take it off their websites. This is a tricky problem. I believe that there should be some limited right to retract information, especially for minors, though developing the contours of such a right would require a much lengthier exposition than is possible here.

Another issue when it comes to self-exposure is the degree of exposure. Suppose a person discloses information on a Facebook page that is set up so that only the person's friends can view it. Suppose the person has fifty friends. Is the information still private? I believe there is a good argument that it is.[26] Even though the data is disseminated to quite a few people, it is clear that the person has explicitly limited the visibility of the information to a select group of people. There should be an implicit understanding of confidentiality in this instance. A stranger who finds a way to pry into the person's Facebook page is committing an intrusion, for she is accessing information she is not authorized to see. If one of the person's friends were to disseminate the information beyond the group of friends, such a disclosure could be understood to be a breach of confidentiality. Abandoning antiquated notions of privacy would be an important first step in working out an appropriate law and policy to deal with situations like these.

One common response to the growing loss of privacy due to online speech is that in the future, Generation Google will develop a much lesser expectation of privacy. Technology has led to a generational divide. On one side are high school and college students whose lives virtually revolve around social-networking sites and blogs. On the other side are their parents, for whom recollection of the past often remains locked in fading memories or, at best, in books, photographs, and videos. For the current generation, the past is preserved on the Internet, potentially forever. And this change raises the question of how much privacy people can expect—or even desire—in an age of ubiquitous networking. For example, Taylor contends in a critique of my calls for greater privacy protection:

> The experience of living online will only become more universalized, giving people more of a basis for judging people and information they encounter there. Privacy will recede from the heights it achieved during our brief period of wealth and atomization. Present notions of reputation will no longer apply; as multiple personas become more difficult to maintain. All this will result in a more accurate and humanized representation: we are who we are, warts and all, and the exposure of actions and beliefs that we now keep under wraps will result in changes in social norms. We need not fear the future, and despite Solove's concerns, the temporary dislocation of the present is no great danger either.[27]

Exposing all our warts, however, will not improve our judgments of others or create a world where the norms people champion yet secretly transgress disappear. People are often hypocritical. Many social norms are idealized standards of behavior. When all our warts are exposed, we might still condemn. It is not clear that exposing people's foibles will change norms—it might just hurt those who get exposed. Perhaps if we had 100 percent information on 100 percent of the people, things might change, but that is unlikely to occur. Whose curtains will get ripped down and whose won't will likely be haphazard. And so a utopia where we all judge each other openly, fairly, and without hypocrisy might never exist. Instead there will be a world where more people are hurt and condemned when their private lives are suddenly exposed.

Moreover, I dispute claims that Generation Google will grow to eschew privacy and love living completely exposed. When members of Generation Google are adults with teenage children, will they celebrate their child's loss of privacy, happily helping them upload their naked pictures to the Internet? Will these parents help edit their children's typos and grammar on their tell-all sex diaries? Or will they be even more cognizant than parents today about the dangers of overexposure? I believe the latter. I believe they will learn the consequences of losing privacy, and they will better educate their own children based on their experiences. Ultimately, only time will tell. Looking back on history, the advent of new technologies frequently raised cries of the inevitable death of privacy. Nevertheless, privacy has persisted as a major social desire and goal. People have long worried that future generations would not care about privacy, but privacy still has not died, and people still care about it.

The Internet is creating new and vexing threats to privacy as people have an unprecedented ability to gather and spread information about each other around the world. To address these problems, we need to rethink privacy for the Information Age. If we fail to do so, we will face severe limitations on freedom and self-development now and in the future.

CHAPTER 2

Civil Rights in Our Information Age

DANIELLE KEATS CITRON

The Internet is a double-edged sword. While it can facilitate the empowerment of people who often face discrimination, it can also be exploited to disenfranchise those very same individuals. Anonymous mobs employ collaborative technologies to terrorize and silence women, people of color, and other minorities. The harassment typically includes threats of sexual violence, postings of individuals' home addresses alongside the suggestion that they should be raped, and technological attacks that shut down blogs and websites. Cyber mobs brand targeted individuals as inferior beings and as sexual objects.

Not surprisingly, the abuse has a profound impact upon targeted individuals. It may intimidate them, chasing them offline. It may convince them to disguise their online identities. When individuals go offline or assume pseudonyms to avoid bigoted cyber attacks, they miss innumerable economic and social opportunities. They suffer feelings of shame and isolation. Cyber mobs effectively deny people the right to participate in online life as equals.

Consider these examples.[1] Kathy Sierra, a programmer and game developer, maintained a popular blog on software development called "Creating Passionate Users." In 2007, anonymous individuals attacked Ms. Sierra on her blog and two other websites. Posters threatened rape and strangulation. They revealed her home address and Social Security number. They posted doctored photographs of Ms. Sierra. One picture featured her with a noose beside her neck; the other depicted her screaming while being suffocated by lingerie. After the attack, Ms. Sierra canceled speaking engagements and feared leaving her yard. She suspended her blog, even though it enhanced her reputation in the technical community. In April 2009, she explained that her "blog [once] was in the Technorati Top 100. I have not blogged there—or anywhere—since."[2]

Posters on a white supremacist website targeted Bonnie Jouhari, a civil rights advocate and mother of a biracial girl. They posted her child's picture and Ms. Jouhari's home address. The site showed an animated picture of Ms. Jouhari's workplace exploding in flames next to the threat that "race traitors" are "hung from the neck from the nearest tree or lamp post." Posters included bomb-making instructions beneath the picture. After Ms. Jouhari and her daughter began receiving harassing phone calls at home and at work, she left her job and moved. Ms. Jouhari has explained that neither she nor her daughter maintains a driver's license, voter registration card, or bank account because they fear creating a public record of their whereabouts.[3]

Many view these attacks as isolated instances of cyber bullying. They characterize them as random pranks or the by-products of soured relationships. But anonymous mobs accomplish something far more systematic than that. Rather than attacking a random mix of individuals, cyber mobs disproportionately target women. The nonprofit organization Working to Halt Online Abuse explains that, from 2000 to 2007, 72.5 percent of the individuals reporting cyber harassment identified themselves as women and 22 percent identified themselves as men. Half of those individuals had no relationship with their attackers.[4] Similarly, the National Center for Victims of Crimes' Stalking Resource Center reports that approximately 60 percent of online harassment cases involve male attackers and female targets. Cyber mobs often target lesbian and/or nonwhite women with particular virulence. They also focus on men of color, religious minorities, and gay men.

These cyber assaults also inflict a wider array of injuries than isolated pranks or fights between adversaries. When online mobs attack individuals because of their race, gender, or other protected characteristic, they damage individuals, their groups, and society in unique ways. Traditional criminal and tort law can reach some of their injuries, such as the tarnished reputations, emotional distress caused by threats, and privacy invasions. But they fall short of a complete response because they fail to address the gender- and race-based nature of the damage.

Civil rights laws are designed to respond to such harm. Antidiscrimination laws guarantee the right to be free of unequal treatment on the basis of race, gender, or other protected characteristics. Cyber mobs violate those guarantees when they shut down income-generating blogs because the bloggers are women or African American. They transgress civil rights laws when they terrorize individuals with rape threats because of their race, gender, or other protected characteristic. Civil rights remedies would combat a cyber mob's interference with individuals' right to work and participate in discourse online as equals.

This essay explores the destructive nature of today's online mobs. It examines how the Internet's features magnify dangerous online mob behavior. It rejects the notion that targeted individuals can, and should, combat cyber mobs on their own. Instead, it offers a comprehensive legal response to combat today's cyber mobs. It emphasizes the important role that traditional criminal and tort remedies would play in addressing the online abuse and acknowledges their limitations. It argues that civil rights laws can compensate for these shortcomings by reaching the damage that a cyber mob's discrimination inflicts upon individuals, groups, and society. I shall then respond to concerns that protecting civil rights online would compromise our commitment to free speech. I explain why a legal response comports with First Amendment doctrine and how a robust protection of cyber civil rights would promote more valuable speech than it would inhibit.

Anonymous Mobs of the Twenty-first Century

Cyber mobs attack women and minorities in several ways. They terrorize individuals with threats of sexual violence and doctored photographs, often encouraging others to physically assault individuals and providing their home addresses. Online mobs invade individuals' privacy, hacking into their personal computers and email accounts to obtain confidential information and then posting it online. Attackers post reputation-harming statements online, accusing individuals of having mental illnesses and sexually transmitted diseases. They send the damaging statements to employers and manipulate search engines to ensure that the statements appear prominently in searches of targeted individuals' names. Attackers use technology to drive targeted individuals offline. Groups coordinate denial-of-service attacks that close sites and blogs. Cyber mobs routinely use all of these tools in their attacks.

In response, targeted individuals abandon income-generating blogs and websites or maintain them under gender-disguising pseudonyms. They withdraw from online discussion groups. They employ passwords to eliminate their websites' connectivity to a wider, and potentially threatening, audience. They close comments on blog posts, foreclosing productive conversations along with abusive ones.

Cyber mobs can be very brutal. In 2007, the social-networking site Auto-Admit hosted group attacks on named female law students. Thirty-nine posters targeted the women on the site's message board. The posters, writing under pseudonyms, generated hundreds of threatening, sexually explicit, and damaging statements about the female law students.[5] Posters threatened them with violence. One poster asserted that a named female student should "get raped." That remark led to many additional threats. A poster promised: "I'll force myself on [the identified student]" and "sodomize" her "repeatedly." Another said that the student "deserves to be raped so that her little fantasy world can be shattered by real life."

Discussion threads suggested that the posters had physical access to the women. A poster described a woman's attire at the school gym. Others mentioned meeting the women, describing what they looked like and where they spent their summer. Some provided updates on sightings of particular women. A poster provided the email address of a female law student under a thread entitled "Mad at [named individual]? Email her."

Posters asserted damaging statements about the women. One claimed that a woman spent time in a drug rehabilitation center. Others remarked that the woman appeared in *Playboy*. Posters claimed that another female student had a sexually transmitted disease. Others provided her purported "subpar" LSAT score. Posters spread the alleged lies offline to ruin the women's reputations. One poster urged the group to tell top law firms about the female student's LSAT score "before she gets an offer." Posters emailed damaging statements to her former employer; they admonished the employer that clients would "not want to be represented by someone who is not of the highest character value."

The posters also engaged in the practice known as "Google bombing" to ensure that anyone searching the female students' names would see the damaging statements. Google bombing raises the ranking of a web page discussing someone if posters link to it in as many other web pages as possible. This helps ensure a web page's prominence because search engines rank a web page highly in a search of a person's name if an overwhelming number of sites link to that page. Posters provided instructions on how to engage in "Google bombing" and made plain their goal: "We're not going to let that bitch have her own blog be the first result from googling her name!"

Posters admitted their desire to intimidate and harm the female students. After one of the women did not get a summer job, a poster asked if the other "bitch got what she deserved too?" Another said, "I'm doing cartwheels knowing this stupid Jew bitch is getting her self esteem raped." A poster explained that the women were targeted "just for being women."

Similarly, a group called Anonymous has devoted itself to terrorizing and silencing hundreds of women on the web. For instance, in 2007, Anonymous used message boards and wikis to plan an attack on a nineteen-year-old woman who maintained a video blog on Japanese language and video games. Group members hacked into her email, obtaining her personal information, and published her home address, passwords, and private medical history on various sites. The group posted a doctored photograph of the woman atop naked bodies. Underneath the photograph appeared the warning: "We will rape her at full force in her vagina, mouth, and ass." Another picture depicted the woman with men brutally raping her. Group members saturated her video blog with sexually violent material and took down her videos. When her live journal or video blog would reappear, Anonymous urged its members to "rape" and "nuke [her site] from orbit."

Anonymous maintains a list of women's issues sites and blogs that it claims to have forced offline. The list includes names of shuttered sites with a line crossed through them and the accompanying message: "[d]own due to excessive bandwidth—great success." When a site reappears online, Anonymous tells its members: "It's back! Show no mercy." The group takes credit for closing more than 100 feminist websites and blogs.[6] Targeted female bloggers and website operators confirm these claims. A victim explained, "[b]eing silenced for over two weeks felt infuriating, stifling, imprisoned by gang rapists just waiting for me to try to get up from underneath their weight so they could stomp on me again."[7]

In August 2008, an online mob attacked a woman who blogged about the film *The Dark Knight*. A poster threatened: "Get a life you two dollar whore blogger, The Dark Knight doesn't suck, you suck! Don't ever post another blog unless you want to get ganged up." Another poster urged: "if you were my wife I would beat you." Others disparaged her intellect: "This is why women are TOO STUPID to think critically and intelligently about film; AND business for that matter" and "Why don't you make yourself useful and go have a baby." The woman explained that of the nearly 200 comments, only three failed to mention her gender in a threatening and disparaging manner. To stop the harassment, she closed the comments and deleted fifty of the most violent ones.[8]

Online mobs target African American and Hispanic women as well. As blogger "La Chola" explains, women-of-color bloggers consistently receive horrific emails and comments threatening violent sexual assault, death, and attacks against family members.[9] After the author of "Ask This Black Woman" posted commentary about a video game, anonymous posters attacked her on her blog and other sites. She received death threats. Posters told her to "[g]et back into the cotton fields, you filthy [n***r]" and threatened to overrun her blog.[10]

Cyber mobs inflict serious injuries. Targeted people who curtail their online activities or go offline incur serious costs. They lose advertising income generated from blogs and websites. They miss opportunities to advance their professional reputations through blogging. They cannot network effectively online if they assume pseudonyms to deflect the abuse. As technology blogger Robert Scoble explains, women who lack a robust online presence are "never going to be included in the [technology] industry." Moreover, damaging online statements can destroy reputations because employers use Google results in assessing candidates. They may decline to interview or hire someone because the statements suggest that the person attracts unwanted controversy.

Online harassment also produces serious emotional and physical suffering. Targeted individuals feel a sustained loss of personal security. They fear that online threats of sexual violence will be realized. Their anxiety is particularly acute as the posters' anonymity vanquishes any cues that might alleviate their concerns. Their emotional distress often produces physical symptoms, such as anorexia nervosa, depression, headaches, and suicide. Posts providing individuals' home addresses alongside the suggestion that they should be raped or killed have led to offline stalking.

The Internet's Role in Aggravating Cyber Mob Behavior

Social science research on group behavior suggests that the Internet will intensify the destructiveness of gender and race-based harassment. It identifies several factors exacerbating the dangerousness of groups. Groups with homogenous views tend to become more extreme when they deliberate.[11] Their members gain confidence in their preconceived ideas as discussions tend to feature many arguments supporting them and few tilting the other way. Hearing agreement from others bolsters group members' confidence, entrenching and radicalizing their views.

Group members often lack a sense of personal responsibility for their acts.[12] According to one school of thought, this occurs because people in groups fail to see themselves as distinct individuals. Another school of thought explains that people behave aggressively because they believe that when immersed in a group they cannot be observed and caught.

Groups are more destructive when they dehumanize their victims.[13] When group members view victims as devoid of humanity and personal identity, they feel free to attack without regret. They are also more aggressive when authority figures support their efforts.[14] Social scientists emphasize a perceived leader's role in accelerating dangerous group behavior. Southern newspapers in the early 1900s explicitly legitimated violence by reporting that lynch mobs included prominent members of the white community. Federal authorities implicitly encouraged the Ku Klux Klan by failing to enforce civil rights laws.[15]

The Internet magnifies the dangerousness of group behavior in each of these respects. Web 2.0 platforms create a feeling of closeness among like-minded individuals. Because online group members tend to affirm each other's negative views, they become more extreme and destructive. Individuals do and say things online they would never consider doing or saying offline because they feel anonymous and do not fear getting caught. Cyber mobs also see victims as digital images that can be eviscerated without regret.

Moreover, site operators who refuse to dismantle destructive posts reinforce, and effectively encourage, negative behavior. Their refusal can stem from a libertarian "You Own Your Own Words" philosophy or irresponsibility bred from the belief that they enjoy broad statutory immunity from liability for the postings of others. In turn, negative posts that remain online constitute calls to action that generate others in a snowball effect. In cyberspace, the accelerants of dangerous group behavior are pervasive, deepening the problem of today's abusive cyber mobs.

Some suggest that the market can solve this serious social problem. They assert that targeted individuals can defeat destructive cyber mobs by recruiting advocacy groups to defend them. They envision women's groups coordinating efforts to rebuild a targeted individual's reputation online by engaging in "Google bombing" to optimize positive posts produced in a search of a victim's name. They point to groups like Reputation Defender that have helped cyber harassment victims establish an online presence to offset destructive postings.

Such a response, however, would be inadequate. It would not remove the threats and lies that terrorize and silence individuals. In defamatory attacks, it is inconceivable that all of the damage will be erased. Because so many people will see the material, some will inevitably miss the individual's response while others will not believe, or only partially believe, it. This is especially true when dealing with attacks on someone's character because the targeted individual does not have an affirmative case she is trying to convey—she is only seeking to dispel the harm from the mob's attack. Moreover, people seeing a disproportionate number of her rebuttals will not counterbalance those who have seen none.

The efforts of advocacy groups may be unable to drown out the assaults of cyber mobs. Consider the case of Nicole Catsouras, who died in a horrific car crash. Gruesome photographs of the carnage appeared on the Internet, spreading to over 1,500 sites. Posters urged cohorts to harass her family and facilitated this harassment by providing the family's home address. The woman's family asked sites to remove the pictures but to no avail. Tracking down anonymous posters proved impossible for the family, and the pictures remained online.

Countermeasures also run the risk of sustaining the life of the attacks rather than slowing them down. Because the very purpose of many online attacks is to force individuals off the web, mobs are likely to respond with venom against those who not only stay online but try to fight back. A targeted individual would likely conclude that more people will see the defamatory or threatening material if she responds than if she does not.

This view ignores the social harm resulting from an online mob's attacks. If working and expressing opinions online subjects someone to the risk of assault, even if the damage is only temporary, the result will change the kind of people who engage in cyber discourse. Members of a targeted group will experience stigma and go offline. These attacks undermine our commitment to full and equal participation in public life in a manner that victims cannot, and should not, address on their own.

A Comprehensive Legal Approach to Cyber Mobs

Because private mechanisms cannot provide a meaningful solution to today's cyber mobs, a legal response is in order. A comprehensive response would include traditional criminal prosecutions, tort remedies, and civil rights actions. Supplementing traditional criminal and tort law remedies with civil rights ones is crucial to reach all of the harm that cyber mobs inflict.

Traditional criminal and tort law remedies can address some of the harm that targeted individuals' experience. Criminal law would punish a cyber mob's members for sending code that shuts down someone's blog. It criminalizes online harassment. For instance, the Violence Against Women Act (VAWA) punishes anyone using a telecommunications device without disclosing his identity and with the intent to "abuse, threaten or harass any person who receives the communication."[16] Some states criminalize posting messages with the intent to urge or incite others to harass a victim.[17] California authorities obtained a guilty plea from a defendant who terrorized a woman by impersonating her in chat rooms and bulletin boards, where the defendant posted the victim's home address alongside the suggestion that she fantasized about being raped.

Tort law would provide redress for a cyber mob's faulty actions. Individuals can sue cyber mobs for defamation if online lies injure their reputation. They can seek money damages for emotional distress that cyber mobs intentionally or recklessly cause. They can also bring privacy claims against cyber mobs that publicly disclose private facts that would be "highly offensive to the reasonable person."[18]

These traditional remedies have an important, yet limited role in combating cyber mobs. They express society's disapproval of online threats, computer crimes, and tortious conduct. They punish cyber mobs for socially unacceptable conduct, such as harassment and computer crimes. They secure compensation for damaged reputations and emotional distress. They serve as a deterrent when cyber mobs see that the cost of their conduct exceeds its benefits.

Now, let's explore the limitations of traditional remedies. Traditional criminal and tort law cannot reach the harm experienced by individuals, their groups, and society due to cyber mobs' interference with their right to equal treatment. Traditional remedies simply are not designed to redress the suffering caused by discrimination, both to individuals and to the public at large. Defamation law, for example, remedies a plaintiff's reputational harm caused by online falsehoods. It does not, however, redress the harm inflicted upon the person's group or society. Nor does defamation law address the stigma and economic injuries that individuals experience when they are targeted because of their race, gender, or other personal characteristic.

Civil rights laws compensate for these shortcomings. They respond to harms inflicted when cyber mobs deprive individuals of their right to equal treatment. They address the unique harms suffered by targeted individuals. Civil rights laws respond to a cyber mob's interference with a person's work because of her race, gender, or other protected characteristic. They would tackle the professional sabotage perpetrated by the anonymous posters whose threats of violence and doctored photographs drove Ms. Sierra and Ms. Jouhari offline. They would respond to the anonymous posters' technological attacks that shut down women's issues websites because the site operators were female. Whereas traditional criminal and tort law fail to address the economic harm caused by discrimination, civil rights laws do.

Civil rights laws also address the corrosive stigmatization of targeted individuals. They recognize victims' feelings of humiliation and inferiority.[19] They redress the alienation that individuals experience when they assume gender-disguising names or downplay stereotypically female attributes, such as compassion, to deflect a cyber mob's abuse. Civil rights laws prevent, punish, and redress this psychic damage.

Civil rights laws respond to the harm experienced by a targeted individual's group. Nontargeted group members often experience cyber attacks as if they happened to them personally. When anonymous posters threatened to rape Ms. Sierra, other female bloggers felt targeted and at risk. When a cyber mob threatened to kill the author of the "Ask This Black Woman" blog and told her to "[g]et back into the cotton fields, you filthy [n***r]," the website operator wasn't the only one who felt threatened. African American readers felt intimidated and threatened. Nontargeted group members may go offline or assume pseudonyms to avoid being targeted. This has psychic and economic costs that civil rights laws recognize and remedy.

Civil rights laws address the harm that cyber mobs inflict upon society. The public experiences a serious loss when targeted individuals and nontargeted group members stop contributing to our online marketplace and discourse due to cyber mobs' abuse. It suffers because online mob attacks entrench gender and racial hierarchy in cyberspace. Sexually demeaning comments and rape threats suggest men's power over women. They reinforce gendered stereotypes, casting men as dominant in the bedroom and at work and women as subservient sexual objects who are not fit to work online. Threats laden with racial epithets operate in a similar fashion, suggesting that African Americans are inferior to white individuals. These messages stake out the Internet as a space for white men. Civil rights laws respond to this systemic harm.

Federal and state antidiscrimination laws offer various means to combat cyber mobs. They would criminalize some of a cyber mob's abusive behavior. The Civil Rights Act of 1968 punishes "force or threat[s] of force" designed to intimidate or interfere with a person's private employment due to that person's race, religion, or national origin.[20] Courts have sustained convictions of defendants who made death threats over employees' email and voice mail.[21] A court upheld the prosecution of a defendant who left messages on an Arab American's voice mail that threatened "the only good Arab is a dead Arab." Similarly, a jury convicted a defendant under this statute for sending an email under the name "Asian Hater" to sixty Asian students that read: "I personally will make it my life career [sic] to find and kill everyone of you personally."[22]

Current law should be amended to criminalize online threats made because of a victim's gender or sexual orientation. VAWA is a profitable place to begin this effort. Although the Supreme Court struck down VAWA's regulation of gender-motivated violence on the grounds that such criminal conduct did not substantially affect interstate commerce to justify congressional action under the Commerce Clause, Congress could amend VAWA pursuant to its power to regulate an instrumentality of interstate commerce—the Internet—to punish anonymous cyber mobs that threaten individuals because of their gender or sexual orientation. The Department of Justice would presumably support such a development as it currently encourages federal prosecutors to seek hate crime penalty enhancements for defendants who subject victims to cyber harassment because of their race, color, religion, national origin, or sexual orientation.[23]

Civil rights laws also sanction private lawsuits against cyber mobs for their discriminatory actions. Section 1981 of Title 42 of the U.S. Code guarantees members of racial minorities "the same right in every State . . . to make and enforce contracts . . . as is enjoyed by white citizens."[24] Section 1981 permits lawsuits against private individuals without the need for state action because Congress enacted the statute under its power to enforce the Thirteenth Amendment. Courts have allowed plaintiffs to bring Section 1981 claims against masked mobs that used tactics of intimidation to prevent members of racial minorities from "making a living" in their chosen field.[25]

Women can sue a cyber mob's members under Title VII of the Civil Rights Act of 1964 for preventing them from making a living because of their sex.[26] Title VII actions can be asserted against private actors because Congress enacted Title VII pursuant to a valid exercise of its power to regulate interstate commerce. Just after Congress passed Title VII, courts upheld discrimination claims where masked defendants engaged in intimidation tactics to prevent plaintiffs from pursuing their chosen careers.[27] Although recent Title VII decisions focus on employer-employee relationships, courts should look to those early cases in deciding whether women can bring sex discrimination claims against anonymous cyber mobs that interfere with their online work because of their gender. Doing so would honor Title VII's goal of eliminating discrimination in women's employment opportunities.

Congress recognized the dangers that anonymous mobs pose to individuals' right to equal treatment during Reconstruction. It enacted the Ku Klux Klan Act of 1871 to reach the destructive conduct of Klan members who conspired to deprive individuals of their basic rights under the cloak of anonymity. Section 2 of the 1871 Act, now codified at Section 1985(3) of Title 42, allows damage suits against two or more people who conspire or go in disguise on the highway to deprive any person of the equal protection of the laws.[28] Section 241 of Title 42 similarly establishes criminal penalties for "two or more persons [who] go in disguise on the highway" to hinder a person's "free exercise or enjoyment of any right or privilege" secured by the Constitution or federal law.[29]

Today's anonymous cyber mobs go on the information superhighway to deprive individuals of their essential rights to engage in discourse and participate in society as equals just as masked Klan members went on public highways to interfere with victims' basic rights. Nonetheless, efforts to apply these statutes to online mobs face formidable obstacles. In 1875, the Supreme Court narrowed their reach by requiring state action.[30] Although relaxing this ruling somewhat in 1971,[31] the Court more recently held that Sections 1985(3) and 241 only cover private conspiracies "aimed at interfering with rights that are 'protected against private, as well as official, encroachment.'"[32] For the Court, freedom of speech is not such a right.

The Court noted that Congress "no doubt" can proscribe private efforts to deny rights secured only against official interference, such as free speech, under its power to regulate interstate commerce, but held that Section 1985(3) was not such a provision. Congress should follow this suggestion and enact a law that would proscribe an anonymous cyber mob's conspiracy to deprive individuals of their right to exercise free speech under its power to regulate interstate commerce. Congress should permit targeted individuals to bring damage suits against cyber mobs, much as Section 1985(3) supplements Section 241.

Some may insist that regulating a cyber mob's attacks would interfere with our commitment to free speech. This is simply not the case. A cyber civil rights agenda comports with First Amendment doctrine and free speech values.

First Amendment jurisprudence would not immunize a cyber mob's conduct from regulation. The Supreme Court has held that the First Amendment permits restrictions on speech that offers "such slight social value as a step to truth that any benefit that may be derived from [it] is clearly outweighed by the social interest in order and morality."[33] This is equally true for threats, defamation, intentional infliction of emotional distress, and civil rights violations.

The First Amendment does not prohibit states from using criminal and civil law to forbid threats. Threats fall outside of the First Amendment's protection and for good reason. Consider an uncontroversial example. Suppose a person tells another that he will kill her the next time she leaves her house. While he makes this threat by speaking, that fact does not provide him with a defense to either criminal prosecution or civil suit. A threat of violence is both a crime and a tort, even though it is accomplished via words. All speaking is not protected, despite the seemingly blanket promise of the First Amendment that "Congress shall make no law abridging the freedom of speech." Bribery, blackmail, and threats are commonplace examples of speech that is not only forbidden but criminalized. Threats of violence made via new technologies are not immunized from penalty on free speech grounds.

These issues become more complicated with crimes that are interwoven with arguably expressive activity. Is the burning of a cross on the lawn of an African American family best characterized as a threat? Or is the expression of a view about race, though noxious, protected by the First Amendment? In Virginia v. Black, the Court answered these questions when it held that a state may ban cross burning if the defendant carried it out with the intent to intimidate. As the Court explained, the First Amendment does not protect "true threats" that communicate a serious intention to commit violence against particular individuals. The Court noted that the speaker need not actually intend to commit a violent act because the prohibition of "true threats" protects individuals from the fear of violence and the disruption that such fear engenders. It distinguished cross burnings done with the intent to intimidate, which it deemed a proscribable "true threat," from cross burning for other purposes, which it held constituted a protected expression of viewpoint.

The Court's reasoning is important here. A cyber mob's postings can constitute "true threats" if they convey a serious intention to inflict bodily harm upon the targeted individual, even if they combine the threatening language with protected offensive views. The anonymous posters arguably conveyed a serious intention to inflict bodily harm upon Kathy Sierra with their rape threats, doctored photographs, and revelation of her home address. The same is true for the individuals who posted a picture of Ms. Jouhari's workplace exploding in flames next to a warning that "race traitors" will be lynched. These threats, and others like them, are afforded no protection under First Amendment law.

The First Amendment does not protect falsehoods that damage reputations.[34] A cyber mob cannot avoid defamation liability on the grounds that their comments are too outrageous to be believed.[35] To the contrary, reputation-harming falsehoods enjoy no First Amendment protection if they assert or imply facts. For instance, the claim that a female law student had an infectious disease or mental illness is a fact that could be proved true or false for defamation purposes. Although public figures such as Kathy Sierra must prove defendants acted with "actual malice" if defamatory statements concern matters on which the public has a justified and important interest, they need not do so here because the public has no important and justified interest in rape threats, Social Security numbers, and doctored photographs.

The First Amendment does not bar antidiscrimination actions even though civil rights violations often communicate bigoted views. As the Supreme Court has held, the First Amendment poses no obstacle to civil rights claims because they proscribe defendants' unequal treatment of individuals and the unique harm that such discrimination inflicts, not the offensive messages that defendants send.

Wisconsin v. Mitchell demonstrates this point. There, the Court considered a First Amendment challenge to a Wisconsin statute enhancing the penalty of certain crimes if the perpetrator selected the victim because of race, religion, color, disability, sexual orientation, national origin, or ancestry.[36] The

Court unanimously rejected the defendant's claim that the statute punished him for his racist views. It explained that the statute did not transgress the First Amendment because it penalized the defendant's discriminatory motive for his conduct, not his bigoted ideas.

The Court analogized the Wisconsin statute to federal and state antidiscrimination laws, which, it explained, were immune from First Amendment challenge. It specifically pointed to Title VII and Section 1981 as civil rights laws that do not infringe upon defendants' First Amendment rights because they proscribe discriminatory motive (e.g., Title VII's prohibition of employment discrimination "because of" a protected characteristic), not the expression of bigoted ideas. The Court deemed both statutes "permissible content-neutral regulation[s] of conduct." It emphasized that the state was justified in singling out bias-inspired conduct due to the great individual and societal harm that it inflicts.

The *Mitchell* Court specifically distinguished R.A.V. v. City of St. Paul,[37] a case involving a city ordinance that criminalized conduct an individual "knows or has reasonable grounds to know arouses anger, alarm, or resentment in others on the basis of race, color, creed, religion, or gender." *R.A.V.* found the ordinance unconstitutional because it discriminated on the basis of the expressions' content—certain bigoted expressions were proscribed by the ordinance, yet those that gave offense in other ways were not. The *Mitchell* Court explained that "whereas the ordinance struck down in *R.A.V.* was explicitly directed at expression (*i.e.*, 'speech' or 'messages'), the [Wisconsin] statute in this case is aimed at conduct unprotected by the First Amendment." It concluded that Wisconsin's desire to address bias-inspired conduct "provides an adequate explanation for its penalty-enhancement provision over and above mere disagreement with offenders' beliefs or biases." In short, the *Mitchell* Court made clear that the First Amendment erects no barrier to the enforcement of antidiscrimination laws that regulate bias-inspired conduct and the special harm it inflicts, whereas it prohibits laws that discriminate on the basis of the ideas expressed like the one addressed in *R.A.V.*

Applying civil rights statutes to the attacks of cyber mobs falls clearly on the *Mitchell* side of this line. The statutes' proscriptions turn on an online mob's choice of victim and the distinct harm to victims, their communities, and society that a defendant's abusive conduct produces, rather than on the opinions that either the victims or the attackers express. Intimidating Ms. Sierra with rape threats and sexually demeaning comments so that she shuts down her income-generating blog is equally offensive, and equally proscribed, no matter the anonymous perpetrators' specific views. This is true when a cyber mob prevents a woman of color from securing gainful employment with sexual threats, damaging statements, and lies. Many online attacks have included racist, sexist, or other bigoted language; others have not. When law punishes online attackers due to the special severity of the social harm produced by targeting individuals because of their gender or race, and not due to the particular opinions that the attackers or victims express, it does not transgress the First Amendment.

Not only does a cyber civil rights agenda comport with First Amendment doctrine, it is consistent with prominent free speech theories that emphasize the importance of autonomy, political deliberation, cultural innovation, and the promotion of truth. Let's address the notion that protecting free speech promotes individual autonomy. On this view, free speech facilitates self-mastery, allowing people to author their own narratives and engage in political discourse. Autonomy and dignity require equitable and effective participation in political self-government, and thus the regulation of certain speech, such as racist and sexist speech, is a necessary prerequisite to secure equal citizenship.

Restraining a mob's most destructive assaults is essential to defending the expressive autonomy of its victims. Preventing mobs from driving vulnerable people offline would advance the reasons why we protect free speech in the first place, even though it would inevitably chill some speech of online mobs. Free from mob attacks, individuals, such as Ms. Sierra, might continue to blog, join online discussions, and express themselves on public issues. Protecting them from discrimination, defamation, threats, and technological attacks would allow them to be candid about their ideas.

Although online mobs express themselves through their assaults, their actions directly implicate their targets' self-determination and ability to participate in political and social discourse. Self-expression should receive little protection if its sole purpose is to extinguish the self-expression of another. As Owen Fiss argues, sometimes we must lower the voices of some to permit the self-expression of others.[38] Similarly, Cass Sunstein contends that threats, libel, and sexual and racial harassment constitute low-value speech of little First Amendment consequence.[39] Rarely is that more true than when one group of voices consciously exploits the Internet to silence others and to hide themselves to escape social responsibility for their actions.

Now, let's discuss the argument that expression deserves protection when it involves deliberation about public issues. A cyber mob's threats, lies, and discrimination, however, do not involve discussion of issues related to public life. Quite the contrary, they deprive vulnerable individuals of their right to engage in online discussions of public issues.

On a different note, democratic culture theorists like Jack Balkin argue that free speech promotes "democracy in the widest possible sense, not merely at the level of governance, or at the level of deliberation, but at the level of culture, where we interact, create, build communities, and build ourselves."[40] Freedom of expression permits innovation in a networked age where people join together to create works of art, gossip, and parody online. It can dissolve unjust social barriers of rank and privilege. Similarly, Diane Zimmerman highlights the role of gossip as generating intimacy and a sense of community among disparate groups.[41] She explains that gossip provides people a way to learn about social groups to which they do not belong and fosters relationships by giving strangers the means to bridge awkward silences when thrown together in social situations.

To be sure, online mobs engage in gossip. But their attacks have little to do with building bonds among disparate communities. Instead, rape threats, lies, damaging photographs, and denial-of-service attacks preclude connections among differently minded group members and sever a victim's connections with her own community. An online mob's attacks inflict serious social harm rather than generating ideas in popular culture or enforcing positive social norms. Defeating such discrimination outweighs any contribution that online mobs make to our cultural interaction and exchange.

Some may insist upon protecting an online mob's attacks in order to promote truth. On this view, any silencing of speech prevents us from better understanding the world in which we live. Justice Holmes drew from this theory when he articulated the notion of the marketplace of ideas: "that the best test of truth is the power of the thought to get itself accepted in the competition of the market."[42] The marketplace-of-ideas metaphor places no special premium on political discussion, but rather captures the idea that "truth must be experimentally determined from the properties of the experience itself."[43]

An extreme version of truth-seeking theory might insist the market should sort out online mobs' deceptions and assaults. Though to do so, the theory would have to consider a Social Security number a truthful fact that contributes to an understanding of that person. A more plausible vision of truth-seeking theory, however, is not served with the disclosure of a person's personal identifying information. Rather than revealing a fact to be tested in the marketplace, a Social Security number is simply a key to a person's credit and bank accounts. In this context, it is a weapon, not a truth or half-truth to be tested in the marketplace. Rape and death threats similarly tell us nothing about the victims—no truths are contested there. This is equally true of denial-of-service attacks. Even where online mobs make factual assertions, the anonymity of online communications prevents the marketplace of ideas from performing its curative function. And as Daniel Solove notes, "truth isn't the only value at stake."[44]

Although members of an online mob may transgress a variety of laws, victims are often unable to press their claims against posters who cannot be identified. This can occur when posters use anonymizing technologies that break the link between their IP addresses and real identities and when websites hosting attacks fail to track IP addresses. To be sure, it is sometimes possible to figure out the identity of posters. All too often, however, abusive posters cannot be identified.

Efforts to rein in online mobs may falter if the posters cannot be held responsible for their civil rights violations, crimes, and torts. Generally, the operators of destructive websites either have information that could help identify abusive posters or have made a conscious decision not to obtain or retain that information. Some website operators function as crowd leaders, influencing the mobs' destructiveness. Deterring websites devoted to abusive attacks on individuals plays a crucial role in inhibiting a destructive mob's coordination and efficacy. Thus, holding accountable the operators of websites that facilitate anonymous attacks may hold the key to protecting the civil rights of individuals set upon by online mobs.

Nonetheless, current law provides a barrier to website operator liability. Courts have broadly interpreted section 230 of the Communications Decency Act to immunize website operators from liability for content created by others.[45] Despite the fact that Section 230 promises "[p]rotection for private blocking and screening of offensive material," courts nonetheless read it to shield operators of sites purveying such material. These efforts to read a sweeping immunity into Section 230 have prevented courts from exploring what standard of care ought to apply to ISPs and website operators.

Broad immunity for operators of abusive websites eliminates incentives for better behavior by those in the best position to minimize harm. As Daniel

Solove explains, such immunity can "foster irresponsibility."[46] With blanket immunity, site operators have no reason to take down false or injurious material or to collect and retain identities of posters. As a result, objectionable posts remain online and searchable by employers, often migrating across the web to become effectively irretrievable, while plaintiffs continue to be unable to find and recover damages from wrongdoers. As judges, legislators, activists, and scholars begin to devote attention to online threats to civil rights, they should reconsider this sweeping immunity of website operators.

Cyber mobs inflict serious injuries that law must address. Combating their cyber assaults requires a comprehensive approach, one that includes traditional criminal prosecutions, tort remedies, and civil rights actions. Together, traditional remedies and antidiscrimination laws have great potential to deter, punish, and remedy the abuse of online mobs.

The Internet has two faces. One propels us forward with exciting opportunities for women and minorities to work, network, and spread their ideas online. The other brings us back to a time when anonymous mobs prevented vulnerable people from participating in society as equals. We can harness law's coercive power to reverse the backward-looking trend without sacrificing our commitment to free speech.

CHAPTER 3

The Internet's Anonymity Problem

SAUL LEVMORE

As social problems go, juvenile and destructive communications on the Internet are a modest matter. These communications are often offensive and noisy, and at times they are defamatory. They are likely to attract viewers in search of amusement, but repel those looking for information. In venues where juvenile and false communications come in great volume, they may discourage or camouflage serious contributions. There are media, and especially Internet websites, where such communications predominate, and others where they mingle with more valuable contributions that might well be lost if strong steps were taken to eliminate those deemed odious. When offensive communications are dispatched by identified senders they do not seem to present a new problem, even when the medium is the Internet with its remarkable reach. The sender's reputational interest, the law of defamation and harassment, and the influence of our tradition of free speech create an environment that is not much different from that found in other media. The same is often true where the sender is unidentified, but where a publisher or other intermediary is responsible. It is anonymous and pseudonymous communications, particularly in the blogosphere where such speech is routine, that are more problematic. One can be the victim of soapbox invectives, crude thoughts recorded on a bathroom wall, malignant lines printed in a letter to the editor of a newspaper, hurtful statements or footage broadcast on television, or the same nasty words written in a comment on a blog site. The likelihood of injury seems greatest in the last of these settings, and it is there that the injured party is least protected by law.

But does the Internet require special legal attention? Novelty often raises the questions of whether new law is required and whether law ought to be neutral in a competitive environment. Infant industries often make claims for special treatment, and the evolution of law is in part the story of law-makers' coming to terms with claims of novelty. Lawyers may overestimate the effect of legal rules on reality, but lawmakers are inclined to exaggerate the need for new rules when they observe new realities. Few politicians campaign on the claim that change is unnecessary, much as few law schools boast that they teach old law for new environments. And yet new terrain is often governed well by old rules. Security interests in airplanes are essentially the same as security interests in ox carts. When we turn to the development of the Internet, we can be sure that a judicial opinion, academic contribution, or legislative initiative will make the rhetorical move of emphasizing the Internet's ubiquity, speed, and multi-jurisdictional reach. But novelty is itself ubiquitous, and we ought to value stability in law, be wary of interest groups, and careful not to impose law in a way that distorts competition among industries. By sketching the level of regulation we find in competing media, as well as the cases for and against regulation, I show that the Internet is not only the most hospitable medium for offensive communications, but also that it does not deserve the lightest touch among the media.

One method of evaluating claims of novelty is to turn to a favorite tool of law and economics, and to ask what a hypothetical bargain among users, or all citizens, would look like with respect to the regulation of these communications on the Internet. I grapple with the question of whether the interest in, or legal rule protecting, free speech trumps this democratic, or market, bargain. I intend to leave the reader with the conclusion that novelty and free speech claims have probably protected the Internet from legal regulation in a manner that has generated excessive costs to the targets of offensive speech and perhaps to Internet entrepreneurs as well. Non-anonymity, or identifiability, is one route to reducing these costs; privileging a notice-and-takedown policy is another.

The Internet and Its Competitors

The Internet is hardly the medium with the highest density of anonymous or offensive communications. A high school's bathroom stalls may be the winner in that category. But Facebook, or a similar Internet site visited and easily discovered by the same high school's students, may well be the canvas of choice for the contemporary offensive graffitist. It is useful then to compare these, and then other media, in order to think about the legal environment in which juvenile—as well as mature but false—communications take place.

Environments, or media, can be compared from the perspective of the law or from that of the communicator. For one who wishes to communicate nasty remarks about a classmate, employer, or competitor, considerations of social standing, legal consequences, audience size, interactvity, and effort are all likely to play roles. A juvenile posting will have real bite—whether on an Internet site, on handbills left around a building, or on the bathroom wall—if something more than a simple slur is produced. Details can generate a defamation claim, unless author and publisher can remain unknown, and they also make possible the communication of socially useful, if painful, information. "Amy X is a slut"[1] is quintessentially juvenile, especially as a signal of interest, and no fun for Amy X or her true friends to read. Still, it is not clear that anyone suffers grave harm, not just because of the familiar aphorism about sticks and stones but also because of the irony that the more commonplace such taunts are, the less seriously anyone will take them. One response to the slut slur is for one's friends to shout out a thousand claims of that status attached to all sorts of people in order to diminish further the value of the first communication. The alternative and not unknown reaction is for an informed or well-intentioned passerby to attempt to expunge the offensive message so that it is not further communicated. Such short messages are typical of bathroom wall postings, and do not even attempt to convey much information. In contrast, "Y stole $150 from me" or "Z loved a dog behind Bartlett Hall," are slight rewordings of observed markings, and I hesitate to be so crude as to refer to them in print except that they are unusual. The details make these claims slightly more memorable and even credible, though not for the usual reason that details facilitate falsification. The claim that Y is a thief, if true, is a good example of an anonymous insult that might provide socially useful information—either because it deters other thieves, who fear shaming, or because it warns others to be wary of Y. The same cannot easily be said for the other comment. I hesitate to label these as unusual examples of *effective* juvenile communications because we do not know the authors' aims or knowledge. Each author ran the small risk of attracting vandalism or defamation charges, or perhaps even revenge by an informed target. Revenge may well be the most serious risk; it is ironic that the target will have more success in identifying the culprit if the original claim is detailed and true, or at least based on some real events. I return to accuracy and social utility below, but for now let us assume that the communications are exaggerations or outright falsehoods and, at best, a juvenile reaction to something about Y or Z that the writer finds distasteful.

When the offensive graffitist uses the bathroom wall he runs up against the medium's constraints; the Internet now provides a superior medium for one who wishes to spread juvenile or malicious speech. One can scratch or spray paint a wall for a variety of reasons, but the audience for that speech is limited, and the greater the offense with respect to both content and audience, the more quickly the communication will be erased. Moreover, the juvenilist who works on the bathroom wall with paint or knife must work quickly to avoid detection and prosecution. Thus, a longer and often more credible message is hard to cast. In obvious contrast, the juvenilist on the Internet is empowered by the ability to communicate in leisurely fashion and to do so from afar. The old-fashioned graffitist risks disciplinary action in a school or workplace, and police attention elsewhere, because in a real environment the graffitist has committed a crime—namely vandalism— even as he is open to a claim of defamation. On the Internet there is no vandalism and, with respect to defamation, the risk of detection and social sanction is close to zero so long as the author chooses a site where anonymity is secure.

The bathroom wall is a noteworthy precursor of the Internet, not only because such graffiti has surely decreased since the Internet came to life, but also because vandalism and defamation claims threatened those graffitists who could not be certain that they would remain unidentified. The same is true for graffitists in more public places, where their work can have great political and artistic significance. Anonymity is important in order to avoid prosecution, and in some cases to escape unpleasant social sanctions. In any event, the Internet has emerged as the site of choice for many users. Whether the goal is to injure with offensive speech or to spread socially useful information about another, the Internet is more appealing than the table or the wall; anonymity is more assured, it has the potential to reach a larger audience, it keeps messages alive, and it is searchable by interested parties who can then reproduce what they like for further publication. Cutting in the other direction is the fact that the Internet does not always offer a site densely visited by a target audience. This remaining advantage of conventional graffiti is, however, certain to disappear, as the Internet's capacity to host new sites, specializing in audiences with a variety of common interests, is limitless.

The Internet, the bathroom wall, and most other media have in common the ability of an intermediary[2] to comply with a request that an offensive comment be deleted. The intermediary may adopt one of several practices. It may choose to avoid litigation or injury by practicing a notice-and-takedown policy, so that complaints bring about a kind of (automatic but slightly delayed) censorship. The intermediary may also monitor the site and pre-emptively remove communications it fears give offense. Alternatively, the intermediary may seek to distance itself from the activities that take place on its site, holding itself out as something of a utility provider rather than responsible manager. Even if the intermediary is otherwise proactive, it may be disinclined to erase when to do so leaves it vulnerable to claims of censorship. Facebook, for example, declines to play the role of arbiter of that which shall be deemed offensive. Similarly, a site like Ripoffreport.com encourages consumers to "get justice!" and share information by posting their complaints about merchants; this intermediary's business model makes no allowance for monitoring or removing false information. Noncommercial sites may also be passively managed, albeit for different reasons. In the case of a university-run blog, for example, interventions run the risk of bad publicity because the industry is one in which free speech is especially exalted.

The juvenilist prefers an inactive intermediary, much as the graffitist prefers a landlord without paint or cleanser. But even if the intermediary is on guard, the author is worse off than the traditional graffitist only in the sense that cleansing can be quick and cheap. The owner of a marked-up wall might delete graffiti in order to discourage yet more graffiti, to avoid offending customers, or to avoid legal claims by those who are slurred. The intermediary might fear liability because there is, in principle, legal liability for the failure of a tavern keeper, for example, to remove defamatory graffiti when it can be viewed by others and in this way further "published."[3]

The Internet is the natural and well-evolved successor to the bathroom wall. Some offending authors must value the tactile experience, spontaneity, or even risk of the restroom, but most modern juvenilists and commercial warriors can be counted on to prefer the rhythm of the keyboard, the reduced probability of detection, and the enhanced, searching, and often easily targeted audience. This preference for the Internet is not entirely the product of legal rules, but it is apparent that laws, or the absence of effective laws, pertaining to vandalism, defamation, and owner liability contribute to the emergence of the Internet as the medium of choice for a variety of communications we might rather do without.

It would be possible to argue that the bathroom wall deserves less legal oversight than the Internet, inasmuch as the wall is more easily cleansed and its small audience implies less harm. But the law favors the Internet, and so the questions then are whether it similarly favors some other media, and whether the case for regulation is weaker or stronger elsewhere. There is no need for a full catalogue here, but a few items of comparison are revealing. Moreover, an exhaustive comparison is unlikely to convince all readers that the Internet is particularly favored, because there are factors that militate for and against regulation in each medium, as well as in others not included here.

Consider, next, radio and television, where the case for regulation—whether in the form of content controls or equal access rules—derives from the scarcity of airwaves and, for some advocates, the presence of children in the audience. The case for lighter regulation (than on the Internet) might come from the greater need for advertiser or subscriber support in these broadcast media, inasmuch as both groups would exercise influence over content. In any event, radio and television stations could broadcast more anonymous messages, but they do not, and the threat of legal intervention plays some role in this state of affairs.[4]

Newspapers have also come to eschew anonymity. They occasionally withhold the names of letter writers, especially where there is a plausible case for whistle-blower protection and, of course, reporters carefully protect the identities of some sources. But, again, these are cases where the danger of anonymity is reduced by the presence of an active intermediary, subject to suit. The reporter's and editor's reputation allows for the anonymity of a source; in contrast, even the intermediary may be anonymous on Internet gossip sites. When the intermediary is passive, as the owner of the bathroom wall might be, there is no vouching for the anonymous source. In print and other media, the legal system might well decide to favor political speech by rarely asking for the identity of a confidential source, but it is clear that the anonymous juvenilist, or for that matter the complaining consumer, does not find a comfortable home in print media, and especially not in any with wide circulation. Note that bookstores, newsstand owners, and logging companies go unregulated when it comes to offensive communications they make possible, but the law's selection of a (different) least cost-avoider intermediary is nothing new.[5]

In each of these comparisons, the low cost of entry on the Internet is striking. In the case of newspapers and magazines, the cost of paper, publication, and distribution surely cause the intermediary to screen content. An Internet site might choose to incorporate all comments on a subject, perhaps because the cost of screening exceeds the implicit cost of losing audience members who do not want to wade through low-quality or offensive contributions. Except perhaps for the case of a very local newspaper, one that did not screen submissions for publication would not only lose readers' attention but also would need to absorb the cost of printing and distributing the unwanted communications. On the Internet, many readers might wish for less, but in the case of newspapers we worry that there are too few voices rather than too many, or at least we did so before the arrival of online "newspapers." Scarcity of this sort means that the intermediary can be counted on to eliminate juvenile speech, and this in turn means that there is less need for legal regulation. An argument for legal intervention is easiest to advance with the claim that in such an environment the government should be neutral, lest the scarcity empower the very government at which valuable, critical speech might be directed.

It is useful to include the soapbox in this sketch. There is something charming about free speech as practiced on that stage, especially when it is observed as a tourist and directed at governments and persons one hardly knows. In terms of comparison to the Internet and other media, there are social sanctions for offensive speech on the soapbox because the speaker is identifiable. In addition, the speaker normally addresses a small audience, and potential listeners cannot search for subjects of interest. Along all these dimensions, we would expect more regulation on the Internet than on the soapbox—and yet it is the soapbox orator who is removed if deemed to cause a disturbance or to be defamatory.[6]

It is plain that the Internet is an outlier, nearly free of regulation. Offending speakers find it easy to communicate anonymously and thus to avoid any direct defamation or other legal claims. A substantial number of hospitable Internet providers promise to protect Internet protocol, or IP, addresses and other threats to anonymity. Under the terms of the Communications Decency Act of 1996 "no provider or user of an interactive computer service shall be treated as the publisher or speaker of any information provided by another information content provider."[7] To the extent that the original reason for this immunity was to allow the new medium to flourish and experiment, it seems that a reasonable test period has now passed. The absence of effective legal regulation on the Internet has made it the preferred medium for juvenile communications, and perhaps for unfiltered communications more generally.

Targets of slurs are not the only ones injured by an unfettered medium like the Internet. Any medium with neither access cost nor legal intervention will generate a high noise-to-signal ratio and most communications will be of low value. Thus, a free wall for graffitists, without periodic cleansing, will be of low value to readers and juvenile authors alike, because the volume of junk will reduce the audience.

It is, therefore, unsurprising that sites like Amazon.com and Cnet.com work to delete juvenile and even superfluous contributions. The policy requires effort, some automated and some expensive, but it is necessary in order to keep a valuable, popular site alive, especially when the site is intended to provide a very particular kind of service.[8] If the Internet's first anonymity problem is represented by the costs imposed on Amy X, then its second anonymity problem is that Internet entrepreneurs with interactive sites are essentially obliged to spend resources in order to control the content of these sites, lest a high noise-to-signal ratio destroy the value of the medium to its users. The problem is ironic because one of the Internet's claims to singularity is the low barrier to entry for provider and user alike, and it is this very feature that makes juvenile communication so easy. The problem is that juvenile communications destroy the low-cost resource. Even if the entrepreneur-intermediary requires identifiability, and even if that greatly reduces the noise, the intermediary must police its own rules. In some settings law can help, as it does with trespass on property, for example. In other cases we may see sites emerge that predicate access on the provision of credit card numbers—not to guarantee purchases but rather to identify the participants.

I suspect that in the long run law will settle on some sort of intermediate identification regime in which IP addresses are made available to those who claim injury, and wish to sue or make demands of offenders, if these claimants can overcome some modest hurdle. Note, however, the perverse feature that these claimants risk further injury by drawing attention to themselves for bringing suit. Consider, once again, Ripoffreports, where a potential consumer can search for negative reports about businesses. Juvenile or otherwise false reports both harm the target and reduce the value of the site, but the Communications Decency Act probably protects the provider. It is interesting that on this site those who complain usually provide their given names and hometowns; some angry consumers provide complete personal information. It is possible that they do so in order to signal reliability, but also plausible that they do so in the hope of extracting appeasement from offending businesses. My intuition is that these consumers do not need anything like whistle-blower protection, so that anonymity, and the withholding of *their* IP addresses, is not an important feature of the information exchange.

When an intermediary does require speakers to identify themselves, or where it screens offensive comments, another provider can try to satisfy the demand for offense or anonymity by appealing to the same audience with a parallel site. JuicyCampus.com, a now-defunct website, was one such innovator. The site promoted "online anonymous free speech on college campuses," and it used anonymous servers to assure users that they would not be identified. The content was occasionally informative but very often malicious and salacious. JuicyCampus provided a venue that even better-targeted sites, namely university websites, declined to provide. Universities have their own websites, of course, and they limit access and control uses. A class discussion group may be anonymous or not, depending on which the teacher thinks will be more productive.[9] In the event of an offensive comment, the webmaster will delete the remark; if the author is identifiable, there will probably be a sanction. JuicyCampus operated outside any university's control but was organized and searchable by school name, as is its successor. In theory, these websites could support intellectual threads, unvarnished discussion of events at named universities, and frank advice for prospective students. In fact, they quickly evolve into mere collection points for juvenile gossip and worse. I like to think that JuicyCampus failed because it could not attract sufficient advertising revenue; advertisers hesitate to attach their names to filth, and too much noise reduces readership. JuicyCampus "improved" on the bathroom stall by accommodating longer messages and by enabling searches of its contents, but the bathroom stall serves another, mundane purpose, and its construction and maintenance are thus subsidized for reasons unrelated to its role in the communication of information. Other sites, and especially those arranged around subjects of common interest, like law school admissions or law firm gossip, are positively learned compared to JuicyCampus, and they may survive with modest advertising revenues, or simply as hobbies. Still, where there is no active censor, comments often sink to the lowest common denominator. A site might provide information about law firm salaries or college political groups but then also seek nominations for the "hottest associate" or the "most hypocritical libertarians." Few people are deeply offended by inclusion on such lists, but personal recognition is often one step removed from additional, ruder comments. Participants appear to self-select on these sites; in some settings a juvenile majority emerges, and the silent majority ignores the site or samples the minority's handiwork from a distance. In many more settings, the civil majority silences the crude minority, which then congregates on a very few sites.

I have emphasized that one cost of Internet anonymity is that a successful site must monitor and censor in order to inhibit what might become overwhelming noise. A complete bar on anonymity is costly both because of enforcement costs and because anonymous provocateurs may attract a valuable audience. Law could help with both by extending defamation law and by enforcing contracts. Requiring and enforcing identifiability would not, of course, reduce a provider's costs to zero. Even if a newspaper receives only signed letters, it would bore readers if it published all that it received. A plausible long-run equilibrium involves some mix of identifiability and central control. One compromise strategy for newspapers as well as the Internet is to permit some known participants to communicate at will, while others are funneled through a gatekeeper. In a newspaper this reflects the difference between a reporter's sources and letter writers. On the Internet, such a site would have more posts and fewer comments than we have become accustomed to observing. One elaborate version of this mix is found on Wikipedia. This ever-changing online encyclopedia thrives through a combination of informed posts, or entries, followed by numerous modifications, or comments, made by many readers, some of whom make a hobby, or even a life, of Wikipedia. The product reflects both the wisdom of crowds as well as the hard work of more skilled labor than a conventional encyclopedia can possibly employ—even in a virtual edition where it too could provide subscribers with ongoing updates and improvements. Wikipedia does attract vandals and ideologues, but their marks can be expunged by subsequent improvers, some of whom seem to take responsibility for selected topics. The good soldiers are remarkably vigilant. Apparently, juvenile or noisy posts are commonly excised on weekends, suggesting that much of the "central control" is accomplished by volunteers, numbering perhaps 75,000, who are otherwise occupied on workdays. But there is more than a dedicated workforce behind the site's success. Even when it was more hospitable to vandals or juveniles, Wikipedia flourished; it has improved by eliminating anonymity in ingenious fashion.

Any contribution or revision made to a Wikipedia entry is recorded on a separate, linked history page. This page details the substance of the revision, the date and time it is made, and some information about the contributor. Contributors to Wikipedia essentially agree to be identified on the history page by their IP addresses, and this identification discourages misbehavior. Any reader can, with some effort, locate the author of an offensive comment; there is no need to bring suit against an Internet forum provider who is disinclined to reveal the identity of its subscribers. Alternatively, a regular contributor can register with Wikipedia, and then be known by his or her chosen moniker, while only the central monitor, a Wikipedia insider, knows the user's true identity, or IP address. Wikipedia can take action if such a contributor's edits or contributions are unwanted; in some cases, Wikipedia will reveal a registrant's IP address. With these and other rules of participation (including rules against multiple personalities that might be used to develop false consensus)[10] Wikipedia has flourished, even though it must be a tempting target for juvenilists. And yet, this success is uninspiring because it is built on an expensive strategy with volunteers, dispute resolution mechanisms, and some central control.[11]

Anonymity can, of course, be privately and socially useful, and anonymous communications are sometimes encouraged by the intended audience. Thus, a manufacturer might encourage feedback by seeking anonymous reviews of its products, and politicians appreciate anonymous polls. A university's website is unlikely to accommodate negative information about a professor because that might discourage applicants or supportive alumni, but the same university is apt to encourage anonymous student evaluations of its faculty's teaching, and then permit or encourage fellow students to read these evaluations. Moreover, the university is probably the most efficient collector of these evaluations. It can solicit information from those who are registered for a course; it can set aside class time or even deny grades until evaluations are completed; and it can best exclude the noise that might be generated by "evaluations" submitted by those who did not really take the course in question.[12]

The great promise of anonymity is that important information or viewpoints might be chilled if authors know they will be identified. Only an uncensored site, open to anonymity, would report that "Amy X is a slut who gave me an STD." It might appear that we are confronted with a trade-off that is familiar in the free speech literature. Even if most communication of a certain kind is useless or offensive, the free speech advocate opposes regulation because it might chill or eliminate some valuable communications. In this case, regulation runs the risk of eliminating the remarks about sexually transmitted diseases—some of which might be true and therefore valuable.

This description is, however, insufficiently sensitive to the availability of alternatives. Altruists or angry victims who seek to communicate their knowledge can contact public health officials, or in some cases a university administrator, who would speak with the alleged agent of infection. At a minimum, an official would communicate the possibility of tort liability. The gossip approach may deter others from contact with the reported source of infection, while the local health official is inclined to focus on the disease and thus on the person providing the information as well as on persons said to have transmitted the infection. It is possible, but unlikely, that the first strategy is superior to the second from a social point of view, but that is something the local authority may have decided against. Lawmakers appear to have calculated that the goal of disease prevention is better served by a tool other than broad-gauge disclosure, or gossip.

Similarly, the consumer who posts on Ripoffreports has other options. In both cases, the Internet provides a low-cost method of spreading information and in both cases it can be seen, optimistically, as a check on lawmakers. It is difficult to see why anonymity should be more valuable for commerce than for disease. But even in the former instance, a responsible intermediary, with the capacity to disclose the IP address associated with what turns out to be a *false* report, would seem to improve the exchange of information.

There is no reason to think that anonymity ought to play the same role in different media, because each has unique characteristics. If one wants to argue for present law, which is to say for Internet forum provider immunity, then one points to the cost of monitoring by the provider, the difficulty of collecting revenues in order to offset this cost, and the ability of an unhappy audience to steer clear of a site.[13] But if one wants to argue for regulation, then one emphasizes the low cost to the juvenilist or speaker of falsehoods, the gravity of the injuries, the harms propagated under the current regime, the ease of giving up (at the very least) IP addresses in order to make direct lawsuits or social sanctions possible, and the ease of following a notice-and-takedown policy—a strategy that I return to below.[14] This last option is neither costless to the intermediary nor an unambiguous social benefit, but it is a useful reminder that while it is catchy to say that the Internet has an anonymity problem, the real problem is one of offensive or noisy information, and the challenge is to devise low-cost methods of improving the exchange of information.

Bargaining for Non-Anonymity or More

I have suggested that we ought to be less distracted by novelty and more concerned with using familiar legal rules to solve identifiable social problems. Defamation and other law might be applied to an Internet provider much as it is to a newspaper publisher or the owner of a graffiti-laden wall. The case for owner immunity, and certainly for Internet exceptionalism, is a weak one. Moreover, the striking thing about the Internet is the low cost of entry, and this characteristic can be used to argue for and against legal regulation. For this reason I have hinted, if only by the title of this essay, that near immunity for Internet forum providers might be maintained in return for law, or perhaps social practice, "requiring" Internet providers to do their best to reveal or make available the identity of speakers. Non-anonymity would surely reduce the problem of juvenile communications as well as that of vengeful rather than informative consumer (and other) reactions. If so, identifiability will raise the value of the medium to most users. There are alternatives to identifiability that might better level the playing field among media, and there are remedies that might suit providers or posters who have little capacity to monitor communications. But the immediate task is to make the case for some regulation of these Internet sites. My strategy is to resort to the well-known guidepost of a hypothetical bargain among participants, or all citizens. Such a mechanism, or metaphor, might be especially apt if we think of the Internet provider as a fairly passive entrepreneur.

Begin with juvenilism, and consider the community of all who are affected by the anonymity problem. The group includes juvenilists as well as those who are plausible targets of the various communications. Participants in a communal bargain or vote need not be certain of their future roles or preferences when they bargain for prices or rules. We might imagine 1,000 people, with most deriving some pleasure from gossip about acquaintances, and a subset enjoying gossip about persons they do not know. A minority of 200, say, gain some pleasure from inflicting emotional harm on others; and a very few persons so enjoy attention or pity that they gain utility when they are the object of derision. It might be fun for some to read, and for a few to write, that "Amy X is a slut," and even if they think this improbable, the communication may help them imagine it so. In this market, Amy X may be harmed. Some targets do not mind such communications, or they may believe that ignoring slurs is the surest way to decrease their cost. But if the target feels injured, she might pay for the taunters to cease, especially if repeated publication increases the sting. She might feel emotional pain or be anxious that the taunts will reduce her future social and economic prospects. If Amy X's loss exceeds the aggregate gains of her taunters, even if added to the small gains of the passive onlookers (minus the losses from other interested parties), then it is easy to see that there could be a bargain to forego taunts. But even if not, so long as the target's loss is significantly greater than any single taunter's or onlooker's gain, then the bargain will be the same, as many of the onlookers and taunters reason that they might themselves be targets in a subsequent round. At the time of the imagined bargain, before the identity of the target is known, there must be many more persons who prefer not to slur and be slurred than who like the opportunity to behave in juvenile fashion toward others.

The simple argument for legal intervention is that there is probably a market failure. Amy X cannot locate her anonymous or pseudonymous taunters in order to pay them to cease their activity; she certainly cannot locate them in advance, before any harm is done. Moreover, if the bargain could be arranged, there is the hazard that extortionists will taunt, or threaten to taunt, in order to extract payments. The obvious analogy is to physical assault. Every legal system makes it actionable for A to kick B. We do not say that, without legal intervention, an unhappy B could simply pay A to stop kicking. Again, the problem with relying on market transactions is that it would be easy to threaten B with a kick in order to extract payment. Legal systems choose the baseline of a kick-free existence because there are surely more people who dislike (and more money would be paid to prevent) being kicked than who would gain from kicking. If the liability or property rule were reversed, there would be threats—even by persons who gained no utility from kicking—and even something of a moral hazard as opportunistic players taunted and kicked simply to establish their reputations as persons requiring payment.

The market failure is not easily solved. A forum provider cannot simply offer a choice between a free-for-all and a taunt-free, sanitary environment because it must have a means of dealing with those who choose to offend the taunt-free rule. In a world without legal sanctions nothing stops people from taunting those who choose the sanitary site. We might interpret the behavior of some celebrities as an implicit endorsement of such a two-tier scheme for specialized publications and websites. Put differently, for some people the hypothetical bargain may plausibly produce a different outcome from the civility suggested here. A Hollywood celebrity might tolerate or welcome attention to such a degree as to prefer to pay for more attention rather than less, even if the attention is sometimes hostile on its face. PerezHilton.com is one such site, and tabloids, like the *National Enquirer,* are thus its competitors. The law of "public figures" implicitly recognizes this fact when it allows more criticism and comment regarding public, rather than private, persons.

Even private citizens are not safe on websites like AbovetheLaw.com, though they might be more protected in a legal regime that followed the hypothetical bargain model. When that website, a favorite of law firm associates and law students, asks "Who is the hottest associate at firm Z?" the responses might be appealing to many of those who are mentioned without their consent, both because they might have agreed (hypothetically, at least, and in advance) to participate in the game and because exposure to harshness is sometimes the price of flattery. Anonymity and the absence of a consent process may indeed generate utility for the subjects. If the cost of legal intervention, perhaps in the form of a ban on complete anonymity, is the decline of "hottest associate" contests, I doubt this will be a stain on the legal system or the social fabric. In other contexts, broad consent may reduce any such losses. Thus, a college may normally require identifiability on Internet sites it controls, but it may encourage anonymity where course evaluations are at issue—perhaps by asking all instructors to agree to the anonymous responses and posts.

I do not claim that a hypothetical bargain of the sort described here would necessarily produce an agreement to ban anonymity. Anonymity might elicit valuable communications, and certainly more passionate expressions of support for various positions. Moreover, as we have seen, identifiability and reliability can require an army of volunteers or other resources. It is plausible that some bargains or votes would result in an agreement to bar interactive communication, to require the registration of those who wish to communicate in a forum, or to deploy what amounts to a notice-and-takedown policy. Each of these comes with costs. A notice-and-takedown policy is probably the most expensive of these to execute, though less costly than ongoing censorship.[15] It does not help targets who will not quickly know they have been maligned. Nor can they be easily protected through an opt-out policy. Juvenile communications often identify their targets by given names, or description and location. A sensitive subject, Y, will thus find it difficult to arrange in advance for the absence of comments about Y.

Notice and takedown is more attractive in some settings than in others. If the Internet's anonymity problem includes commercial slurs on a site like Ripoffreports, then it is important to see that the notice-and-takedown alternative is problematic. Information on the site is of little value if a business can merely ask the intermediary to remove any complaint against it. It is of little value to users if the site asks them to balance complaints and compliments, if only because the compliments might be planted by the targeted business. And if the intermediary must evaluate the complaint in order to decide whether to maintain or remove it, then the high cost of intermediation is obvious and the apparent technological leap of the Internet largely lost.

Finally, the hypothetical bargain approach runs the danger of underestimating the taste for taunting, much as speed limits may underestimate the preference of some citizens for speed and danger. If so, it may be useful to contemplate a site in which these speedsters and taunters can congregate with like-minded peers. There are fraternities that can be thought of as implicitly coordinating around such a norm, and there is no reason to deny the possibility or health of a virtual community of this kind. But Amy X and other targets need not be taunted by this group, any more than they need to be kicked by someone, and it is hard to see how a bargain would lead to an equilibrium in which she would be willing to be slurred without personally knowing about it. Amy X's future social and economic prospects are diminished even by slurs of which she is unaware.

When Law Trumps Bargains

In many cases it is a small leap from hypothetical bargains to laws. Laws are produced by popular and legislative votes, or by the voters' agents, and will often reflect the same preferences, and intense preferences, that produce bargains. Still, there are plainly situations where constitutional rules trump the market or the majority will. Many constitutional protections, like those that discourage warrantless wiretapping or torture of citizens, probably do track majority sentiments, but others do not. In the case of communications and expression, the majority has much less patience for something like flag burning or a "F____ the Draft" logo than does the law.[16] It is unlikely that there would be a bargain for the current, constitutional result. It is noteworthy, however, that where law is tolerant of such unpopular speech, the speaker is remarkably identifiable. My claim here is that the bathroom wall and its successors will provide more useful communications if some policy, including one requiring the identification of authors or vetting by intermediaries, reduces noise—and juvenile offense—in the process. It is difficult to see why this majoritarian-supported policy need offend constitutional law if it, or a comparable convention, does not do so in other media.

One barrier to bringing the Internet into line with other media is that citizens who like high-quality speech, and who think they might get more of it with *more,* or at least some, regulation are dispersed and unlikely to form political pressure groups. Law often comes about, and indeed overreacts, because politicians or litigants respond to the appearance of a social problem. Cyber bullying may be a social problem that energizes politicians, perhaps in the direction of anti-anonymity, but there will also be interest groups that press for Internet exceptionalism, even as they do not argue for the deregulation of competing media. It is therefore not obvious that the problem of the virtual bathroom wall will be solved by law.

One easy step for law would be the repeal of Section 230 of the Communications Decency Act, so that an Internet provider would be like a newspaper publisher. It is easy to imagine a compromise in which the provider retains immunity by promising to enforce non-anonymity or, in some settings, a notice-and-takedown rule or a notice-and-response (by the target or other interested parties) convention.

It is interesting and unfortunate that well-developed Internet networking sites do not yet provide sophisticated speech and information exchanges. Facebook and other social-networking sites make it easy for J to find K's friends, but not for J and L to get together because they share an interest in humanitarian relief in Darfur. Even Ripoffreports is surprisingly unhelpful, though there are sites, like Angie's List, that share positive and negative recommendations of vendors. But on all these sites there is a great deal of noise; there is no incentive to file reports, or accurate reports; and many searches yield no information. One cannot use Facebook to find others who used a given auto repair shop. It is not yet about these communities of interest, perhaps because, with the current architecture, it would be overwhelming to deal with the hundreds or even thousands of interests we each have.

There is, of course, the prospect of change through private action rather than through legal regulation. Over time, I anticipate that more Internet entrepreneurs will limit participation or require identification. There will remain a few sites that remind us of JuicyCampus, occupying a niche like that in which we find porn shops in city centers, at the periphery of most social interaction. The effort law takes to limit their poison to consenting adults will rise and fall. "Respectable" sites will require identification (non-anonymity) and this will severely limit sites where people comment on a professor or classmate's anatomy or alleged promiscuity. There will be some loss of opportunities to flatter, criticize, and convey information. But inasmuch as this information would have been lost in the midst of much noise, most of us will not and should not mourn the loss.

CHAPTER 4

Objectification and Internet Misogyny

MARTHA C. NUSSBAUM

> Beati in regno coelesti videbunt poenas damnatorum, ut beatitudo illis magis complaceat.
>
> Blissful, in the kingdom of heaven, they will see the sufferings of the damned, so that their bliss should be more delightful to them.
>
> Thomas Aquinas, Summa Theologiae,
> quoted in Nietzsche, *Genealogy of Morals*[1]

Internet Objectification

Much of the damage done by the spread of gossip and slander on the Internet is damage to women. A significant proportion of the harmful material involves what feminists have called "objectification": treating women as objects for men's use and abuse. Getting clear about the concept of objectification is important as a prelude to seeing what is morally and legally problematic about some common forms of expression on Internet gossip sites.

Objectification has long been a cherished feminist concept, but it has not always been analyzed with the requisite clarity and complexity. I have argued that it is properly seen as a cluster concept, with no single set of necessary and sufficient conditions.[2] If, however, we want to understand what is wrong with objectification in the context of gender relations, we will do well to focus on the idea of (mere) instrumental use: the objectifier treats the objectified as a mere tool of his ends, not as an end in herself.

To objectify, further, always involves conferring on the object a spoiled, or stigmatized, identity, a compromised status. To objectify publicly is a variety of shame punishment. Pursuing that connection helps us to understand the specific type of objectification that occurs on Internet gossip sites.[3]

But what is really going on, when a woman is objectified, hence stigmatized, in an objectionable way? I argue that we can understand the malice underlying much male objectification of women on the Internet by pondering (a version of) Friedrich Nietzsche's analysis of *ressentiment* and the "slave revolt" in morality. People who feel themselves to be weak or inadequate vis à vis some other group of people seek to validate themselves by creating an entire world in which these people are no longer glorious, autonomous, or happy, a world in which they themselves enjoy complete power over those who formerly held power over them.

Beginning with the objectification of female celebrities and moving to the objectification of fellow law students, the essay studies the operation of ressentiment on the Internet, looking at how relatively powerless people gain enormous power over the lives of particular women by using the specific properties of the Internet: its ability to create a whole world in which an objectified version of the person replaces the real person; its ability to disseminate this spoiled identity widely and rapidly; and its ability to cause large-scale disruptions in the real world, as the abuse colors daily life and the spread of the hostile material through search engines such as Google affects job opportunities.

Finally, asking what sort of weakness or injury drives this massive outpouring of ressentiment, I turn to a psychological study of teenage boys in America that explains widespread aggression in terms of a pernicious overgrowth of shame about weakness and need, together with a diseased norm of masculinity that exalts total control and penalizes need and compassion.

Objectification: A Cluster Concept

The concept of objectification has been often used in feminist theory without clarification. In order to get clear about the harms involved in objectification we need to do more analysis.[4]

To objectify a person is to treat her as a thing, an object, although, being a person, she is not really a (mere) thing. So far so good. But there are many different ways in which a woman's human personhood may be denied, and objectification should therefore be viewed as a cluster concept, involving seven distinct ideas, seven ways to treat a person as a thing:

1. *Instrumentality:* the objectifier treats the object as a tool of his or her purposes.
2. *Denial of Autonomy:* the objectifier treats the object as lacking in autonomy and self-determination.

3. *Inertness:* the objectifier treats the object as lacking in agency, and perhaps also in activity.
4. *Fungibility:* the objectifier treats the object as interchangeable (a) with other objects of the same type, and/or (b) with objects of other types.
5. *Violability:* the objectifier treats the object as lacking in boundary integrity, as something that it is permissible to break up, smash, break into.
6. *Ownership:* the objectifier treats the object as something that is owned by another, can be bought or sold, etc.
7. *Denial of Subjectivity:* the objectifier treats the object as something whose experience and feelings (if any) need not be taken into account.

These different ways of objectifying a human being can be seen both in the context of sexual relations and in other contexts (slavery, labor relations, etc.). The seven are distinct notions, giving rise to different types of objectification, interrelated in a variety of complicated ways. We should think of the concept as involving a family of interweaving criteria, rather than as having a single set of necessary and sufficient conditions.

In the context of gender and sexuality, however, the key feature that makes objectification morally objectionable is instrumentality, the use of a woman as a mere means to the objectifier's ends. The treatment of a woman not as an end in herself but as a mere tool of the ends of others is the central target of feminist criticisms of objectification, and the idea of use as a mere means typically explains the presence of some of the other features, insofar as they are present in an objectionable form. Objectification is thus a notion at home in the world of Kantian ethics, whose key contrast—between treating humanity as an end and treating it as a mere means—it captures well.

Both Kant and Catharine MacKinnon are mistaken in suggesting that objectification, in the context of sexual relations, can be assessed on the basis of an isolated piece or episode of behavior.[5] A full moral assessment requires an understanding of context and relationship. In the context of an overall relationship of intimacy and reciprocity, it may be fine, or even great, to treat the person, at times, as a nonautonomous animal body. Kant suggests that focusing on a person as an animal body entails, in and of itself, a morally objectionable denial of humanity, which a relationship of trust and care can render relatively harm-free, but never morally appropriate. (Thus he thinks that what goes on in sex is always morally bad, although marriage can make it less harmful.) I argue that this view is wrong. The overall context of an instance of objectification may justify the conclusion that the behavior, though certainly involving objectification, is not morally objectionable, and it may even be wonderful, involving an embrace of the body that often eludes us in daily life.

In standard pornographic examples of objectification, however, the larger context (insofar as there is one) does not remove the moral worry in the way that a respectful and loving relationship would. Even if a pornographic film or novel has a thin story line, the woman is presented throughout as a mere thing who exists only as a tool of male desires, and who may be manipulated with impunity. Often this manipulation involves the deliberate infliction of pain.

In her new book *Sexual Solipsism*,[6] feminist philosopher Rae Langton proposes several additions to this analysis. In addition to my seven varieties of objectification, she proposes adding:

8. *Reduction to Body:* one treats it as identified with its body, or body parts.[7]
9. *Reduction to Appearance:* one treats it primarily in terms of how it looks, or how it appears to the senses.
10. *Silencing:* one treats it as silent, lacking the capacity to speak.[8]

These are valuable additions. Langton's Reduction to Body is a central feature of many of my examples. (Indeed, it is that very identification with body that I hold to be a potentially valuable part of sexual objectification in the context of respect and trust.) I failed to single it out as a separate category because I took it to be implicit in several of the others, such as Denial of Autonomy and Denial of Subjectivity, but Langton seems correct when she says that it deserves separate recognition. Reduction to Appearance is also an important one to focus on, suggested by several of the others on my list but surely not entailed by any of them. Both Reduction to Body and Reduction to Appearance turn out to be key aspects of Internet objectification, so it is important to recognize them explicitly. So often, high-achieving women are treated, on Internet gossip sites, as if they are no more than a photo, or a set of body parts. Finally, Silencing is surely linked closely to the categories of autonomy-denial and inertness, but again, it is a distinct idea, and an important one to add when we consider Internet harassment, since one of its most persistent effects is to prevent women from expressing feminist views or maintaining feminist websites.

Another suggestion of Langton's is also valuable, both in general and in the Internet context. She suggests that autonomy-denial has two species that need to be carefully distinguished.[9] One case is the failure to *ascribe* autonomy in the first place, as with a child or a domestic animal. A very different case is what she calls *autonomy-violation:* the objectifier forcibly removes, or curtails, the woman's autonomy. Autonomy-violation is pervasive in pornographic sexual objectification. Langton's distinction is implicit in some of my examples, but I do not give it the theoretical weight that it deserves. I would, however, qualify Langton's analysis in the following way: sometimes the sexual objectification of women involves simple *autonomy-denial*—as when a woman is infantilized, treated as a lower species, or is simply not accorded full adulthood. That sort of autonomy-denial figures in pornography, prominently including Internet pornography.

Nonetheless, as Langton says, the more common pornographic scenario involves autonomy-violation: the scenario represents the woman as an agent, attempting to control her own destiny, and the man removes that freedom; sexual pleasure is found in the ability to exert control over the woman's options, removing her ability to refuse consent, to depart from the situation, and so forth. This distinction is particularly important when we think about Internet defamation, for often what is resented is a woman's freedom, agency, and good name, and pleasure is taken in destroying these things—first in fantasy, and then, given the Internet's power to affect job opportunities, in reality. The objectifier puts the objectified person in a position of helplessness. Not knowing where the abuse is coming from or how to stop it, but affected by it pervasively in her daily activities, she loses agency and employment opportunities.

In the spirit of Langton's analysis, I think we should add a similar distinction in the area of subjectivity. Sometimes one may deny subjectivity by treating a person as a thing that has no inner world, a mere automaton. That happens at times in pornographic scenarios, and it happens ubiquitously in human treatment of nonhuman animals. There is also, however, *subjectivity-violation*, in which pleasure is taken in invading and colonizing the person's inner world. Threatening and demeaning behavior often has the effect of taking over someone's thoughts, making the person unable to focus on work and friendship in the usual way. A great deal of the harm caused by pornographic Internet attacks on women involves subjectivity-violation.

Objectification and Shaming

To objectify is to treat as a mere thing, a tool of the purposes of the objectifier, an entity whose subjective feelings need not be taken into account, or whose feelings, like her autonomy, may be willfully violated. Given that the objectified is a human being, objectification confers a spoiled, or stigmatized, identity, and is thus a species of shaming.[10]

All societies inflict shame on relatively powerless groups, asking them to blush for what they are. Penalties based on the idea of shame are one common manifestation of this tendency: people are asked to wear a sign, or a symbol, identifying them as bearers of a stigmatized identity, or placed in an undignified position (i.e., in the stocks or pillory) for public viewing. Shame justice is justice by the mob: the dominant group are asked to take delight in the discomfort of the excluded and stigmatized.

Women, so often an underclass in many societies, are stigmatized in many ways, but gender-based objectification is one very prominent form of social shaming. Objectification says, "You claim to be a full human being, but you are much less than that. You are a mere thing, because I can use you that way. Your autonomy can be snatched away, your feelings ignored or violated." Despite its ubiquity, objectification is a very extreme form of shaming. Shaming always involves giving someone a stigmatized, spoiled identity. But the gap between human and thing is vast, so objectification involves an extreme form of spoiling: a statement that the person no longer counts in the universe of the human.

As both Langton and Andrea Dworkin have observed, women are often objectified, thereby spoiled, by being identified with their body parts ("Tits," "Cunt"). Brian Leiter has documented that AutoAdmit has nearly 300 threads with "cunt" in the subject line. The very fact of having those female parts is taken as sufficient to confer a spoiled identity, which can then become the object of pornographic ridicule. Typical examples of this sort occur all over Internet gossip sites, but perhaps it will suffice to focus on the site AutoAdmit. Here are several examples from the complaint filed by two female students at Yale Law School, which details the harassment they endured on that site:

> [Doe II] of YLS has huge fake titties.
> YLS 1L [DOE II] has huge fake titties and is universally hated.
> [DOE I] is a dumbass bitch and [DOE II] is a slut.

Just don't FUCK her, she has herpes.

I wish to rape [DOE I} and {DOE II] in the ass.

Such examples, utterly typical of what AutoAdmit purveys, show a real person being turned into a set of body parts, and diseased body parts at that.

Often, as we see in the last example—extremely common on the AutoAdmit site—the objectification takes the form of rape-fantasy, where pleasure is derived from violent autonomy-violation. "Jill" is written about as follows:

I want to brutally rape that Jill slut.

I'm 98% sure that she should be raped (if only in Internet Land).

She's a normal-sized girl that I'd bang violently.

Maybe you'd have to kill her afterwards [this in a thread titled, "Be honest, everyone here would FUCK THE SHIT out of Jill Feministe"].

A perceptive writer, Jill reflected about her abuse, later, on a feminist site. She notes that objectification moves in two directions: If the woman is agreed to be ugly, she is pilloried as an ugly set of body parts. If she is pretty, then she becomes a bimbo or a whore. "When you're held up to a subjective physical standard, to people who have no personal investment in you as a person, *you cannot win*."[11] (Notice that the reason you can't win is that you're already reduced to appearance: you've lost subjectivity, autonomy, and the moral status of being an end.)

In daily life, there are some barriers to a woman's conversion from "whole and usual" into a mere set of stigmatized organs. The woman is there in three dimensions, and she does things that may disrupt the objectifying fantasy. She might do something kind; or make a good argument; or show a capacity for empathetic understanding; or get mad and protest. At least sometimes, such signs of humanity have an impact on male objectifiers. The Internet is different. The whole world of gossip sites is a construct, and the woman is present only insofar as the male objectifier puts her there. She is even less real than the models in *Playboy*, airbrushed though they are: they at least have faces that rather resemble the faces of real women. The Internet world is a self-enclosed, self-nourishing world that is remarkably resistant to the reality outside. Indeed, it prides itself on being *its own reality*, by contrast to the merely fictitious world of friendship and human interaction. Of DOE I, a poster calling himself Spanky wrote, "Clearly she deserves to be raped so that her little fantasy world can be shattered by real life."

At the same time, the shaming inflicted by Internet objectification spills back into the real world, damaging women's employment prospects and their self-esteem. Autonomy-violation in the fantasy becomes autonomy-violation (and silencing) in reality. The AutoAdmit lawsuit carefully details the way in which threads on the site get onto Google, and impact a woman's job search. The impact on identity in daily life is at least as severe. "Jill" continues:

> I'm a fairly self-confident person. I don't usually feel like I'm being evaluated on my looks. . . . But for the last two months of school, I was absolutely neurotic, glaring at anyone I didn't know who made eye contact with me, and doing my best to not let myself check that stupid board to see what they were saying.

Notice here the importance of the idea of subjectivity-violation. Jill's subjectivity was not simply ignored. That would be bad enough. But the aim, and the "achievement," of the objectifiers was to take over her mind, make it impossible for her to think happy thoughts, to do her work in the normal way, to pursue friendships and sexual relationships with confidence. In that way, Internet abuse is very similar to stalking, or is, perhaps, a form of stalking.

Objectifying Famous Women

Why? What is going on when (some) men treat women they don't even know as bearers of a spoiled identity, as mere tools of their fantasy, violating their autonomy and hijacking their subjectivity?

Some objectification of women might be called merely traditional. Throughout human history, women have been treated as objects of possession and exchange, the way men treat a cow or a sports car. Men seem to be reared, in so many times and places, to think of women as sets of body parts, beautiful or ugly, and to speak of them as if they were not autonomous or feeling beings. So it's the man who manages to perceive a woman as a whole human being who requires explaining, in many cultures at least.

To say, "It's traditional," and "It's part of culture" is not to dispense with the need for an account. But perhaps we should begin with the more obviously malign cases, asking where their malice comes from, and later ask how deeply rooted in culture and tradition it is. So: what is the cruelty of AutoAdmit all about?

Objectification of women, both on the Internet and in other media, often focuses on women who are public figures: actresses, politicians, sports figures, and so on. Endless gossip surrounds their divorces, their sexual escapades, their drug use—and in the typical cases the treatment of these story lines involves all the classic features of objectification. The woman's story is used as a tool of fantasy, and her feelings are not taken into account. Both men and women objectify the famous, treating them as fantasy objects, and both men and women are objectified, but there is a recognizably distinct strand of the phenomenon that partakes of the general characteristics of male objectification of women, involving a pornographic delight in the misadventures of female celebrities.

When men objectify the models in *Playboy*, there is little obvious cruelty involved, and how could there be? These women don't have a story, they are just models, and any suffering or hurt they experience in life is concealed from view. Even a frown will not be shown, so skillfully airbrushed is the usual photograph. When, by contrast, a man objectifies Britney Spears, or Marilyn Monroe, the narrative of suffering and reversal is central to the pleasure that he experiences. The reader of objectifying star fiction cannot actually influence the life of the star. Somehow, though, the idea of the powerful being brought low is integral to the sexiness of these reports and the type of sexual fantasy that they evoke. Significantly, one sad event in a famous person's life that is never the occasion for objectifying eroticization is *loss of celebrity*. To many celebrities, this might be the worst loss of all, but if the world at large has become bored with someone, the porno world is too.

Now I turn to Nietzsche. Here I do not pretend to be doing Nietzsche scholarship. I want only to extract a set of ideas from *The Genealogy of Morals* and to use them to explain what underlies the objectification and shaming of famous women.

Ressentiment is a reactive emotion inspired by the feeling of weakness. A group feels itself weak and inadequate, in a world that values certain attributes that its members don't have. Another group of people in the society does have those attributes, and the goal of ressentiment is to bring those people down and get power over them. Unable to win on the terms of the strong (unable, say, to beat Homeric heroes in a contest of strength), the weak find another way to get power. They create a system of values that ranks them high and the powerful low. In the case of Nietzsche's Christians, they create moral values of altruism and self-denial that they are capable of exemplifying, and then use these values to denigrate the behavior of the heroes. So it's the hatred of the powerful that explains the creation of the new set of values.

On one common account, ressentiment is strategic: the weak want to get power for themselves and to punish the powerful. According to R. J. Wallace's perceptive reconstruction, however (and let's not worry whether it is really the right account of Nietzsche), there is something deeper going on: the weak need to affirm themselves, relieving the psychic distress that comes with subordination, by creating a virtual world, an expressive world, in which they hold sway.[12] (Wallace notes that the ascetic priests described by Nietzsche probably do take a purely strategic approach to the new values: without really believing them, they use them to get power over those who previously held power over them.)

The revenge of the powerless is merely imaginary, in the following sense: they do not really have physical or social power, they are still economically and socially oppressed. But in fantasy, they dominate the world. As Nietzsche graphically shows, the Christian world picture creates a universe in which the weak indeed inherit the earth, in the sense that Christian eschatology informs them that they will be rewarded in heaven, and will even be able to witness the penalties of the damned. Nietzsche makes much of this feature of the Christian world, suggesting that the fantasy of vindication in the afterlife is a source of psychic affirmation and pleasure in this one.

Now let us return to the objectification of famous women. And let us consider objectification not simply of the fan-mag sort, but the more aggressive and sordid pornographic objectifying that often takes place on the Internet when well-known people are discussed. (As I've noted, the fan-mag sort involves men as well as women, but the more pornographic variety is primarily directed at women by men.) Here we see something like a "slave revolt": the powerful are depicted as suffering, powerless, prone to disasters of all sorts (and yet somehow sexy and glamorous. Meanwhile, the unknown person who fantasizes about them can feel affirmed and empowered. In fantasy, he creates a world in which celebrities are no longer autonomous, or happy, or free, a world in which he enjoys power over those who once held power over him. It's not just their troubles he imagines, he imagines himself having sexual power over them.

This is a slave revolt of sorts: and yet it does not create new values. There's a veneer of that, in that fame is taken to be a source of disaster, obscurity of safety—but the gaze of the pornographer remains fixed on fame, not obscurity, and the things that celebrity brings with it—glamor, money, nice clothes, fancy cars—these things are not really repudiated. And the pornographic blogger still does not have them. So his fantasy of having power over those who in the real world have power over him is unstable, always subject to unmasking. It hasn't really remade the world.

Moreover, the pornographer doesn't really impinge on the celebrity's world, or not for long. He can blog to his heart's content, but it's very likely that Julia Roberts will never know of his fantasies and they will have no impact on her life. So that's another way the fantasy is vulnerable: it just doesn't work, it doesn't really do anything to the self-confidence of the powerful, the way that Nietzsche's slave revolt eventually, over time, did have an impact on the self-confidence of the former master types. Objectification is directed at power, but it succeeds only to the extent that the powerful are vulnerable.

The objectifier might do better with a minor celebrity, because someone who is only a little bit famous may take the trouble to read what is said about her, and to get upset by it. Some minor celebrities are addicted to Googling themselves, and fasten on any abuse and get obsessed with it. And if the minor celebrity is part of the same narrower world as the pornographer—a law firm, a university—the objectifier may be able to feel satisfaction at having the power to disrupt the well-being of people who in daily life have fame and autonomy and achievements that he does not have.

Here, then, we are moving closer to the slave revolt. Achievement, glamor, literary productivity, and other forms of worldly power are reconfigured as sources of vulnerability to abuse, and the obscure position of the objectifier is reconfigured as a position of immense power.

Note that this power of the obscure to disrupt the lives of the powerful has been immensely magnified, more or less created, by the Internet. Before the emergence of our Internet-suffused environment, if you didn't like some big shot in the university, or in some other profession touching on your life, you had the power to insult and objectify that person in personal fantasy, and perhaps to circulate that porno vision to a few friends, but you could not spread it very far, or get that person's attention. You would have to hesitate before publicizing your abuse, or mailing it to the person, because you would put yourself in a vulnerable position by so doing. Now, by contrast, your view of the target circulates all over the world, and such publicity often has a major impact on the life of the target. Meanwhile, you are protected by anonymity.

The Internet has this power because of its ability to circulate information rapidly, at little to no cost, to every corner of the globe, and also because of its own quite autonomous existence, a virtual world set over against the world of reality, and frequently impervious to protests from that other world. Search engines magnify that power. A pernicious statement on a website might have little or no effect; but if it becomes highly ranked on a Google search of the target's name, it assumes in the reader's mind an importance disproportionate to its relevance. Nietzsche's Christians achieved that kind of insulation from critique only by arduous efforts of conversion and political/military conquest. After spreading their vision of the afterlife around the world by conversion and bloodthirsty battle, they could enjoy their fantasy of viewing the punishments of the damned to their hearts' content. But that took centuries of work. By contrast, the Internet objectifier doesn't have to convert anyone or go to war against anyone: he has only to know how to get his vision of a person onto Google, and presto, it flies around the globe. Who needs the Crusades? With a little savvy he can create a world in which his target exists only as a thing, a spoiled identity, and he, the spoiler, has complete power.

Objectification of Fellow Students

Now we arrive at the case of AutoAdmit, and other cases like it. The women objectified on AutoAdmit are not famous at all. At most, they are locally known as attractive women, or good students, or whatever. The anonymous commentators objectify them, treating them as mere sets of body parts, mere appearances. This treatment shames them, giving them a spoiled identity. They are also constructed as violable, threatened with rape and other violence.[13]

But there's a difference between celebrity objects and these other targets: what the objectifier does can really change the woman's life in major ways. When the objectified is Julia Roberts, the porno world is smaller and weaker than the real world. When it is Professor X (some big shot in the world of scholarship, but relatively unknown outside it), the porno world is large enough, perhaps, to get the attention of Professor X, but still is not very large. When the target is DOE I, the porno world can define her in the eyes of the entire world, because there's no counterweight, no other way she exists in the eyes of the world at large. So, the analogue to Nietzsche's picture of Christian eschatology is far closer. Through the power of Internet connectivity, the objectifier can create an entire world in which DOE I exists as a mere thing, a cunt, a set of tits. And then he can watch with malicious delight as this construct damns DOE I in the eyes of employers, clients, and prospective friends and lovers. (As with all objectification, the assault presupposes that DOE I is not really just a set of tits, that she has feelings and autonomy to be violated.) Thus the objectifier violates both DOE I's autonomy and her subjectivity far more effectively than he ever would be able to violate the humanity of a celebrity. In effect he hijacks her agency more or less completely, by colonizing her mind, her social relationships, her access to employment.

Many real-world consequences follow. In law schools, women who are the targets of Internet objectification may stop participating in class. (One Harvard law student whom I won't name told me that she entirely stopped attending her discussion section as the result of anonymous Internet harassment, on the section blog, clearly from a member of the section.) In many other related ways, their relationships with faculty and peers may be affected. When they begin to look for work, employers may learn of the material circulated about them. Even if prospective employers are clear that they are victims and that the rumors are false, knowing the pornographic depictions may taint their view of these women, just as knowledge of a rape victim's identity often colors people's associations with her. DOE I and DOE II, good students at Yale, got no job offers.

Is this objectification motivated by ressentiment, and, if so, of what? In the case of the celebrity, it is easy enough to identify the targets of ressentiment: fame, money, glamor, sexiness, achievement. But what is it that makes DOE I and DOE II the objects of misogynistic hatred, and can it be analogized at all to the case of the celebrity? Well, what seems to set these men off is competitive achievement: much turns on fabricating lies about the students' LSAT scores, for example. These women are high achievers in a world of tremendous male anxiety, and they are attractive and independent as well. This may be enough to make anxious, highly competitive men want to blot them out, spoil their identities so that they will no longer be out there as part of the competition. Insecure about their own futures in law, they delight in the spectacle of pain inflicted on those uppity women who dare to compete with them for grades, jobs, and clerkships.

In effect, these men are restoring the patriarchal world before the advent of sex equality, the world in which women were just tools of male purposes. In the real world, women today are threats to male autonomy, job security, and pride (as newly freed slaves were to lower-class whites in the Reconstruction South). In the fantasy world of the Internet, there is no such threat, because men have total power over women's futures, their self-esteem, their relations with others. So in a deep sense there is something like "revaluation of values" going on here, far more, in fact, than in the celebrity case, only it is retrogressive: the objectifier restores the world of yesteryear, in which women had no right to be more than tits and cunt. And then he makes this revaluation real and effective in the real world, through the pervasive power of the Internet over multiple dimensions of human opportunity.

According to Wallace's Nietzsche, the gratification of the rebelling slaves is achieved in fantasy, albeit a fantasy so powerful that it can completely dominate a society's picture of human relations, as Christian eschatology did, thus indirectly influencing social relations in the real world. The Christian's pleasure is one of anticipation, as he foresees the time when the weak will gloat over the damnation of the strong.

In the case of AutoAdmit, the gratification is still subjective, as all gratification is, but it does not require much anticipation, since the deleterious effects on the prospects of DOE I and DOE II begin as soon as slanders are published. The Internet, moreover, blurs the distinction between fantasy and reality, in that the objectifier's fantasy is out there, a piece of every reader's reality, and it also shapes reality.

What is distinctive about the Internet is that it is its own world, and a world in which values can be remade, in something like the way in which Christian eschatology creates a world of value inversion. The person who was free, happy, and autonomous can be turned into a thing there and damned, silenced, violated for all the world and all time. Meanwhile, the objectifier, anonymous and hidden, becomes like the blissful in Christian heaven, safely shielded from accident or pain, as secure as in the womb, watching the penalties of the damned. As in the passage from Aquinas that Nietzsche quotes, his awareness of the torments of the damned make his own security from shaming more delightful to him.

What Lies Beneath

What lies behind the ressentiment of the Internet objectifier? At this point all diagnoses are speculative, but mine has some solid empirical work to back it up. In *Hiding from Humanity*, I argue that all human beings suffer, to some extent, from an emotion that I call *primitive shame,* a shame at the very fact of helplessness. From blissful completeness in the womb, human beings are born into a world that they do not control. The precocious cognitive maturity of the human infant, combined with its extreme physical helplessness—a combination unknown in any other species—leads to long periods during which a child can fasten on wanted objects but can do nothing to ensure their arrival. Growing awareness of this situation leads not only to fear (lest the objects not arrive) and anger (at those who withhold them), but also to a feeling of helplessness that contrasts painfully with the expectation of being attended to constantly, which all children form to some extent—what psychologists call "infantile omnipotence." The thought is, "I am the center of the world—and yet, here I am, cold, hungry, and wet." A painful emotion arises. Primitive shame, like all shame, is a pain at not having some desired trait or perfection. What makes it primitive shame is that the state inspiring pain is imperfect humanity itself, the ills and incompletenesses that are a part of our worldly condition, since we do not live in the womb.

As life goes on, primitive shame may be transformed in various ways. Children learn that they are part of a world of interdependent beings, and that they can help one another out. They also learn to fend for themselves, and to be less helpless. All of this diminishes shame. Nonetheless, to the extent that completeness and fullness are still craved, shame will remain on the scene, since no human being is ever in total control. When people become aware of mortality, something nobody fails to want to control and surmount, shame at lack of control increases.

So, all human beings feel shame at a very deep level in their personalities—some more, some less. And one very handy way of discharging primitive shame is to turn some other group of people into the shamed ones. The shaming of others creates safety for the shamer.[14]

A social fact that augments shame is the tendency of some societies to define the ideal adult as self-sufficient, independent, lacking in deep needs with respect to others. In many societies, such pictures are held out to young people—but far more often to males than to females. The idea of the "real man" as someone who is never weak, never dependent, always in control, is a very common feature of developmental patterns in countless societies, but certainly in ours, which so strongly valorizes the lone cowboy who can provide for himself without the help of any others. Women, by contrast, are more often taught that maturity includes interdependency with others.[15] Thus lack of control will be more alarming to someone who has bought into the male myth than someone reared on a different norm.

But of course the idea of total control is a myth, unmasked every day by life itself. So an undercurrent of shame runs through the psyche of any person who lives by that myth: I'm supposed to be the "real man," controlling everything, but I feel that I don't control my own world, in countless ways. Psychologists Dan Kindlon and Michael Thompson have spent years studying disturbed adolescent boys in the United States. They conclude that a "dominant image of masculinity that requires strength and stoicism" leads to the formation of a "culture of cruelty," in which the shame boys feel at not being totally in control is turned outward toward the humiliation of others.[16] "With every lesson in dominance, fear, and betrayal, a boy is tutored away from trust, empathy, and relationship."[17] This peer culture is reinforced by the use of shame as a motivator in sports, as players must strive to avoid humiliation.

Meanwhile, patterns of talk about emotions in the culture enhance the growth of shame and aggression, since adults, very much including mothers, typically assume that boys are not interested in talking about emotions, whereas girls are far more interested.[18] So boys don't learn a language to name and reflect on their own insecurities, and this makes it all the more likely that they will turn them outward in the form of aggression. Repeatedly, Kindlon and Thompson found that boys could not talk about their feelings, or imagine how their actions affected those of others.[19] Thus skills that might have helped boys come to terms with their own weakness, diminishing shame, remain uncultivated, and primitive shame, augmented by the culture, lurks, unaddressed.

This undercurrent of shame then leads to a vicious ratcheting process: whenever inner reality signals to the boy his own failure to exemplify the desired (but impossible) norm, the need to humiliate someone else becomes more acute. But this project of domination is itself fraught with anxiety; ultimately it increases shame rather than diminishing it.

At just the time when the "culture of cruelty" is reaching its height, boys are going through puberty and experiencing constant sexual arousal. The peer culture now tells them that kindness and empathy are "soft" feelings and that only domination is good. They now learn from other boys that sex is all about control, and that tenderness and softness are bad.[20] Boys are very anxious about sexual performance, and yet they cannot show fear or pain to other boys. What they can show is hostility and anger. Real intimacy, the psychologists note, requires "sensitivity, respect, and tenderness." And yet, just as they are becoming interested in girls, boys are subjected to a culture that stigmatizes these qualities as feminine, and teaches them that "power, dominance, and denial of sensitivity" are the good qualities.[21]

Meanwhile, boys masturbate frequently, and they find that experience satisfying in part because it is an experience that they can control. But the culture of cruelty shapes a boy's fantasies, building up "a library of sexual memories" in which he is in complete control over women who, in real life, may terrify him.[22] Given the way in which his culture values control, he soon learns to prefer the fantasy world, in which women are objects he can manipulate. He then seeks to replicate that fantasy world in reality by treating women as mere objects and attempting to dominate them. The ubiquitous presence of pornographic images reinforcing that way of treating women strengthens the habit of viewing women in this way.

In short, what Kindlon and Thompson find as a result of their detailed empirical study is very much what my analysis of "primitive shame" has suggested. All human beings feel anxiety and shame about lack of control, in various areas of life. Sexuality is one area where these anxieties are extremely prominent. But culture greatly influences how those anxieties develop and whether shame will be to some extent renounced in favor of compassion, or converted into aggressive objectifying behavior.

This is where the males of AutoAdmit are coming from. They fit perfectly into the Kindlon/Thompson analysis, and we can see how the Internet facilitates a young man's aggressive response to women, viewed as powerful, secure, and out of reach. In fantasy, he can dominate and punish them, remaining utterly secure himself. Shaming comes from shame, untutored and even augmented by a culture of maleness that teaches that any status short of total control is weak and shameful.

Law?

Does this analysis have any implications for law? First of all, it suggests the urgent importance of figuring out how to make it possible for plaintiffs like DOE I and DOE II to win. At present it is very difficult for them to do so, and this situation needs everyone's attention. Beyond this, my analysis suggests that the behavior of the anonymous AutoAdmit writers is best understood as a gender-based hate crime. That way of understanding what is happening may or may not lead to any concrete steps for law and policy:

much depends on one's view of the whole category of hate crime, and the justifiability of treating it as a separate category.

As Saul Levmore's essay argues, the anonymity of the AutoAdmit writers is a major source of their freedom to create for themselves a shame-free zone in which they can inflict shame on others: so my analysis suggests the importance of requiring identification as a condition of posting. Such requirements are already in force on many university sites, and it would be good if this became the norm of good practice everywhere. There will still be irresponsible outliers, but their outlier status would be plain, and both readers and employers would beware of the information they received there.

Removing anonymity goes to the heart of the "slave revolt": for the ability of the bloggers to create a new world in which they exercise power and the women are humiliated depends on their ability to insulate their Internet selves from responsibility in the real world, while ensuring real-world consequences for the woman. The world of AutoAdmit can accomplish the goals of ressentiment precisely because it is sealed at one end and not at the other, so to speak: the real watcher, securely masked, enjoys the real-world torment of the target woman that flows from her torment in cyberspace.

More generally, my analysis suggests that we should be much less deferential to this sort of anonymous speech in close-knit communities (such as law schools) than in the broader public sphere. Julia Roberts is unlikely to suffer serious harms from Internet abuse. The harms suffered by DOE I and DOE II are real and major. We need to prevent this unhealthy phenomenon from corrupting the climate of instruction and conversation in our university communities, though perhaps we need not be as vigilant about the public sphere more generally. Regulation must consider the size of the community, the status of the objectified victim, and the likelihood of serious damage, both to individuals and to the community.

The more general conclusion suggested by my analysis, however, is cultural rather than legal. The culture of shame/domination that leads to the world of AutoAdmit is not immutable. Changing it, however, requires not just reining in some pathological bad apples: it requires changing pervasive cultural patterns of thinking and talking about masculinity. Part of this change may be produced through more responsible images of masculinity in the media and the public culture.

Most of the work, however, can be implemented only on the individual level. As Kindlon and Thompson conclude:

It is the responsibility of people who raise boys to train them specifically to be good, empathic partners to girls and women. It can be done, by fathers who model respect for women in the family and in the wider world, by mothers who help sons understand a girl's point of view, and by anyone in a boy's life who helps him see his connectedness to others as a positive thing. What will not work is to ignore this need for guidance, leaving boys to their own devices, winking at their dominating and reckless behavior, and forcing girls and women to pay the price for this cultural and personal negligence.[23]

That's easy to say, hard to do—particularly in the midst of a culture that values aggression and domination and devalues empathy and connection. Can it be done one family at a time? It is difficult for parents to counteract the tremendous influence of the peer culture. A boy who is connected and loving at home soon enters the culture Kindlon and Thompson describe, and is very likely to learn, there, to feel shame about the "soft" and "feminine" values he has been exhibiting at home. Families sometimes prevail: not all male law students become AutoAdmit objectifiers. Universities and law schools can also play their part in shaping culture. Nonetheless, it is not enough to call the behavior exhibited on this and other sites pathological, or the work of isolated nuts. It is rooted in American culture itself, and in one form or another in most cultures of masculinity in the world.

Above all, however, what we really need is what Nietzsche, I am sure, would have hated most of all: a true "slave revolt," a "revaluation of values" that would put the "morality of pity" (i.e., a morality centrally based upon compassion for weakness and suffering) in place of the will to power as a key social aspiration. Or, even more radically, a revolution that would show that the need to dominate is a form of weakness, the ability to allow another person to be whole and real a sign of strength. *Pace* Nietzsche, this "slave revolt" would not be inspired by ressentiment. It would be an attempt to undo the work of ressentiment, and it would be inspired by compassion, respect for the dignity of each human individual, and a sense of human interdependence. (Mohandas Gandhi was one leader who successfully conducted such a "slave revolt" for a time, convincing his followers that respect and compassion are stronger and more manly than aggression. But then, of course, he was shot by someone who described himself as motivated by feelings of humiliated masculinity on behalf of all Indian males—who were being lured, as Nathuram Godse saw it, into an unmanly and shamefully nonaggressive style of life.)

The culture of gender-based objectification is tenacious, and the Internet has made it more difficult to combat. Many individual men are wonderful, but the culture of masculinity around the world, and perhaps especially in America, remains deeply diseased. Andrea Dworkin wrote in 1974: "[W]omen are objects, commodities, some deemed more expensive than others—but it is only by asserting one's humanness every time, in all situations, that one becomes someone as opposed to something. That, after all, is the core of our struggle."[24] As we consider Internet norms, we must, then, ask: How can we facilitate those assertions of humanness? And how can we ensure that the voices who make those assertions will not be silenced by pornographic hate?

PART II

Reputation

CHAPTER **5**

Believing False Rumors

CASS R. SUNSTEIN

With the rise of the Internet, false rumors are ubiquitous. Many of them involve famous people. For example, numerous Americans have believed that Barack Obama is a Muslim, that he was not born in the United States, and that he "pals around with terrorists." False rumors are pervasive about the allegedly terrible acts, beliefs, and motivations of public officials and about the allegedly scandalous private lives not only of those officials, but of many other people with a high public profile.

In the era of the Internet, it is easy to spread false rumors about almost anyone. A student, a professor, a banker, an employer, an insurance broker, a real estate agent—each of these is vulnerable to an allegation that can have a painful, damaging, or even devastating effect. If the allegation appears on the Internet, those who Google the relevant name will immediately learn about it. The allegation will help to define the person. The false rumor can involve organizations—the Central Intelligence Agency, General Motors, Bank of America, the Boy Scouts, the Catholic Church—as well as individuals. And because material on the Internet tends to have considerable longevity, and may even be permanent (for all practical purposes), a false rumor can have an enduring effect.

My goal here is to specify some of the mechanisms that lead to the acceptance of false rumors, even destructive and bizarre ones. When people believe false rumors, they are often perfectly rational in the sense that they are led, quite sensibly in light of their existing knowledge, to accept falsehoods. This problem is especially acute on the Internet. Rumors often arise and gain traction because they fit with, and support, the prior convictions of those who accept them.

As we shall see, false rumors end up spreading through two processes: social cascades and group polarization. People often rely on what other people believe, or seem to believe, and the informational signals given by others can ensure widespread belief in false rumors. The discussion has a straightforward implication for politics and law: the processes that underlie the "marketplace of ideas" sometimes work poorly because they ensure that many people will converge on falsehoods rather than truth. It is not at all clear what, if anything, the law should or can do about the matter, but it is reasonable to conclude that a "chilling effect" on the transmission of destructive falsehoods about human beings and their institutions can be highly desirable. Without such an effect the marketplace of ideas will predictably lead many people to accept damaging falsehoods about both individuals and institutions, sometimes to the detriment of democracy itself.

Rumors as Informational Cascades

To see how informational cascades work, imagine a deliberating group that is deciding whether some person or group has engaged in unfair or even outrageous conduct, warranting disapproval or some kind of punishment or reprisal.[1] Assume that the group members are announcing their views in sequence. From his own knowledge and experience, each member has at least a little private information about what that person or group has done. But each member also attends, reasonably enough, to the judgments of others. Andrews is the first to speak; perhaps he is a propagator of the rumor. Starting or spreading a rumor, he suggests that bad conduct has indeed occurred. Barnes now knows Andrews's judgment; it is clear that she too should certainly conclude that there was such conduct if she agrees independently with Andrews. But if her independent judgment is otherwise, she would—if she trusts Andrews no more and no less than she trusts herself—be indifferent about what to think or do, and she might simply flip a coin.

Now turn to a third person, Carlton. Suppose that both Andrews and Barnes have said that outrageous conduct has occurred, but that Carlton's own information, though not conclusive, suggests that they are wrong. In that event, Carlton might well ignore what he knows and follow Andrews and Barnes. It is likely, after all, that both Andrews and Barnes had reasons for their conclusion, and unless Carlton thinks that his own information is better than theirs, he should follow their lead. If he does, Carlton is in a cascade.

Now suppose that Carlton is speaking in response to what Andrews and Barnes did, not on the basis of his own information, and also that subsequent deliberators know what Andrews, Barnes, and Carlton said. On reasonable assumptions, they will do exactly what Carlton did: accept the view that bad or outrageous conduct has occurred regardless of their private information (which, we are supposing, is relevant but inconclusive). This will happen even if Andrews initially blundered. That initial blunder, in short, can start a process by which a number of people participate in creating serious mistakes. This sort of process happens on the Internet every day.

If this is what is happening, there are two major social problems. First, people will believe a falsehood, possibly a damaging one. They might well disapprove of a third party, or favor punishment or some kind of sanction against that person, even if the rumor is baseless. Second, those who are in the cascade do not disclose any information or doubts that they privately hold. In the example just given, the judgment of group members will not reflect the overall knowledge, or the aggregate knowledge, of those within the group—even if the information held by individual members, if actually revealed and aggregated, would produce a better and quite different conclusion. The reason for the problem is that individuals are following the lead of those who came before.

With respect to rumors, of course, people start with diverse levels of information. Most or many will lack any relevant information at all; they might simply follow the informational signals of their predecessors, including the propagators. Other people will have some relevant information, but not enough to overcome the signal given by the shared beliefs of many others, at least of those others are trusted. Still other people will have some relevant information, but are nonetheless motivated to accept or to reject the false rumor. When rumors spread, it is often through a process in which they are accepted by people with low thresholds for acceptance, and eventually through others as well, simply because most people think that so many people cannot be wrong. A tipping point can be reached in which large numbers of people accept a false rumor even though it is quite baseless.

Informational cascades often do occur in the real world. For a seemingly distant example, offering illumination on the mechanisms of rumor transmission, consider a study of music downloads. Matthew Salganik and his coauthors[2] created an artificial music market, with 14,341 participants who were visitors to a website popular with young people. The participants were given a list of previously unknown songs from unknown bands. They were asked to listen to a brief selection of any songs that interested them, to decide which songs (if any) to download, and to assign a rating to the songs they chose. About half of the participants were asked to make their decisions independently, based on the names of the bands and the songs and their own judgment about the quality of the music. The other half could see how many times each song had been downloaded by other participants. These participants were also randomly assigned to one or another of eight possible "worlds," with each evolving on its own; those in any particular world could see only the downloads in their own world. Two key questions were whether people would be affected by the choices of others—and whether different music would become popular in the different "worlds."

Informational cascades developed. In all eight worlds, individuals were far more likely to download songs that had been previously downloaded in significant numbers, and far less likely to download songs that had not been so popular. Most strikingly, the success of songs was quite unpredictable, and the songs that did well or poorly in the control group, where people did not see other people's judgments, could perform very differently in the "social influence worlds." In those worlds, most songs could become very popular or very unpopular, with much depending on the choices of the first downloaders. The identical song could be a hit or a failure, simply because other people, at the start, were seen to choose to download it or not. As Salganik and his coauthors put it: "In general, the 'best' songs never do very badly, and the 'worst' songs never do extremely well," but (and this is the remarkable point) "almost any other result is possible."[3]

We can easily see an analogue to the domain of rumor transmission. Alleged facts do spread from one "world" to another—and in different worlds, people will believe different "facts." Rumor propagators will have terrific success in some worlds but none at all in others. Quality, in terms of correspondence to the truth, might not matter a great deal. We can see in this light why some social groups will hold, quite tenaciously, to false rumors, while other groups will treat them as implausible or even ridiculous. The differential success of rumors provides a real-world analogue to the science fictional concept of "parallel worlds." Consider in this regard the existence of widely divergent group judgments about the origins and causes of AIDS—with some groups believing, falsely, that the first cases were observed in Africa as a result of sexual relations between human beings and monkeys, and with other groups believing, also falsely, that the virus was produced in government laboratories.[4] Consider also the existence of widely divergent views, including rumors, about the causes of the 9/11 attacks—views that attribute the attacks to many sources, including Israel and the United States.

The multiple views about AIDS and the attacks of 9/11 are products of social interactions and in particular of cascade effects. False rumors often spread as a result. When groups come to believe some alleged fact about the egregious misconduct of (say) the United States, or the foolishness or terrible misdeeds of a public or private figure, an informational cascade is often at work. Indeed, cascadelike processes are sufficient to explain divergences across groups—but as we shall see, divergent prior beliefs are important as well.

Rumors as Reputational Cascades

In a reputational cascade, people think that they know what is right, or what is likely to be right, but they nonetheless go along with the group or the crowd in order to maintain the good opinion of others. Suppose that Albert suggests that a certain political figure is corrupt and that Barbara concurs with Albert, not because she actually thinks that Albert is right, but because she does not wish to seem, to Albert, to be ignorant or indifferent to official corruption. (Albert may or may not be a propagator.) If Albert and Barbara say that the official is corrupt, Cynthia might not contradict them publicly and might even appear to share their judgment—not because she believes that judgment to be correct, but because she does not want to face their hostility or lose their good opinion.

It should be easy to see how this process might generate a cascade. Once Albert, Barbara, and Cynthia offer a united front on the issue, their friend David might be reluctant to contradict them even if he thinks that they are wrong. The apparently shared view of Albert, Barbara, and Cynthia carry information; that view might be right. But even if David is skeptical or has reason to believe that they are wrong, he might not want to take them on publicly. The problem, of course, is that the group will not hear what David knows. Reputational cascades often help to account for the spread of a false or disgusting rumor. Especially when people live in some kind of enclave, they may silence themselves in the face of an emerging judgment or opinion even if they believe it to be wrong. Often, people will be suspicious of a rumor, or believe that it is not true, but they will not contradict the judgment of the relevant group, largely in order to avoid social sanctions.

In the actual world of group decisions, people are of course uncertain whether publicly expressed statements are a product of independent knowledge, participation in an informational cascade, or reputational pressure.

Much of the time, listeners and observers often overstate the extent to which the actions of others are based on independent information rather than social pressures. False rumors spread and are sometimes quite robust as a result. And here too, of course, diverse thresholds matter a great deal. Jones may not silence himself, or agree with the relevant group, unless the reputational pressure is intense; Smith might more easily be led to go along with the crowd. But if most of the world consists of people like Smith, then Jones might eventually yield.

Rumors and Group Polarization

As we shall now see, deliberation among like-minded people often entrenches false rumors.[5] The explanations here overlap with those that account for social cascades, and here too we can understand why some groups will believe rumors that seem ludicrously implausible in others.

The Basic Finding

What happens when group members deliberate with one another? A standard answer is *group polarization:* Like-minded people typically end up in a more extreme position in line with their pre-deliberation tendencies.[6] In keeping with the subject at hand, let us focus on beliefs about facts, rather than values. If, for example, people tend to believe that the nation's leader is a criminal, or that some corporate executive is a scoundrel, their belief to this effect will be strengthened after they speak together. In the context of rumor transmission, the implication is simple: if group members begin with an antecedent commitment to a rumor, internal deliberations will strengthen that belief. The antecedent commitment might involve a specific claim, including a bit of gossip. Or it might involve a more general belief with which the rumor easily fits. The key point is that internal deliberations should entrench the rumor.

With respect to group polarization, the initial experiments involved risk-taking behavior. What happens when risk-inclined people talk with other people who are risk inclined? The answer is that they become still more risk inclined.[7] Consider, for example, the questions whether to take a new job, to invest in a foreign country, to escape from a prisoner-of-war camp, or to run for political office.[8] For many decisions, members of deliberating groups became significantly more disposed to take risks after a brief period of collective discussion. On the basis of such evidence, it became standard to believe that deliberation produced a systematic "risky shift." For a significant period, the major consequence of group discussion, it was thought, was to produce that risky shift—a thought that would bear on many parts of social life, because groups are often asked to decided whether to take a gamble or instead to take precautions.

But later studies drew this conclusion into serious question. On many of the same questions on which Americans displayed a risky shift, Taiwanese subjects showed a "cautious shift."[9] On most of the topics just listed, deliberation led citizens of Taiwan to become significantly less risk inclined than they were before they started to talk. Nor was the cautious shift limited to the Taiwanese. Among Americans, deliberation sometimes produced a cautious shift as well, as risk-averse people became more reluctant to take certain risks after they talked with one another.[10]

At first glance, it seemed hard to reconcile these competing findings, but the reconciliation turned out to be simple: *the pre-deliberation median is the best predictor of the direction of the shift.*[11] When group members are disposed toward risk taking, a risky shift is observed. Where members are disposed toward caution, a cautious shift is observed. It follows that the striking difference between American and Taiwanese subjects is not a product of any cultural difference in how people behave in groups. It results from a difference in the pre-deliberation medians of the Americans and the Taiwanese on the key questions.[12] Thus the risky shift and the cautious shift are both subsumed under the general rubric of group polarization.

In the behavioral laboratory, group polarization has been shown in a remarkably wide range of contexts, many bearing directly on transmission of rumors.[13] How good-looking are people in slides? Group deliberation produces more extreme judgments about that question: if individuals think that someone is good-looking, the group is likely to think that that person is devastatingly attractive.[14] (Movie stars undoubtedly benefit from this process.) Group polarization also occurs for obscure factual questions, such as how far Sodom (on the Dead Sea) is below sea level.[15] Even burglars show a shift in the cautious direction when they discuss prospective criminal endeavors.[16]

In the domains of rumor transmission, several studies are especially relevant (though they do not involve factual claims). After deliberation, groups of people turn out to be far more inclined to protest apparently unfair behavior than was their median member before discussion began.[17] Consider, for example, the appropriate response to three different events: police brutality against African Americans; an apparently unjustified war; and sex discrimination by a local city council. *In every one of these contexts, deliberation made group members far more likely to support aggressive protest action.* Group member moved, for example, from support for a peaceful march to support for a nonviolent demonstration, such as a sit-in at a police station or city hall. Interestingly, the size of the shift toward a more extreme response was correlated with the initial mean. When people initially supported a strong response, group discussion produced a greater shift in the direction of a support for a still stronger response. This finding is standard within the literature: the extent of the shift is associated with the strength of the average person's starting point.[18]

People often make individual judgments about fairness and unfairness, including about whether particular people have behaved unfairly; they also make those judgments in groups. What happens to our judgments about unfairness when we speak with one another? The answer should now be clear: when we are individually inclined to believe that unfairness has occurred, our discussion will intensify our beliefs and make us very angry.[19] The most relevant studies had a high degree of realism. People were asked to engage in certain tasks, designed to simulate activities that might actually be undertaken in a business setting—such as classifying budget items, scheduling meetings, and routing a phone message through the proper channels with assignment of the proper level of priority. Good performance could produce financial rewards. After completing the tasks, people were able to ask for their supervisors' judgment and to receive feedback from them. Some of the answers seemed rude and unfair, such as "I've decided not to read your message. The instructions say it's up to me . . . so don't bother sending me any other messages or explanations about your performance on this task," and "If you would have worked harder, then you'd have scored higher. I will not accept your message on this round!"

People were asked to rate their supervisors along various dimensions including fairness, politeness, bias, and good leadership. The ratings occurred in three periods. The first included individual ratings; the second included a group consensus judgment; and the third included individual ratings after group judgment. It turned out that group judgments were far more negative than the average of individual judgments.[20] In many cases, group members decided that the behavior was really very unfair, even though individuals believed that the behavior was only mildly unfair. Interestingly, the groups' conclusions were typically more extreme than were people's individual judgments after deliberation. But such judgments were nonetheless more negative, and thus more extreme, than pre-deliberation individual judgments.

This study does not exactly involve rumor transmission, but it bears directly on that subject. Often, people think that some person or institution has engaged in unfair or outrageous behavior, and when they speak to one another that belief intensifies. False and terrible rumors become entrenched as a result.[21] If people begin with a belief that person X might well have said or done Y, they will become more committed to that (false) belief as they speak with one another. And even if people begin without a clear belief about Y, it may well suffice if they start with some negative judgments about X. Once it is suggested that X said or did Y, the group's antipathy toward X may well be enough to ensure that group polarization entrenches the false rumor.

Why Polarization?

To understand how group polarization solidifies and spreads rumors, we need to ask why like-minded people go to extremes. There are three important reasons:

The exchange of information intensifies preexisting beliefs. The most important reason involves information.[22] People tend to respond to the arguments made by other people—and the pool of arguments, in any group with some predisposition in one direction, will inevitably be skewed in the direction of the original predisposition.

Suppose that you are in a group of people whose members tend to think that Israel is the real aggressor in the Mideast conflict, that eating beef is unhealthy, that some person did in fact engage in sexual misconduct, or that same-sex unions are a good idea. In such a group, you will hear many arguments to that effect, and considerable support for reports, including rumors, that support these tentative thoughts. Because of the initial distribution of views, you will hear relatively fewer opposing views. It is highly likely that you will have heard some, but not all, of the arguments that emerge from the discussion. After you have heard all of what is said, you will probably move further in the direction of being anti-Israel, opposed to eating beef, accepting the claim of sexual misconduct, and favoring civil unions—and you will probably be more inclined to accept supporting rumors. And even if you do not move—even if you are impervious to what others think--most group members will probably be affected.

Corroboration breeds confidence, and confidence breeds extremism.   Those who lack confidence and who are unsure what they should think tend to moderate their views.[23] Suppose that you are asked your view on some question on which you lack information—say, whether some rumor is true. You are likely to avoid an extreme position. It is for this reason that cautious people, not knowing what to do, are likely to choose the midpoint between the extremes.[24] But if other people seem to share their views, people are likely to become more confident that they are correct. As a result, they will probably move in a more extreme direction.

In a wide variety of experimental contexts, people's opinions have been shown to become more extreme simply because their initial view has been corroborated, and because they have been more confident after learning of the shared views of others.[25] Suppose that other people share your view that the United States is not to be trusted, that the attacks of 9/11 were staged, or that Iran poses a serious threat to the rest of the world. If so, your own view will be more deeply felt after you hear what they have to say.

What is especially noteworthy here is that this process—of increased confidence and increased extremism—is often occurring simultaneously for all participants. Suppose that a group of four people is inclined to distrust the intentions of the United States with respect to foreign aid. Seeing her tentative view confirmed by three others, each member is likely to feel vindicated, to hold her view more confidently, and to move in a more extreme direction. At the same time, the very same internal movements are also occurring in *other* people (from corroboration to more confidence, and from more confidence to more extremism). But those movements will not be highly visible to each participant. It will simply appear as if others "really" hold their views without hesitation. As a result, our little group might conclude, after a day's discussion, that the intentions of the United States, with respect to foreign aid, cannot be trusted at all.

We have a clue here about the immense importance of social networks, on the Internet and in ordinary life, in transmitting rumors and in creating movements of various sorts. Social networks can operate as polarization machines, because they help to confirm and thus amplify people's antecedent views.[26] Consider the fact that in one army camp, "the rumor that all men over thirty-five years of age were to be discharged traveled like lightning—but almost exclusively among men over that age."[27] A far more serious example is provided by Islamic terrorism, which is fueled by spontaneous social networks, in which like-minded people spread information and discuss grievances, with potentially violent results.[28] At certain stages, "the interactivity among a 'bunch of guys' acted as an echo chamber, which progressively radicalized them collectively to the point where they were ready to collectively join a terrorist organization. Now the same process is taking place online."[29] The major force here is not websites, which people read passively; it consists of listserves, blogs, and discussion forums, "which are crucial in the process of radicalization."[30] Of course many factors contribute to terrorist behavior, but there is little doubt that social networks, spreading false rumors, play a significant role.

These are examples from the political domain, where rumors run rampant; but there are many other illustrations. Why are some foods enjoyed, or rumored to be especially healthy, in some places, whereas the same foods are disliked, or rumored to be unhealthy, in other places? "Many Germans believe that drinking water after eating cherries is deadly; they also believe that putting ice in soft drinks is unhealthy. The English, however, rather enjoy a cold drink of water after some cherries; and Americans love icy refreshments."[31] A less innocuous example: In some nations, strong majorities believe that Arab terrorists were not responsible for the attacks of September 11, 2001. According the Pew Research Institute, 93 percent of Americans believe that Arab terrorists destroyed the World Trade Center, whereas only 11 percent of Kuwaitis believe that Arab terrorists destroyed the World Trade Center.[32] With respect to daily life, a great deal of what we believe, like, and dislike is influenced by the processes of information exchange that I am exploring here.

People's concern for their reputations can increase extremism.   A third explanation involves social comparison. That explanation begins with the claim that people want to be perceived favorably by other group members, and also to perceive themselves favorably. Sometimes our views are, to a greater or lesser extent, a function of how we want to present ourselves. Of course some people are more concerned with others than with their self-presentation. But once we hear what others believe, some of us will adjust our positions at least slightly in the direction of the dominant position, to hold onto our preserved self-presentation. We might contain our opposition;

we might voice somewhat more enthusiasm for the majority view than we really feel.

Some people might want to show, for example, that they are not cowardly or cautious, especially in an entrepreneurial group that disparages these characteristics and that favors boldness and risk taking. In business, people often want to seem to be risk takers. In such a group, people will frame their position so that they do not appear cowardly or cautious by comparison to other group members. And when they hear what other people think, they might find that they occupy a somewhat different position, in relation to the group, from what they hoped. They will shift accordingly.[33] This might be because they want others to see them in a certain way. Or it might be because they want to see themselves a certain way, and a shift is necessary so that they can see themselves in the most attractive light. The phenomenon occurs in many contexts, including acceptance and transmission of rumors.

The Chilling Effect Revisited

In discussions of possible restrictions on free speech, it is standard to speak of, and to deplore, the "chilling effect" that is created by the prospect of civil or criminal sanctions.[34] Libel law, for example, might chill speech about public figures and public issues, in a way that could damage democratic debate. And if there is a "marketplace of ideas," we should be especially concerned about the risk of a chilling effect, because it will undermine processes that will ultimately produce the truth.

Everyone should agree that a chilling effect can be exceedingly harmful to a system of free expression, and that it is important to devise methods to reduce that effect. But the discussion thus far raises doubts about these standard claims, which seem, in their most extreme forms, to be based on empirical blunders and an indefensible optimism about the actual operation of information markets.

There are two points here. First, the chilling effect may be desirable insofar as it reduces damaging and destructive falsehoods, including falsehoods about individuals, famous or not famous, and institutions, public or private. To be sure, some falsehoods are helpful for producing the truth. But many false rumors are not merely damaging but also entirely unhelpful to those who seek to know what is true. Second, the marketplace of ideas will not work well if social influences ensure that false rumors can spread and become entrenched. As we have seen, one consequence of cascade effects and group polarization is to make false rumors widely believed in relevant communities. Under certain conditions, it can be exceedingly difficult to dislodge those false rumors.

Claims about the risks associated with the chilling effect should note that any society needs not an absence of "chill," but an optimal level. To decide on the optimal level, it is necessary to have an understanding of the relationship between the marketplace of ideas and the emergence of truth. Such an understanding would require a great deal of empirical work, which I have not attempted to undertake here. But I hope that I have said enough to suggest that especially in the age of the Internet, the marketplace of ideas will often ensure widespread acceptance of falsehoods.

There are several puzzles here. The first involves the Condorcet Jury Theorem, which shows that under certain conditions, crowds can be extremely wise.[35] To summarize a complex story: If each member of a group is more likely than not to arrive at the right answer, the likelihood that the majority of the group will be right expands to 100 percent as the size of the group expands. We might conclude that in this light, small groups will believe false rumors, but large groups will be able to handle them, in the sense that they will be able to separate error from truth. Undoubtedly this is so under some conditions, and the Condorcet Jury Theorem helps to explain why. But without exploring all of the complexities here, we should notice a single point, which is that the optimistic result of the theorem follows *only if group members are more likely than not to be right.* Suppose, by contrast, that group members suffer from a systematic bias and are hence more likely than not to be wrong. If so, the logic of the theorem suggests a pessimistic result: as the group becomes larger, the likelihood that the majority will be wrong approaches 100 percent. In many contexts, the very mechanisms described here guarantee that group members be more likely than not to be wrong. For this reason, large groups can go astray and crowds will be foolish rather than wise, not in spite of the theorem but by its own logic.

Two of the most important empirical puzzles are these: To what extent do people believe false rumors on the Internet? To what extent are such rumors subject to correction? On a pessimistic view, many or most people follow a simple heuristic, to the effect that people generally do not say things unless they are true. If it is reported that some student or professor engaged in terrible misconduct, or that a candidate for public office is corrupt, many people may be likely to think that the report would not have been unless it had some basis. On this view, there is fire wherever there is smoke. And even if people do not think exactly that, the presence of the bad rumor can leave a residue of suspicion, a kind of negative effect that can ultimately affect beliefs and behavior.

On an optimistic view, there are two safeguards against widespread belief in false rumors, especially in the era of the Internet. The first is the sheer existence of numerous rumors, many of them false. With so much falsity, it might be thought, people will increasingly discount and distrust what they read and hear. Internet "scams" were more effective ten years ago than today; when you read that you have won the lottery, you are unlikely to believe it, even if you might have thought "maybe!" a decade before. Perhaps the culture will generally move toward greater skepticism, especially when the Internet ensures that propagators can easily reach a large audience.

The second safeguard is the greater ability to produce instant corrections. A political figure is able to say, immediately, that the false rumor is false, and to reach numerous people in doing so. Even a private person, lacking any kind of celebrity, may be able to do the same thing. Taken together, the two safeguards might provide a strong correction against belief in false rumors. In my view, this judgment is too optimistic, but it bears empirical testing.

Lives, Pieces of Lives, and the Truman Show (for Everyone)

For democratic discussion about actual and prospective public officials, existing evidence suggests that there is a genuine problem. The Internet is full of reports about what people (supposedly) did and said, and about what they (supposedly) believe. Sometimes those reports are false and are based on nothing at all, other than a desire to obtain attention or to promote or to defeat a cause. Sometimes those reports are false but based on a shred or a kernel of truth, but they produce a palpably incorrect impression, one that harms not only individual people but also institutions that might benefit from their participation.

There is a larger point in the background. People's lives consist of a number of statements and actions, and over a period of years it is nearly inevitable that a particular person will have said something, or done something, that might trigger concern or perhaps even opprobrium if it is broadcast to the world. One of the great risks in the era of bloggers and YouTube is that statements and actions are so closely monitored that any particular one, taken out of context, might seem representative of the whole, or a clue to something dark and bad.

To see the concern, imagine a world, not so very different from what seems to be emerging in our own, in which many lives are monitored and filmed, not by government but by technologies that permit them to be recorded. (This is a generalization of the 1998 movie, *The Truman Show*.) Of course recording would present serious risks to individual privacy.[36] But this is not my concern here; we could suppose that in this imaginable world, recording occurs only for events or statements that are in some sense public. The problem, in any variation in such a world, is that single incidents can obtain real salience. And if this is so, the processes that I have described can greatly magnify that salience. For public figures and members of public institutions, this is a serious problem. It is also a problem for self-government insofar as citizens obtain a false understanding of those people. Of course my topic is false rumors, not true but misleading ones. It is difficult to "chill" reports on particular events that provide a deceptive understanding; the law itself cannot and should not become involved here. But at least we can say that in terms of social norms there is an optimal level of chill on deception as well; and that it is exceedingly important to attempt to convey a social understanding that particular events and statements may badly mislead, even or especially when they become salient.

There is also a problem for ordinary people, who can be greatly injured by false rumors, and all the more easily by virtue of the Internet. Friends, employers, and even family members might well encounter those rumors, based perhaps on a misreading of a single statement or incident. That statement may well come to be taken as representative of some whole, if only because of the operation of human attention; recall the importance of focusing. A chilling effect, at least via social norms, can achieve a great deal of good. The more tractable issue, for purposes of both analysis and policy, involves falsehoods. As we have seen, they can be persistent, not in spite of the marketplace of ideas but because of it.

Of course nothing said here is sufficient to justify any reform of existing practices, even with respect to false rumors. As I have said, any chilling effect on falsehoods is likely to affect truths as well. What counts as a false rumor or true one is often greatly disputed, and we might not trust our institutions to tell the difference with sufficient reliability. Perhaps our norms and our practices will ensure that we discount, to an increasing extent, what we hear. But at the very least, we should be able to see that in the age of the

Internet there is no reason for easy confidence in the power of the market-place of ideas to produce truths, especially when we consider the all-too-comfortable relationship, much of the time, between prior convictions and acceptance of false statements.

Conclusion

False rumors are pervasive on the Internet, and otherwise sensible people believe them. Self-interested and altruistic propagators spread rumors about prominent people and institutions. Such rumors cast doubt on their subject's honesty, decency, fairness, patriotism, and sometimes even sanity; often they portray public figures as fundamentally corrupt. Those who are not in the public sphere are similarly vulnerable. In a matter of seconds, it is easy to portray almost anyone as some kind of wrongdoer, and in that sense to injure their reputation, if only because of the easy availability of information on the Internet. The Internet, then, has two important effects. It allows information to be provided to the world, in an instant, and it allows easy discovery, by anyone, of that information, also in an instant.

Rumor transmission frequently occurs as a result of cascade effects and group polarization. Indeed, rumors spread as a textbook example of an informational cascade: imperfectly or entirely uninformed people accept what they hear from others. Sometimes reputational cascades are involved as well, as people appear to accept rumors, not because they actually believe them but so as to curry favor or not to face opprobrium. Group polarization also plays a large role, as people strengthen their antecedent commitment to a rumor simply because of a process of internal deliberation. When employers come to believe something about an employee, or teachers about a student, or students about a teacher, or voters about a public official, group polarization is typically at work.

I have said little here about how to respond to the existing situation, either through social norms or through legal institutions. The risk of a chilling effect must be taken seriously. But it should be plain that the market-place of ideas will often fail to produce the truth; the very mechanisms explored here ensure that any marketplace will lead many people to accept damaging and destructive falsehoods. A clear conclusion is that some kind of chilling effect on false statements of fact is important—not only to protect people against negligence, cruelty, and unjustified damage to their reputations—but also to ensure the proper functioning of democracy itself.

CHAPTER 6

Reputation Regulation:
Disclosure and the Challenge of Clandestinely Commensurating Computing

FRANK PASQUALE

There are many reasons to worry about the unsubstantiated rumors, opinions, and evaluations now polluting cyberspace. Viral culture online has made literally true the old bromide, "A lie can be halfway 'round the world before the truth has got its boots on." Although the emancipatory potential of digital connectivity is clear, critical Internet studies have illuminated its role in reinforcing old structures of unfair disadvantage and unearned privilege. Regulation may be necessary to check these trends.

For years, search engines have tried to reassure us that diligent "vanity searching"—that is, entering one's own name as a search query, in order to see what comes up—is the key to good "online hygiene." If an objectionable result comes up about a person, she can litigate against its publisher, or try to "drown it out" with rival information designed to drive the unflattering material to less salient positions in search results. Companies like Reputation Defender offer such services, acting as twenty-first century "reverse private detectives" who specialize in concealing or obscuring damaging information.

The self-help approach always had many shortcomings. Defamation lawsuits are expensive and uncertain projects, especially in the United States. Litigation can backfire, increasing the salience of provocative material if the suit garners media attention. Even the best search engine optimizer cannot guarantee the success of an effort to "bury" unflattering results with other material. But these tactics at least offered some means of trying to "clear one's name" online by detecting, deterring, and occasionally obscuring slurs and innuendo viewable to all.

New search technology has now fatally compromised self-help strategies. As personalization advances, there is no single set of "search results" for a person's name. One searcher may see a collection of positive or neutral results about an individual; another might be presented with compromising material. Screeners within human resources or credit-approval departments may order specialized software that scours the Internet for the most troubling material about any applicant. It is unlikely that the applicants they evaluate will have access to similar software.

In the United States, expansive interpretations of the First Amendment undermine even modest proposals for regulating the results of search engines. However, promoting individuals' access to the Internet results obtained by those making important decisions about them would pass constitutional muster. It would also reduce the reputational "unknown unknowns" that can wreak havoc on careers, credit, and educational opportunities. To the extent that key decision makers know more about us, we need to know exactly what data they have and how they are using it. As David Brin predicted in *The Transparent Society,* further disclosure from corporate entities needs to accompany the scrutiny we all increasingly suffer as individuals.[1]

Reputational systems can never be rendered completely just, but legislators can take two steps toward fairness. The first is relatively straightforward: to ensure that key decision makers reveal the full range of online sources they consult as they approve or deny applications for credit, insurance, employment, and college and graduate school admissions. Such disclosure will at least serve to warn applicants of the dynamic digital dossier they are accumulating in cyberspace. Effective disclosure requirements need to cover more than the users of reputational information—they should also apply to some aggregators as well. Just as banks have moved from consideration of a long-form credit report to use of a single commensurating credit score, employers and educators in an age of reputation regulation may turn to intermediaries that combine extant indicators of reputation into a single scoring of a person. Since such scoring can be characterized as a trade secret, it may be even less accountable than the sorts of rumors and innuendo discussed above. Any proposed legislation will need to address the use of such reputation scores, lest black-box evaluations defeat its broader purposes of accountability and transparency.

Internet-Driven Decision Making

In developed countries, having an online presence is a near inevitability for all but the most marginalized. Classes routinely complete projects online, and profiles on social-networking sites are becoming not only a social but a professional necessity. An individual need not try to create a web presence for herself—detractors or admirers can instantly catapult her into micro-celebrity with or without her permission. Blogging also creates both professional opportunities and dangers, as Heather B. Armstrong, the author of the blog "Dooce," learned when she was fired by her employer for her online commentaries. She ultimately had the last laugh: "getting Dooced" became a slang term for being fired for blogging, and she was able to support herself from advertising as the site became more popular. But many others with online presences may never discover the adverse impact of the "digital person" they appear to be online.[2]

Search engines and social networks offer a tempting trove of data for decision makers. In the college admissions context, "a recent study by the University of Massachusetts-Dartmouth found that 25 percent of college admissions offices admit to using search engines such as Google, Yahoo, and MSN to research potential students and that 20 percent look for the same information on social networking sites such as Facebook and MySpace."[3] Employment lawyers routinely offer guidelines to employers who plan to Google job applicants.[4] There is evidence that "as many as 50% of employers and 77% of job recruiters concerned about alcohol/drug abuse, violence, and similar problems check out potential employees on the Web."[5] Sources for online scrutiny range from Google, Facebook, eBay, and Yahoo to PeopleFinders .com, Local.Live.com, Zillow.com (real estate purchase and sale data), Feed ster.com, Technorati.com (to search for blogs), and Opensecrets.org and Fundrace.org (to search for campaign donations).

Legal efforts to ensure the fairness and accuracy of such reputation-affecting information have not caught up to technological advances in producing it. For example, if a human resources department has "personalized" its results to ensure that the most damaging information available about a person (from its perspective) comes up first, that applicant has no right to learn what information the office considered as it made its negative decision. The applicant would have to avail himself of the same personalizing software to be fully aware of all the negative information such a personalized search was generating. Yet trade secrecy and contracts could easily prevent him from ever accessing an exact replica of the programs used by the educators, employers, landlords, bankers, and others making vital decisions about his future. Even as health reform legislation makes it harder for insurers to discriminate against individuals on the basis of health status, employers or other entities may start to consult personal health data on sites including "Patients Like Me" if users fail to adequately secure their information.[6] Online openness can lead to permanent records of one's weight, health status, and mental health issues.

In popular books like Ian Ayres's *Super Crunchers* and Stephen Baker's *The Numerati,* legal scholars and journalists have celebrated data-driven decision making as a cornerstone of future advances in productivity.[7] However, the individual who is an *object* of such "super-crunching" may fear that a crucial decision about her is being made on the basis of a misunderstanding—an unfair reduction of a complex person to one trait, fact, or record.

In *The Politics of Recognition,* Charles Taylor explores the claims of individuals who felt that they were treated unfairly—or, worse, degraded and subordinated—on account of their ethnic identity.[8] Taylor advanced discussion of multiculturalism by articulating the harm of *misrecognition*—of being understood by others in an untrue or insultingly unflattering light. For example, women are routinely treated unfairly (and even brutally) solely on the basis of gender-based stereotypes.[9] Those dogged by digital scarlet letters may find whole new modes of discrimination blocking their professional or personal advance.

Of course, employers, colleges, and banks have a right to reject or approve applications as they see fit. But while it is one thing to be judged on an identified fault, it is a different experience altogether to to suffer a negative judgment for an unknown reason. While such a problem might seem unlikely now, personalized search technology makes it increasingly possible in the future. As any individual uses a search engine, he gradually trains it to prioritize certain types of results and de-prioritize others.[10] This translation of behavior into a "database of intentions" helps searchers a great deal—but can create uncertainty and anxiety once one is the object searched.[11] While the investigative consumer reports (ICRs) generated by credit-reporting agencies (CRAs) are subject to several strictures, personalized searches are not regulated in the United States.[12] The regulatory framework surrounding extant background checks may unfairly induce the use of informal, digital methods that increase the chance of mis-recognition and reductionism. It is time to develop a consistent regulatory approach for credit bureaus and other sources of reputational information. Antidiscrimination norms may well lead us from legislating against aggregate stereotyping to creating opportunities for individuals to correct misinformation.

Background on the Fair Credit Reporting Act

Much like today's Internet, the files of pre-Fair Credit Reporting Act (FCRA) credit bureaus were often contaminated with irrelevant and inaccurate information, or innuendo. Their dossiers included judgments laced with prejudice; for example, "in 1972, a man in San Francisco discovered that a consumer report about him for life insurance policy included the comment that he used 'his hands in an effeminate manner, also talks in an effeminate manner.'"[13] Senator William Proxmire translated public concern about "erroneous and selective credit reporting" into hearings about credit industry practices and eventual passage of the FCRA.[14]

Congress passed the FCRA in 1970 to protect consumers and regulate the consumer credit-reporting industry. The Congressional findings associated with the act describe the sorry state of the industry as it existed before the passage of FCRA.[15] Congress intended the law "to require that consumer-reporting agencies adopt reasonable procedures . . . for [compiling] consumer credit, personnel, insurance, and other information in a manner which is fair and equitable to the consumer, with regard to the confidentiality, accuracy, relevancy, and proper utilization of such information."[16]

The act regulates the preparation of consumer credit reports by "credit-reporting agencies," as well as the disclosure of those reports, and procedures associated with the maintenance of consumer credit information.[17] When the act applies, it establishes the permissible uses for which an agency may release a report or disclose information, such as by consent of the consumer or for insurance and credit applications. The FCRA also requires that agencies make reasonable efforts to verify information, including the identities of consumers, to increase accuracy.

CRAs must remove information from a report after a certain period of time to reduce the likelihood of reporting obsolete information. If incorrect or inaccurate information is reported, a consumer has the right to dispute the record, at which point the agency must reasonably investigate at no cost to the consumer, and must delete inaccurate data. In addition, consumers are supposed to benefit from mandatory disclosure after an adverse action is taken against them based on a credit report, which gives them the opportunity to dispute inaccuracies under the FCRA. When an agency fails to comply, the FCRA provides a cause of action for civil liability.[18]

Scholars have addressed the policy behind the "second chances" that FCRA mandates are meant to ensure. While "practical obscurity" used to occlude transgressions over time, the CRAs' data storage technology necessitated a legal requirement to restore the old balance between obscurity and publicity. Updating its mandates for the digital age, Jonathan Zittrain has proposed a form of "reputational bankruptcy," giving individuals the ability to block out some features of their online identity.[19] Viktor Mayer-Schonberger's book *Delete: The Virtues of Forgetting in the Digital Age* takes up the difficult task of specifying technical standards for this type of monitoring.[20] Each of these proposals fits into the framework of Danielle Citron's model of "technological due process"—ensuring that the de facto adjudications and rule makings made by software programs live up to some standards of reviewability and revisability.[21]

To complement proposals for "editing by deletion," I have proposed an "annotation remedy" designed to give a more complete picture of persons who object to certain hyperlinks in search results.[22] Such a remedy would permit individuals to add an asterisk to the offending hyperlink, directing web users to their own comment on the objectionable result. Google has recently adopted an "online profiles" program that is one small step toward such annotation rights.[23] My proposal is inspired by Helen Nissenbaum's characterization of privacy as "contextual integrity"—a social condition affording the individual more chances to give a full and complete picture of oneself in a world increasingly driven by scores, snapshots, and sound bites.[24]

Can such ideas be incorporated into a regime like the FCRA? At first glance, the FCRA's focus on the mundane transactional details of credit and debt management has little to offer in the way of solutions to online reputation problems generally. But the very regulatory infrastructure that imposes some minimum standards on credit reports may unfairly elevate the salience of online reputation generators, which can report more provocative (and less vetted) information and rumors. As search engines and other online ratings and rankings entities grow in prominence, some level playing field needs to develop to take into account their roles as data collectors and arrangers. Finland has prevented employers from using Google results (among other unauthorized information sources) in evaluating potential applicants.[25] In this essay, I propose a less draconian solution: requiring important decision makers to reveal the online sources they use in order to evaluate applicants, and revealing the particular information found out about an applicant to that applicant after any decision is made.

A Fair Reputation Reporting Act?

The FCRA is targeted at credit bureaus and the reports they generate. Now that search engines permit anyone to compile a digital dossier on anyone else, can such distributed activity be effectively regulated? Probably not—but at least some elementary steps toward the disclosure of such materials by critical decision makers can curb the most Kafkaesque features of the new reputation systems.

The types of unfairness created by undisclosed reputation dossiers are traditional concerns of three bodies of law: antidiscrimination law, employment law, and fair information practices.[26] None of these laws aspires to cover all human endeavors, and a Fair Reputation Reporting Act would need to be focused, too.[27] Critical decision makers—those with the power to grant or deny applications for employment, credit, insurance, housing, and education—are a logical starting point for such a law. As these decision makers take into account new sources of aggregated information, it would be deeply unfair for applicants not to have a chance to review the digital dossier compiled about them.

Business interests are likely to object to the obligations generated by such a review requirement. However, the same technology that makes so much information available presently can ease the transition to dedicated documentation. As storage costs decline and cloud computing becomes ubiquitous, a decision maker can use software to default to recording the online "leads" pursued as she investigates an applicant. Anyone who has seen a search engine's "web history" knows how revealing and meticulous that documentation can be.

The exact scope of the requirements will need to be worked out by an administrative agency—perhaps the Federal Trade Commission, or perhaps a true privacy regulator to be created pursuant to the proposed act. Regulators will not need to reinvent the wheel. Administrative law has long addressed the record-keeping requirements of government agencies, carefully separating the types of searches for information that constitute forbidden "ex parte contacts" from the run-of-the-mill research no one expects to be recorded.

Though this essay is too brief to flesh out the administrative details of disclosure provisions in a Fair Reputation Reporting Act, it should address three key objections to it. First, while administrative law principles of disclosing the basis of a decision are accepted for government actors, why should the private actors targeted by such legislation also be required to be open about what they are reviewing? Second, should word of mouth or personal recommendations be subject to the same level of review? Third, would the new transparency render reputation reporting as overly positive because individuals will contest negative information, but have no incentive to correct inaccurate positive information?

The first objection merits a layered response. Issuers of credit and insurers are pervasively regulated. As the financial crisis has demonstrated, these entities rely on government as their "ultimate risk manager."[28] After the failure of financial industry deregulation, an ever-closer intertwining of state and the FIRE (finance, insurance, and real estate) industries is a hallmark of the Obama administration.[29] "Coming clean" on the bases of their decisions is a small price to pay for the degree of government subvention they are now receiving.

The case of employers and educators is slightly more complicated. These decision makers are subject to many antidiscrimination laws, and the fair data practices discussed above might better be incorporated into extant regulation on those grounds rather than being a free-standing privacy law. Given the extraordinary targeting of women documented by Danielle Citron and Martha Nussbaum in this volume, there is already a serious civil rights case to be made against indiscriminate reliance on Internet sources.

Citron's documentation of the negative effects of Internet abuse on women is also part of a suite of responses to the second objection. Unlike a recommendation letter written for one or a few readers, or a phone call that is almost never heard by anyone other than the callers, Internet-based rumors and lies are frequently persistent, searchable, replicable, and accessible to any decision maker with access to the right software or database. A negative reference hurts only for as long as a job seeker keeps it on her résumé; a negative comment online is almost always beyond her control. Anyone affected by such expression deserves at least some chance at discovering whether it has been considered by key decision makers.

The third objection above attempts to shift our attention from the rights of the individual to the information environment as a whole. While individuals will likely contest or try to obscure negative data about them, they have no incentive to eliminate incorrect positive information about them. The problem of incorrect positive information has plagued employment references for some time. If decision makers must disclose the reports and research they use to make decisions, the information environment overall could become biased.

To help sort out these problems, it is helpful to examine J. H. Verkerke's work on the law of employment reference practices.[30] Verkerke provides a typology of three problems facing employers and regulators: "falsely negative references, an inadequate supply of reference information, and falsely positive references."[31] At this level of generality, Verkerke's typology also fits the problem of matching customers to insurers and banks, tenants to landlords, and students to schools. Verkerke argues that any effort to improve the quality of references risks reducing the quantity of information available. He concludes that proposed "regulatory measures that would . . . deter [employers] from providing falsely positive references . . . [present an] inescapable trade-off between quantity and quality substantially weakens the case for these reforms." Could the same be said of the fair information practices promoted in this essay? I believe there are many reasons to believe that the information environment and our understanding of reputation have changed sufficiently since Verkerke's piece was published to justify taking special aim at false and negative information.

First, we might want to consider the implications of environmental law for information privacy. Dennis D. Hirsch argues that just as new forms of pollution have caused extraordinary damage to the natural environment, "the digital age is causing unprecedented damage to privacy . . . [as a] 'faceless infrastructure' employs . . . data to deny us jobs, credit, insurance, and other social goods, often without our knowledge."[32] He observes that environmental law has long grappled with the problem of balancing the costs and benefits of regulation. If a given effort to purify the natural environment becomes too costly, state and federal agencies provide many opportunities for feedback designed to subsequently reduce the costs of compliance. Any agency enforcing a Fair Reputation Reporting Act should be open to concerns that its actions have "biased" the information environment, and respond accordingly.

We can already envision some concrete methods of doing so. For example, just as the agency enforcing FCRA could be seen as a guardian of consumers' reputations, a counter-agency dedicated to dispelling false, positive information could arise to assist businesses. Such an agency would investigate suspicious "sock-puppet" behavior designed to create a misleading impression of the authority, talent, or other positive attributes of an individual. Tal Zarsky has noted the problem of manipulative gaming of reputational systems and has recommended deterrence of "gamers" and "sock-puppeteers."[33] The rise of fusion centers and other public-private surveillance initiatives suggests that state actors will assist businesses in such endeavors in exchange for businesses' supplying antiterrorism and other crime-fighting leads.[34]

Even if the state does not become involved on behalf of businesses in this way, information intermediaries can also sniff out false, positive information on their behalf. Verkerke already predicted their rise in his 1998 article, and Lior Strahilevitz has written about their emergence in areas ranging from real estate to insurance.[35] Just as credit bureaus emerged to vet applicants for customers and banks, they and other information intermediaries may start to scrutinize sources of information online. Using algorithms like those employed by Google, they could begin to weight sources of information by reliability in order to give decision makers a clearer sense of exactly how reliable a given positive or negative piece of information is.

Frontiers of Reputation Regulation

Credit bureaus have already gone beyond merely vetting *sources* of information about individuals. They routinely commensurate information into a single score purporting to assess the creditworthiness of applicants for loans. The FCRA may have helped spur the development of this reputation mechanism. After the content of their reports had to be accessible to consumers, credit bureaus became increasingly reliant on opaque credit scoring. Though a credit score is computed via proprietary algorithms protected as trade secrets, it is widely treated as a fair and objective evaluation of an individual's creditworthiness.[36] Disclosure of such secrets can easily amount to a "taking," requiring government compensation for all the business based on it.

After the subprime debacle, the social importance of credit scoring (and its use by predatory lenders) has become more obvious than ever. Nevertheless, the industry remains highly opaque, with scored individuals unable to determine the consequences of late payments, changes in location, or other decisions. Several disturbing reports have alleged racial, geographic, and other inappropriate influences on credit scores. Because of concerns about their unreliability and unfairness, use of credit scores has been regulated by forty-eight states.[37]

Credit scores have also come under attack for having a disparate impact on poor and minority populations.[38] The National Fair Housing Alliance has criticized them as embedding sexist and racist assumptions into an ostensibly neutral process:

> Studies as well as lawsuits continue to demonstrate that African Americans, Hispanics, and elderly women are not treated the same as similarly qualified white males when attempting to purchase products such as cars, or secure mortgage loans or homeowners insurance. The terms and conditions for purchase of these products can be driven by the race, national origin or gender of the consumer rather than by their ability to pay or condition of the home.[39]

The scores themselves may be self-fulfilling prophecies, creating the financial distress they claim merely to indicate.[40] If a scorer determines that one missed $10 payment for a woman with two children earning $30,000 per year lowers her credit score by 200 points, she will be more likely to default because her low score means that she is going to be paying much more in interest for any financing she can find. Since the scores are black boxes, we have no assurance that scorers try to eliminate such endogeneity or whether they profit from such self-fulfilling prophecies.

Could the black-box proprietary models now common in credit scoring spread to reputation scoring? Several Silicon Valley entrepreneurs have already made the connection. For example, Auren Hoffman's company, Rapleaf, offers individuals a bargain—in exchange for plugging in all the details of extant online profiles about them into its system, Rapleaf will give them one-stop access to the information, and will generate a "reputation score" for its members. The Korean site Cyworld has long rated users' "friendliness," "karma," and "sexiness," among other qualities.[41] A company called Gorb "allows, even insists on, anonymous comments and ratings about rated individual's" professional and personal lives.[42] Some of these sites aim not merely to rate the willing, but also to rate everyone within a particular sphere.

So far, the only reported legal case pertaining to such sites has concerned the rating of attorneys by a site called Avvo. As reputation regulation develops, policy makers should examine closely professionals' campaign for accountable rating sites. Though the attorneys ultimately lost their case, physicians have succeeded in forcing insurers that rate them to engage in fair information practices. Both professions' struggles foreshadow future efforts to hold reputation raters more accountable than credit scorers currently are.

In the legal industry, Avvo aims to rate all licensed attorneys within the states it covers.[43] It claims its service gives lawyers the opportunity to increase their exposure and find potential clients. Toward that end, each licensed attorney has a profile on the site. Using public records, Avvo also provides a history of any sanctions or disciplinary measures taken against the attorney. Clients can post reviews of attorneys whose services they have used. Avvo uses this and other information to generate a rating for lawyers, which is a numerical score from 1.0 (the worst—"Extreme Caution") to 10.0 (the best—"Superb"). A rated attorney can add certain information to her profile after "claiming" it by using an identification verification system.

The right to claim the profile is a classic example of Web 2.0 business models. Attorneys listed on the site ignore the profile at their peril, and those critical of Avvo's project are put in a double bind by the profile's very existence. If they ignore the profile, they effectively allow Avvo and others the ability to control this aspect of their online identity. To the extent they tell "their side of the story" on the site, they are feeding data to Avvo and building its reliability. The aggregator acts like Tom Sawyer, inviting others to "paint the fence" by adding to the store of data that increases its authority and comprehensiveness.

Avvo's rating is difficult to assess because the company does not disclose how it is calculated, ostensibly because such disclosure would allow lawyers to manipulate and "game" the rankings in their favor. Avvo does not permit lawyers to pay or purchase ads to help their ratings—however, given the secrecy of its rating algorithm, it is difficult to verify this anti-payola pledge. Partly in order to avoid liability for defamation, Avvo insists that its rankings are merely its opinion, and are not factual.

In 2007, two Washington attorneys filed a complaint against Avvo for violation of the state's Consumer Protection Act (CPA), and sought class certification to include all lawyers rated by Avvo.com. The complaint alleged that "by reporting arbitrary and capricious scores and promoting them to consumers as mathematical calculations and a reliable assessment of a lawyer's competence to handle legal matters, Avvo has engaged in . . . unfair and deceptive acts and practices in violation of" the CPA. The plaintiffs alleged that the rating system treated lawyers unfairly and deceived the consumers who relied on it.

Avvo filed a pretrial motion to dismiss the case, arguing that the complaint was insufficient for several reasons. The court granted the motion, ruling that the "opinions expressed through the rating system . . . are absolutely protected by the First Amendment." The court posited that the site did not deceive consumers because it "contains numerous reminders that the Avvo rating system is subjective," an opinion rather than fact. Since the ratings on the site could not be proven true or false, the court ruled that Avvo was immune from liability for defamation. Avvo did not disclose its algorithm at any time in the suit.

The blanket protection the *Avvo* court would provide for opinions is open to challenge. Internet law expert James Grimmelmann unpacks the leading case on the issue:

> Milkovich v. Lorain Journal Co., while stating the rule that the Constitution shields opinions, leaves in place two significant exceptions. A statement of opinion may imply an underlying fact (the Court's example: "In my opinion John Jones is a liar."), and even a statement of opinion may be false if not honestly held (the Court's example: "I think Jones lied," where the speaker thought nothing of the sort). . . . The relationship of subjective opinion to objective fact . . . is not simple.[44]

Here, the opinion "John Jones is a terrible lawyer" implies certain facts about what Jones did to make him such a rotten attorney. Avvo's disclaimers about its "subjectivity" notwithstanding, no one would take the site seriously if it did not claim to be based on objective and relevant information.

There are examples of challenges to ratings that survived a motion to dismiss,[45] settled out of court,[46] or lost on the merits.[47] These cases demonstrate that there is no absolute First Amendment privilege for opinions or ratings. Therefore, the threat of costly litigation can be used as leverage to persuade raters to accept regulation. This dynamic may have driven resolution of several lawsuits against physician-rating websites.

In the medical field, insurance companies have begun to create "black-box" evaluation, ranking, and rating systems for doctors. Fearing an unfair tiering of its members, the Washington State Medical Association (WSMA) filed suit against Regence BlueShield, an insurance company that evaluated doctors using allegedly inaccurate and outdated information.[48] The doctors claimed that Regence used four-year-old data, small sample sizes, and focused on cost of claims rather than quality of care.[49] The complaint alleged defamation and violation of the CPA, among other causes of action.[50] After ten months of litigation, Regence agreed to settle with the WSMA "in an effort to better understand physician concerns,"[51] voluntarily withdrawing the Select Network program. The settlement agreement, effective for at least two years, promises transparency in evaluations, as well as fair methodology.[52]

In New York, the state attorney general, Andrew Cuomo, launched an investigation of insurers' physician ratings that culminated in settlement agreements in 2007. Cuomo claimed that the evaluation programs were confusing and unfair to both physicians and consumers.[53] After negotiating with his office, insurance companies eventually agreed to follow the ranking guidelines in a national model provided by the Office of the Attorney General (OAG) (in cooperation and consultation with the American Medical Association and other provider trade organizations). The model agreements require "insurers to fully disclose to consumers and physicians all aspects of their ranking system."[54] Since there is mandatory disclosure of all data and methodologies, the problem of the "black-box" evaluation system is reduced under the model agreements. Attorney General Cuomo has advocated the codification of the model based on his written agreements with insurance companies, and several prominent members of the New York legislature have agreed to support the bill.[55] The proposed bill suggests a trend toward transparent, quality-based rankings. CIGNA has agreed to make its rating methodologies public.[56] A "Patient Charter for Physician Performance Measurement" has also emerged as a project of the Consumer-Purchaser Disclosure Project (CPDP). The specific terms of the charter call for evaluations that are "meaningful to consumers" and bar decontextualized ratings based solely on cost.

Comparing Lawyers' Failures and Doctors' Successes in Regulating Reputation Scoring

Professional ranking programs are here to stay, and may play a vital role in pay-for-performance programs designed to rationalize compensation for physicians and lawyers. The CPDP's approach suggests some principles that could govern reputation regulation more generally. However, the failure of the Avvo lawsuit shows that First Amendment defenses can pose a formidable challenge to accountability here. Why have lawyers so far failed where doctors have succeeded?

Some nonlegal differences in the two cases spring to mind. Avvo.com is far smaller than the settling health insurance companies. There is an obvious conflict of interest in the latter situation: insurance companies have a financial incentive to "rank" doctors based on their cost to the insurance company, not the quality of care they offer. An insurance company might profitably purport to evaluate and rank doctors by quality, but then put the physicians who cost the company the least money at the top of its rankings. On the other hand, more subtle and dispersed conflicts of interest permeate Avvo's business model. It has no direct financial interest in the costs of lawyers' work, but it does have an interest in spurring attorneys to "claim" their profiles and supply the site with more information.

Frequently blamed for making heartless coverage decisions, insurance companies are eager to avoid additional bad press. Avvo.com is a new company without the image problems of the private health insurance industry. Moreover, Avvo's prime business model is to rate attorneys, while the insurers' core profit centers lie elsewhere. Though both attorneys and physicians have successfully protected their economic interests, more compressed income distribution among the bulk of physicians may make the "logic of collective action" more compelling to them. Finally, while attorneys ignore their Avvo profile at their peril, and cannot directly deny Avvo business, physicians can pull out of offending insurers' networks.

Yet there are also significant legal rationales for the divergent results of the two lines of litigation. Insurers are part of a heavily regulated industry where government decisions are crucial to their ongoing profitability. Many Supreme Court decisions have permitted agencies to shape the speech of recipients of governmental largesse. In its 9–0 decision in Rumsfeld v. Forum for Academic and Institutional Rights, Inc., the Court allowed the government to condition certain benefits on beneficiaries' compliance with governmental standards. Had the insurers failed to settle, they would likely have seen the doctors merely shift their case from the courts to state insurance commissioners. Avvo, by contrast, is a mere web start-up, with very little contact with or (apparent) reliance on governmental largesse. But as a closer examination of the complex web of laws that govern cyberspace intermediaries reveals, they may well be as vulnerable as insurers to governmental pressure designed to ensure basic protections for the individuals they rank and rate.

Free Speech and the Regulatory State

Internet service providers and search engines have mapped the web, accelerated e-commerce, and empowered new communities. They also pose new challenges for law. Individuals are rapidly losing the ability to affect their own image on the web—or even to know what data others are presented with regarding them. Technology's impact on privacy and democratic culture needs to be at the center of Internet policy making. Regulators should promote individuals' capacity to understand how their reputations— and the online world generally—are shaped by dominant intermediaries.

Heraclitus wrote that "for the waking there is one world, and it is common; but sleepers turn aside each one into a world of his own." In our age of fragmented lifeworlds, narrowcasting, and personalization, Internet searchers are increasingly like Heraclitus's sleepers, each turning to customized reports on the persons and events they take an interest in. While many authors have lamented the effects of the "Daily Me" on politics, and others have noted the Kafkaesque implications of data-driven decision making, few have considered the intersection of these trends. This essay has attempted to do so, and has proposed norms of transparency to ensure that the "watched" have some idea of what type of dossier and scoring the "watchers" are compiling about them.

Because First Amendment defenses have so far quashed many tort actions against raters and rankers, this essay has focused on tailored regulatory responses. Although there is no blanket exception from First Amendment protections for regulations, they appear to be less limited by this constitutional privilege than tort suits. This may be because regulations that promote "the social interest in order and morality" can outweigh the First Amendment concerns that have stymied tort suits.[57] As both Robert Post and Fred Schauer have observed, there are a number of examples of speech-restricting regulations that have not been rendered unconstitutional by First Amendment challenges.[58]

For example, commercial speech is one category of expression frequently regulated by the government. The law "accords a lesser protection to commercial speech than to other constitutionally guaranteed expression."[59] When commercial speech is misleading it can be restricted. . . . For example, regulatory actions banning false advertisements are not prohibited by the First Amendment.

Moreover, when the government has a "substantial interest in regulating" commercial speech, it is not necessarily limited by the First Amendment, even if the speech in question is completely lawful and is not misleading.[60] Copyright and trademark law are two instances where the unfettered right to free speech yields to larger "social interest[s] in order and morality."[61] Provisions of the DMCA strictly regulate what an intermediary like YouTube can keep on its site once it receives a notice that certain material infringes on copyrights. It would be deeply troubling if law could simultaneously be so solicitous of copyright owners (who are able to veto many fair uses, at least temporarily, under the terms of the DMCA), and utterly neglect the interests of those whose reputations are harmed by irresponsible intermediaries.

Just as consumers' interests trump a false advertiser's right to "express himself" with lies about products, so too should certain reputational interests take precedence over the bare right to offer scoring of others' reputations. Norms of due process may throw some sand in the wheels of today's lightning-fast generation of information and scores about individuals. However, fair opportunity in the Information Age depends on accountable rating practices and models. More open and accurate systems of evaluation are a legitimate choice for a culture increasingly disillusioned with clandestinely commensurating computing.

CHAPTER 7

Youthful Indiscretion in an Internet Age

ANUPAM CHANDER

> Instantaneous photographs and newspaper enterprise have invaded the sacred precincts of private and domestic life; and numerous mechanical devices threaten to make good the prediction that "what is whispered in the closet shall be proclaimed from the house-tops."
>
> —Samuel D. Warren & Louis D. Brandeis, The Right to Privacy, *Harvard Law Review*, 1890

A child born in the twenty-first century will have her life documented in digital form. When the records involve benign conduct, such as the fact that her soccer team made it into the regional finals, there may be little cause for concern. But when the conduct revealed to the world is more intimate or embarrassing there is reason for alarm. In this new century of ubiquitous camera phones and digital communications, a youthful indiscretion might become an albatross a person can never escape. The torts for the invasion of privacy were themselves born of technological developments. But the "instantaneous photography" that moved Warren and Brandeis to formulate legal rights to privacy is now coupled with the instantaneous global dissemination platform of the Internet, magnifying the problem immeasurably. The digital form extends the accessibility of the private sphere not only in space, but in time. The Internet Age can place a person's history, or, worse, a fleeting episode from that history, at the world's call. The past might haunt the twenty-first-century child till the end of her days.

Fear of future ramifications might cause individuals to recoil from any practice that might lead to public humiliation or embarrassment in the decades to come. Their hopes for careers as politicians, judges, prosecutors, executives, or doctors may hang in the balance. The youth of the Internet Age may be strait jacketed—teens and young adults at the mercy of the world—living their lives as if in a fishbowl. Decisions in such a life require consideration not only of the reputational consequences vis-à-vis families, friends, and acquaintances, but also with respect to future employers, partners, and even unborn children. The cognitive task required is forbidding. In such a world, we may risk youthfulness in youth.

The youth facing a fishbowl life might be tempted to adopt either of two strategies: excessive caution or foolhardy fearlessness. The first strategy might limit decisional autonomy now, constraining the choices available now. The second strategy might limit decisional autonomy later, constraining the choices available then. We should not tolerate this unnecessary choice between reduced choice set now, or reduced choice set later. Here I will argue that both law and society more generally must ameliorate the risks inherent in a fishbowl life, especially for youth, in the service of autonomy.

With respect to the legal regime, I will argue that judges must reinvigorate the paradigmatic privacy tort—the tort for public disclosure of embarrassing private fact. Many scholars have offered requiems for the privacy torts, victim to changing social attitudes and greater solicitude to free speech. By contrast, I will argue that new technologies make the public disclosure tort more necessary than ever before. In particular, I will argue that the disclosure tort is especially appropriate to regulate the display of nude photographs and videos not authorized for public dissemination. The special power of the image, particularly sexual images, requires the special attention of the law.

At the same time, society should take into account the elephantine memory of the digital medium when fashioning architectures of communication. Educators in particular should be careful when they require students to blog, or post their writing or art online. We might all be careful about what we post about others, and respect reasonable requests to remove information about others. While the problem I describe requires greater adjustment to private and educational practices than to the law, my focus in this paper is on the legal regime.

The dangers of inattention are becoming increasingly evident. A champion swimmer at the Beijing Olympics was humiliated by the publication on the Internet of nude photos of her "seemingly taken in an intimate moment by a lover." "I've been to hell," she told a magazine, adding, "I no longer dared wear a [swimsuit]. . . ."[1] Paris Hilton's liaison with a boyfriend became the stuff of a DVD that the man later sought to peddle for profit. Most readers may feel far from either the celebrity or activity of Paris Hilton and other similarly famous personages, insulated by our own obscurity and protected by our own discretion. But the Internet does not restrict its attentions to the private lives of the rich and famous. Nor can we all be counted on to act discreetly in all circumstances. Paris Hilton and other celebrities become the canary in the coal mine, an early warning of the dangers of this new age for us all. Internet sites collect "revenge porn"— depicting ex-girlfriends in sexual situations.[2] One site promises "Nude and REAL Ex-Girlfriends and Ex-Wives Photo Blog Submitted by Surfers as Revenge or Braggin[g] Rights."[3] The media have identified the rise of "sexting," the sending of sexually explicit photos electronically, primarily between cell phones. Kiss and tell now becomes show and tell.[4]

In one grave case, the publication of photos might even have contributed to a young woman's death. After her former boyfriend distributed nude pictures of her within her high school, Jessica Logan was tormented by classmates: "The girls were harassing her, calling her a slut and a whore." Months later, she committed suicide.[5]

Youthful experiment—including challenge and rebellion—is often central to the process of growing up, of becoming autonomous, independent adults. We should not yield youthfulness to the merciless memory of digital recorders. No less values than autonomy and human development are at stake. The risks are especially grave for women. In the age of camera phones, handheld video cameras, and the Internet, a fleeting encounter can find its way to the prying eyes of the world. Liberalism would leave certain decisions to individual choice, outside the realm of state coercion. If one knows that entering the public sphere by seeking a position of authority might risk a disclosure that will compromise one's bodily modesty, one's autonomy will be adversely affected. In this sense, bodily privacy serves here to advance decisional autonomy.[6] Life in a fishbowl constrains choices, not through the coercive mechanisms of the state, but through the disciplinary mechanisms of social pressures, limiting access to jobs, friends, and positions of authority.

But is not truthfulness a virtue? Disclosures of private behavior can reveal hypocrisy or expose lying. They can undermine or promote confidence in counterparties to a transaction, whether professional or personal. Revelations of widespread transgressions can even make it clear that societal norms against such behavior might be outdated. They might also lead to ennui—becoming so commonplace as to lack any capacity to embarrass. "Been there, done that," in the words of one state supreme court.[7]

Because these objections have force, I do not propose a general right to wipe the slate clean.[8] Instead, my intervention is limited to two purposes: (1) highlighting the general problem, and by so doing motivating reconsideration of the increasingly public nature of youth life; and (2) arguing that, at least with respect to nude images, the privacy interest should generally prevail over the interest in public display. My goal here is not to promote a Victorian Compromise—of high public rectitude and low private misdeeds.[9] Rather it is to suggest that even nonmorally-reprobate behavior can be embarrassing when it is exposed to the world and available for the remainder of our lives. At times, law will need to provide a remedy; at other times, individuals and the institutions we craft will have to recognize the risks involved, and ameliorate them.

Since the rise of the Internet, many have noted the threat posed by the digital realm to our privacy. In this writing, I consider the dynamic effects of the technological change currently under way. How will people change their behaviors in response to this technology? Many may respond by modifying either their private behavior—risking youthfulness—or their public behavior—avoiding positions that might lead to embarrassing disclosures. I note the special concerns arising from the fact that such disclosures are likely to be visual and the possibility that they might have a disparate impact on women in public life. I suggest that there is a partial response available in the common law in the tort for public disclosure of private facts, and I defend that suggestion against anticipated critiques.

The United States has long been the land of fresh starts. Because of a vast frontier, individuals who faced hard luck where they lived could begin anew, putting their past behind them. With both geographic mobility and urbanization came the ability to forget, a power absent in the small villages where one's neighbors remained the same from birth to death. Bankruptcy provided a legal fresh start for financial obligations.[10] Youthful offenses in particular long received given special treatment. Expungement statutes throughout the country require states to destroy criminal records of minors, sometimes automatically.[11] There may be little reason to rehabilitate oneself, if one's past transgression will be forever worn like a scarlet letter—or so the theory goes.

With the advent of computers, attention turned to their prodigious data-gathering and collating capacities.[12] Credit histories were one of the first areas of concern following the database revolution of the 1960s. The Fair Credit Reporting Act of 1970 classified negative information that was more than seven years old (ten years, in the case of bankruptcy) "outdated."[13] Credit agencies can release such information only for limited purposes. Burgeoning databases of personal information, Congress recognized, require us to be careful that people are not burdened with past errors for the rest of their lives.

Privacy law too has sought to assist the "rehabilitation of the fallen."[14] In the classic privacy case of Melvin v. Reid, a woman who had once been a prostitute sued the producers of a movie titled *The Red Kimono*, which told her life story using her name without permission. The court held in her favor, explaining that she had, years earlier, "abandoned her life of shame, had rehabilitated herself and had taken her place as a respected and honored member of society."[15] By allowing individuals to contain public release of certain information, privacy law permits us to avoid being forever tarred by any embarrassing youthful actions. Privacy law also prevents an individual from being frozen in society's view at a particular moment; it allows the individual to grow and to change.

Privacy law has recently demonstrated special solicitude for youth facing a digital future. Concerned that technology now permitted children to speak directly to strangers even without leaving home, Congress sought to give parents control over such communications.[16] It passed in 1998 the Children's Online Privacy Protection Act (COPPA), an act that requires online service providers to obtain parental consent before collecting personally identifiable information from children. The statute goes further to give children and their parents rights to the use of the information: "parents are ascribed a powerful right to veto primary collection, primary use, secondary use, and even maintenance of data."[17] But this statute limits itself to websites directed at children under the age of thirteen. The painful truth is that COPPA leaves youth precisely when they enter that time in their lives where they need it most. The period of our lives that we might least want exposed to public attention is our teens and early adulthood, when we begin grappling with the complications of sex and responsibility. COPPA was designed to protect children from prying adults, but not from themselves.

Disclosures involving sex often receive special attention from the law. Privacy law has long had a special concern with sex. Lawrence Friedman even describes privacy as "the idea that certain things (notably the sexual side of life) had to be kept secret, kept private."[18]

Images of private or intimate behavior, in particular, seem especially problematic. The visceral quality of the photograph or the video, coupled with the rapidity with which a human mind can comprehend an image, make the publication of images of special concern. Indeed, as I described earlier, Warren and Brandeis, writing in 1890, were especially concerned about the advent of the Kodak camera, then just two years old. The compact, portable camera offered the ability to make publicly available scenes that normally would have been viewed by few. The photos provided long-lasting visual evidence that might prove difficult to disprove. It was the publication of the photos from Abu Ghraib, and not the earlier textual reports of torture, that caused a worldwide scandal. Similarly, the video of the beating of Rodney King may have galvanized public attention to the problem of police brutality in ways that words could not. (These two examples, of course, suggest that there may be times that we clearly do not want law to suppress images.)

Federal law pays special attention to the image, criminalizing the *"visual depiction"* of sexual activity involving minors.[19] Federal law now requires publishers of sexually explicit photographs to maintain certifications that the subjects are adults.[20] Some jurisdictions have gone so far as to prosecute children for nude photos they take of themselves under state law, a seemingly inappropriate use of criminal statutes designed to counter the exploitation of children by adults.[21]

The problem of intrusions with respect to sexual privacy may be more grave for women than men, for at least two reasons. First, society has long allowed men greater latitude in sexual affairs than it affords women. "Boys will be boys" is a mantra repeated to excuse behaviors. Second, women are more likely to be the subject of nude photographs.[22] A recent survey suggests that males are catching up, though the survey's methodology makes it unreliable. Of those who volunteered to participate in an online survey on sex, one out of every five teenagers (22 percent of teen girls and 18 percent of teen boys) and a third of young adults ages twenty to twenty-six (36 percent of young adult women and 31 percent of young adult men) stated that they had shared nude or seminude photos of themselves electronically.[23] One might speculate that reciprocal nude photo sharing between couples might hold the possibility of giving each person a compromising photo of the other, and thus offer the possibility of deterring wrongful release through an implicit tit-for-tat strategy.

Perhaps the most important legal tool to protect youthful indiscretions in the Internet Age is the tort for public disclosure of embarrassing private facts. This tort, recognized by some thirty-six states, allows a cause of action for the public disclosure of a private matter that is "highly offensive to a reasonable person." Truthfulness is not a defense. The action turns on the inappropriate public revelation of a matter deemed properly private.

Other privacy torts may be relevant as well, such as the tort for intrusion upon seclusion, though I will not focus on them here. A woman successfully deployed the seclusion tort, for example, against a boyfriend who secretly videotaped a sexual encounter with her in his bedroom.[24] Yet another privacy tort, the false light tort, has been deployed successfully against adult magazines that publish photographs of individuals without their consent.[25]

Two principal legal hurdles exist with respect to the use of the public disclosure tort to prevent a youthful indiscretion from becoming a scarlet letter. First, the indiscretion may itself be of legitimate interest to the public—it may be "newsworthy," in the terminology of the common law. Second, Section 230 of the Communications Decency Act (CDA) might well insulate claims against online service providers for hosting material provided by others. I consider these two difficulties below.

The Restatement of Torts limits the public disclosure tort to disclosures "not of legitimate concern to the public."[26] Harry Kalven noted that newsworthiness is "the privilege that has virtually 'swallowed the tort.'" But recent cases demonstrate that courts will not always sustain a claim of newsworthiness, especially when it comes to sexual images. When an adult video company obtained an explicit videotape of actress Pamela Anderson Lee and singer Bret Michaels, the two sued for invasion of privacy. The video company asserted in its defense that the material was "newsworthy," more so because of the subjects' celebrity status. Judge Dean Pregerson's decision upholding the privacy claim seems on the mark: "The fact recorded on the Tape . . . is not that Lee and Michaels were romantically involved, but rather the visual and aural details of their sexual relations, facts which are ordinarily considered private even for celebrities."[27] Judge Pregerson thus entered an injunction—doing so over claims that it would amount to a prior restraint of speech: "Furthermore, the privacy of the acts depicted on the Tape cannot be restored by monetary damages after the Tape becomes public. The nature of the Internet aggravates the irreparable nature of the injury. Once the Tape is posted on [the distributor's] web site, it will be available for instant copying and further dissemination by [the distributor's] subscribers." The injunction did not extend to disclosures that the tape existed, or to public discussion regarding the tape. Such an approach still allows kiss and tell—it's the *show* and tell that is most problematic.

Newsworthiness is especially tricky in an age of a hundred million blogs. Where earlier courts were likely to defer to the editorial decisions of news intermediaries to determine whether information was truly newsworthy, in the age of the Internet, there may be no editorial function before information is released to the public at large. Where the costs of newsprint and the limited space available in a limited set of papers once required the careful exercise of discretion in decisions about what to publish, blogs are available for free to self-appointed editors who do not face such constraints. Blogworthiness is not the same as newsworthiness.

Like celebrity Pamela Lee, ordinary individuals should be able to take preemptive action against improper disclosures. Individuals could seek a declaratory judgment against an individual who might possess compromising photographs, enjoining against future publication.

But would not a lawsuit merely circulate the undesirable information further? Because of this concern, courts often permit the plaintiff to proceed under a Jane Doe pseudonym. Even while holding that imposing damages on a newspaper for publishing the name of a rape victim violated the First Amendment, the Supreme Court in Florida Star v. B.J.F. adopted the lower state court's decision to use the rape victim plaintiff's initials instead of her name.[28] In a case involving "sexting," the practice of sending nude pictures of oneself over electronic networks, the Alabama Supreme Court similarly used initials for the male and female high school students involved in the case, as well as for their parents, reasoning that naming the parents would effectively identify the students as well.[29] (Another aspect of that decision is more troubling: the Court in dicta declared that a person could not be charged with a *public* disclosure of a private fact unless he or she shared the information with a wide group. This seems unwise, given that sexual pictures once released to a few have a high likelihood of being disseminated widely.)

As in all potential civil cases, the cost of litigation will deter many from filing suit. Perhaps the cease and desist letter, written with or without a lawyer's signature, might do the trick—letting the offender know of his or her potential legal exposure. And like all potential civil cases, there is the risk that the threat of an action or an action itself will be misused. However, these cases are unlikely to offer the possibility of a class action that might attract plaintiffs' attorneys to file suit with the hope of extracting settlements.

Another difficulty is perhaps the most serious: intermediaries can escape demands to withdraw information posted by others because of a special statutory immunity. How intermediaries must respond to requests to remove information varies by the subject matter of the underlying infraction. An online intermediary facing an allegation of copyright infringement must immediately take down the material, or risk losing the safe harbor promising immunity from secondary liability. An online intermediary facing an allegation of defamation or invasion of privacy, however, can refuse to remove the material, finding refuge within the immunity grant of the ironically named Good Samaritan provision of the CDA. The end result is that the online gossip site might escape liability for invasions of privacy conducted through its service. In a case involving the posting of a nude picture of a woman on a widely accessible website without her consent, for example, a district court ruled that the Good Samaritan provision immunized the website from the traditional privacy torts of public disclosure, false light, and the intrusion upon seclusion.[30] Such sites could offer takedown procedures on their own, however. Facebook, for example, allows users to withdraw content they have posted—though an individual has no similar right to withdraw content posted by others about her, unless it infringes on her intellectual property rights.

The law should allow the individual to find information to lead her to the person who committed the privacy invasion. In recent litigation involving defamatory statements made about two Yale law students on the gossip site AutoAdmit.com, a federal district court was willing to enforce subpoenas requiring the site to help identify the individuals who posted that material. In that case, initially titled Doe I v. Individuals, Whose True Names Are Unknown, the court compelled the site to disclose information about the people who posted the material.[31] In the AutoAdmit case, Judge Droney also rejected the motion of a defendant to proceed anonymously even though, as the court noted, naming the defendant might result in "social stigma, embarrassment, and economic harm." The fact that such suits might lead to the public identification of individuals who post malicious material behind a cloak of anonymity might itself cause some to desist from posting such material.

While the risks of technology to privacy are great, we need to be careful to not overreact by creating overprotective law. Rights to stop people from disclosing truthful information raise significant difficulties. Reputations would be meaningless if they could be subject to a legal right to manipulate.

Accountability, Anita Allen reminds us, often relies upon reputation.[32] Equally important, the specter of harm to children is often trotted out to reach the legal result that some adults desire. We do not want to infantilize our society, making everything child safe. This would require adults to live according to rules for children. A public disclosure tort that simply allowed people to remove unflattering but truthful material about them from cyberspace would go too far.

I consider below a handful of arguments against the disclosure tort. I conclude that each of these objections, while raising meritorious concerns and requiring cautious application of the tort, should not stop us from seeking, at least, to contain nude images within the private sphere when the subjects of those images never intended their public dissemination and where their content lacks special news value.

First Amendment.   The disclosure tort clearly bars certain speech, and thus raises significant First Amendment concerns. The Supreme Court considered the conflict between privacy and speech in Florida Star v. B.J.F., a case in which a rape victim sued a newspaper for revealing her name in the course of a story about the rape. In that case, the Supreme Court upheld the paper's right to publish her name, where the paper had obtained the information lawfully, the information was truthful, the crime report (if not the identification of the individual by name) involved a matter of public significance, and there were no compelling state interests mandating criminal liability of the newspaper.[33] As *Florida Star* itself indicates, First Amendment free speech protections are not absolute, but tolerate certain restrictions when justified by other compelling societal interests. The Court preferred a case-by-case analysis: "We continue to believe that the sensitivity and significance of the interests presented in clashes between First Amendment and privacy rights counsel relying on limited principles that sweep no more broadly than the appropriate context of the instant case."[34]

The law is replete with constraints on speech. The Video Privacy Protection Act of 1988, for example, bars truthful disclosures of video rental records.[35] Securities law bars even truthful priming of the markets prior to the effectiveness of the registration statement. Perhaps these regulations would fall under First Amendment scrutiny, but perhaps also a court would hold that the interests of privacy and proper functioning of the securities markets might justify the speech intrusions.

Moreover, there is a long history of regulation for nude images in the United States. Such images may often meet the definition of obscenity, and are often trafficked on websites devoted to collecting such material for prurient interest.

Doing away with the privacy tort in favor of certain speech might itself imperil certain other speech and even legal behavior. We often fail to recognize that there are chilling effects on either side in the privacy/speech clash. On one side, individuals who might have exposed private facts to the public in a context we might have valued may find themselves deterred by the possibility of liability. But there is a less often identified chilling effect as well: without privacy rights, individuals may fear for the consequences of their behavior, and hew to a safe path, a path not likely to draw controversy or scrutiny in the decades to come. This implicates an autonomy interest, but also a speech interest: individuals may share less information privately as well. The Supreme Court recognized this possible risk from inadequate protection of privacy in its recent opinion in Bartnicki v. Vopper: "the fear of public disclosure of private conversations might well have a chilling effect on private speech."[36] In that case, the Court ultimately sided with the public disclosure of illegally recorded private conversations within a union's leadership, where the publisher itself had not been engaged in the wrongful recording. The Court explained that "[i]n this case, privacy concerns give way when balanced against the interest in publishing matters of public importance."

The popular maxim counseling one to fight bad speech with good speech will prove unavailing in many privacy intrusion contexts. What is the proper counter to a truthful disclosure of a nude photograph? "You have flab, too" or "Lots of people have sex, as children attest" hardly suffices to lessen the sting.

There will, of course, be occasions in which free speech values will require publication, even of nude images. Anita Allen writes, "If President Thomas Jefferson took the public position that blacks were morally inferior and unfit for the society of whites and if he was having an intimate relationship with his black slave Sally Hemings, his hypocrisy would have merited disclosure."[37] A picture evidencing such a relationship merits even a place on the evening news, at least with some bits edited out.

Efficient markets.   Markets run better with more information. Richard Posner goes further, observing that "the tax collector, fiancé, partner, creditor, and competitor" might seek private information.[38] Revelations about private behavior can improve information on counterparties—perhaps helping us avoid, for example, the pitfalls of statistical discrimination by allowing more individualized evaluation.[39]

The point is important, though with respect to the fact of sexual conduct, there may be limited value to the information; indeed, to borrow a concept from another legal domain, the information may be more prejudicial than probative. Posner himself suggests that "most people do not like to be seen naked" and that the law properly gives individuals a property right in their own nudity.[40] Posner explains that reticence to reveal one's body publicly imposes little "social costs" and given that transaction costs are low, an individual can contract away her privacy right in this regard.

Furthermore, the market consequences will not be limited to the increased information available to those who hire or otherwise deal with the data subject. The release of such private information might lead the individual to shy away from certain marketplace transactions, embarrassed at the revelations that would likely follow. While lifetime income-smoothing decisions and human capital investment show that individuals can make major decisions in consideration of lifetime consequences, one suspects that cognitive limits on such an exercise might well be reached when they involve decisions related to the minutiae of intimate life. Even when one can consider them, the lifetime consequences for youthful error would magnify a particular decision beyond its reasonable limits.

Society will become inured to the problem. It might be argued that publicizing private behavior will, over time, lead society to accept that behavior as normal, and thus not embarrassing. Society, however, has long been well aware of widespread sexual activity before, within, and outside marriage. Yet, the fascination continues. Embarrassment, or even humiliation, does not turn on whether some activity is out of the ordinary or freakish. Rather human bodily functions can themselves be grounds for embarrassment. Ridicule often takes the form of borrowing ordinary activities and exposing and exploiting them in a public setting.

A related argument, the one most popular among today's youth, is that such behavior will soon be no longer worthy of reprobation, its sting gone. One's own indiscretion will perhaps be lost amidst a sea of similar disclosures. In rejecting a disclosure privacy tort, the Indiana Supreme Court explained, "[W]e do not discern anything special about disclosure injuries. Perhaps Victorian sensibilities once provided a sound basis of distinction,

but our more open and tolerant society has largely outgrown such a justification. In our 'been there, done that' age of talk shows, tabloids, and
twelve-step programs, public disclosures of private facts are far less likely
to cause shock, offense, or emotional distress than at the time Warren and
Brandeis wrote their famous article."[41] In the Indiana case, an individual
sued a fellow postal worker for revealing that he was HIV positive. Whether
such a revelation against the individual's wishes has indeed lost its sting in
contemporary society is unclear. However, when it comes to nude photographs, there is no guarantee that revelations will be treated as humdrum—
entirely unremarkable and without cause for embarrassment. Indeed, to
see the continuing power of such images to embarrass, one need only read
the sordid facts of a case involving explicit photographs that four fourteen-
year-old girls emailed to two male classmates.[42] One picture even appeared
subsequently as " 'wallpaper' on a computer in the sixth-grade computer
lab."

The disclosure tort itself covers only disclosures that are highly offensive to a reasonable person, and thus allows for changes in social standards.[43] If society does indeed believe a particular disclosure to be unob-
jectionable under an objective, reasonable person standard, then no tort
claim will lie.

While it is possible that society will become blasé to such revelations, it
is easy to underestimate the dangers. After all, within the community of
youth, these behaviors may well be common, so much so that anyone not
engaging in them may even be ridiculed as prudish. A natural presumption is that, as the youth age, their peers will share the same past; their
closets will share the same skeletons. It is thus easy for youth to feel comfortable that, given how common these behaviors are among their friends
and acquaintances, there is little cause for concern for future disclosure.
But when one considers that reputation reaches not only one's immediate
peers, but also potential employers, current superiors, and professional acquaintances, the risks may look different. Even while parts of society may
come to find such a revelation unremarkable, there is reason to suspect
that the subject may continue to worry about its impact. What if the individual has children—might she be concerned about what comes to their
attention? What of her parents, grandparents, and relatives? What of the
snickers of opposing counsel or law clerks when they email photos while
a lawyer takes the stand or of business partners when she speaks in a
boardroom? Monica Lewinsky did not take pictures (of which we should

be thankful). A former paramour of the first woman president may not be so discreet.

Futility. Even if a privacy tort is available, is it not futile? Some will argue that legal niceties are hardly likely to staunch the distribution of information in cyberspace. After all, trying to stamp out runaway information in cyberspace is like an endless game of Whack-A-Mole, now gone worldwide and viral. This is clearly true of some information. It may be outside the finances of even Paris Hilton to rid cyberspace entirely of unwanted videos, even if she owns them. But this is not true of more run-of-the-mill events. An individual might contact a person whom she believes might hold intimate photographs, and inform that person that release of that information might subject him to liability. Such an act might deter the individual from disseminating the photograph.

Search engines can do their part by creating methods for permitting individuals to seek to remove images and videos from their indices. Search engines could face secondary liability claims if the individual data subject owned a copyright in the work. Section 230 of the Communications Decency Act might make it difficult to hold intermediaries that do not develop the material liable for privacy invasions, but some have argued for expanding the scope of liability even if intermediaries do not develop the material, but fail to act upon knowledge and appropriate testament from the person alleging the wrong.

Protecting private tyrannies. By demarcating a private realm not readily accessible to the public, society cannot as easily police that realm. Surveillance facilitates enforcement of both government laws and social norms. This has led many to be concerned about the possible tyrannies of private spaces. Privacy, as Martha Nussbaum concisely puts it, protects a "patriarchal sphere of authority."[44] Catherine MacKinnon criticizes the way that the abortion right is constructed, with the result, she says, that it simply reinforces male hegemony: "[U]nder conditions of gender inequality, sexual liberation in this sense does not so much free women sexually as it frees male sexual aggression."[45] She concludes, "Privacy law keeps some men out of the bedrooms of other men."[46]

The disclosure tort, however, does not necessarily create a private zone free from the policing of either the government or society. The tort is not available if the matter is of "legitimate concern" to the public. Private violence and other private behaviors remain available for police and societal sanction. Of course, the tort begs the question of what is of "legitimate concern." Common law judges have elaborated this tort, making difficult and contestable calls between what is of legitimate concern and what is not.

My suggestion is that a narrowly tailored tort can give individuals, including women, a legal remedy if they themselves choose to exercise it. Lacking such a remedy, the risk is that men and women, and particularly women, will take themselves out of the pool of candidates for positions of authority for fear of embarrassing revelations. Thus, autonomy in the public sphere of marketplace employment and politics can be compromised by unwarranted intrusions in the private sphere of sex. Allowing the free dissemination of photos of sexual relations only compounds any patriarchal authority within the bedroom. As Judith Wagner DeCew writes, "While care must be taken to avoid allowing privacy as a cover for abuse, privacy is nevertheless essential for protecting the freedom and independence needed for individuals to develop their identities and values as self-conscious beings."[47] This certainly has been implicit in the stance of the many women plaintiffs in the cases that have thus far been brought. In a Texas case in which an appeals court rejected a woman's claim against a former lover who had exhibited a sexual videotape of the pair, the Women and the Law section of the State Bar of Texas asserted, "If the tables had been turned, and [the female plaintiff] had peddled the videotape as a vignette of [male defendant's] sexual performance . . . , the all-male majority in this case would have reached a decidedly different result."[48]

Many men (and some women) have publicly disclosed private acts to publicly humiliate former lovers or to announce sexual conquests. Granting women (as well as men) a tort for such actions does not reduce women to mere toys of men, but rather grants them a legal right to counter male exploitation.

"Je ne regrette rien." (I regret nothing.) "Je me fous du passe." (I don't give a damn about the past.) Edith Piaf sang these lines with a devil-may-care world weariness. But even if we regret little, we may yet care about the publication of the details.

The public disclosure tort should remain a viable option with respect to, at the minimum, nude images. Courts can weigh the public interest in the disclosure against the harms of subjecting individuals to the invasion of bodily privacy, and decide whether the intrusion is justified. More broadly, the widespread diffusion of the tools for private recording coupled with the Internet's public disclosure and the digital medium's long memory places youth at risk of being haunted by past actions throughout their lives. In our roles as educators, parents, or government officials, we should strive to give youth a measure of decisional privacy.

CHAPTER 8

Academic Administrators and the Challenge of Social-Networking Websites

KAREN M. BRADSHAW AND SOUVIK SAHA

There exists a divide between users and nonusers of social-networking websites. For users, such websites are generally an integral part of social interaction used daily for information sharing, event planning, and reputation building. In contrast, nonusers typically fail to grasp the extent to which social-networking websites influence in-person interactions. Consequently, university professors and administrators who do not participate in online communities may underestimate the extent to which interactions occurring in the virtual realm affect their academic institutions. This divide can produce serious, negative consequences, particularly when students engage in behavior online that would be unacceptable in a traditional, live setting.

Millions of college students are members of social-networking websites and belong to online groups.[1] The majority of groups on social-networking websites are devoted to shared interests, such as a sport or geographical connection. Other groups, however, are focused on individuals, including faculty members and fellow students. Such groups share candid photos and threads of commentary about their targets. Some are complimentary and are of a fan club nature. Others are not. Bitter comments and untruthful rants about students and faculty at a number of educational institutions are easily found using a quick search of social-networking websites. The existence of these groups raises many questions: When does a thread of commentary transform from acceptably critical to abusive? When do unflattering photos taken and posted without permission become a violation of privacy? Why do students feel free to post lewd comments that they would not say in person?

Abusive behavior taking place online, known as "cyber bullying," is easy to dismiss as harmless pestering that is unlikely to affect a serious graduate student or tenured professor. Yet, online communities often engage in targeted hate speech and defamation that academic communities would not accept in a live setting. These abuses have serious consequences, including professional and reputational damage, sexual harassment, and perhaps even increased suicide rates.

What nonusers fail to recognize is the potency of social-networking websites as compared with other virtual communication tools, such as chat rooms or instant messaging systems. Rather than just a means of communication, Facebook and similar websites–like MySpace and Bebo–are functional communities that happen to exist on the Internet. Technological or generational barriers often render these online communities void of administrators and faculty, allowing students to feel removed from the supervision that exists in classrooms or campuses. We argue that, as a result, online communities lack many of the positive social norms found in traditional academic communities. Without these norms, individuals are emboldened to engage in strikingly abusive harassment of students and faculty. Administrators who are not a part of online social networks tend to underestimate the impact online communities have on classrooms and campuses.

In this essay, we survey administrators' attempts to engage with online communities, and argue that many current approaches fail to appreciate that Facebook is a fundamental component of social dynamics among students. Some schools focus on classroom dynamics by limiting or restricting in-class Internet use. Other academic institutions focus more broadly on monitoring and disciplining inappropriate behavior. These approaches are controversial: privacy concerns, free speech issues, and the appropriate reach of institutional authority are all fodder for heated debates. More importantly, continued, widespread cyber bullying demonstrates that these regulations are ineffective as currently applied. In looking to alternative approaches, we argue that methods designed to inject social norms into the online environment and introduce the metaphorical adult into the room are important, achievable steps toward addressing the most blatant online abuses.

Interactions between Online and Academic Communities

We posit that two communities exist simultaneously in the modern academic setting. First, there is the obvious traditional community in which students, faculty, and administrators interact with one another in the physical space of the institution. A second community has arisen among the millions of students who participate daily in social-networking websites. Administrators have yet to fully grasp the extent to which the traditional academic community is affected by what occurs in these virtual communities. Though a multitude of positive outcomes are generated through student participation in online communities,[2] so too are abuses. This essay focuses on two forms of abuse: obvious in-class use of the Internet, and cyber bullying that may impact the academic community even though it occurs outside the physical classroom.

Social-networking websites provide hundreds of millions of users with a forum for online interaction.[3] According to the website of one popular online community, "Facebook helps you connect and share with the people in your life." These websites are stunningly popular and widely used.[4] University students rely on social-networking websites to keep in touch with friends, organize activities, and pursue information and groups that interest them. Social-networking websites are distinct from previous forms of online communications because they do more than facilitate interaction. Unlike chat rooms or instant messaging, social-networking websites continue to convey and send information about participants even when they are not logged on.

Facebook groups are of particular interest because they are an example of online communities that coexist or even supplant traditional communities. Students can create and join groups focused on varied interests. Group "administrators" provide a title and description of the groups and monitor who can join. Members of the group may post pictures, events, and comments viewable by every group member.

Although social-networking websites provide a new forum for interaction, abusive behavior by college students against a particular target is not new. Facebook groups are somewhat like fraternities that engage in targeted rumor spreading and information sharing. Just as fraternity behavior can become abusive toward individual targets–by spreading lies around campus about a fellow student or creating hateful reviews of professors–online groups may also provide a forum that encourages group members to act increasingly abusively toward targeted persons. Such analogies are helpful in contextualizing the problem for administrators, but can minimize the unique features of cyber bullying that can make it especially difficult but important to discourage.

Some features of social-networking websites, particularly the vast audience and constancy of interaction, make them particularly prone to abuse. Social-networking groups constitute a broadcasting mechanism that permits hundreds of students to see the same information simultaneously. The reach of the broadcasting capability is exponentially magnified when coupled with Facebook's ability to synthesize information from multiple sources, such as other groups or applications on Facebook. Unlike traditional academic communities, Facebook groups can span geographical distances, and members may simultaneously view and share information. The number of potential group members is far greater than in physical communities; on Facebook, elementary school friends and potential employers may have access to the same information that would previously have been available only to students in the academic setting. While strangers may care little about a target, people with minimal external context about a person— especially potential employers—may rely upon the information. This becomes especially damaging when the archiving of Internet pages is taken into account; it can take years for negative messages to disappear from search engine results. Combined, these characteristics create a new and powerful communication tool that is different from previous forms of social information sharing.[5]

Educators mistakenly believe that they understand the depth of concerns presented by social-networking websites because the *symptoms* of in-class Facebook use are obvious. Faculty can easily detect inattention, reduced participation, and distraction. It is perhaps too easy to attribute this inattention to Internet use. For example, Norman Garrett, a professor of Computer Information Systems at Eastern Illinois University, wonders: "Are [students] not even in the same universe as I'm in because they're looking at the Internet?"[6] Studies reporting high in-class use of social-networking websites lead administrators to wrongly conclude that the extent of problems caused by the Internet is limited to inappropriate use within the classroom.

Administrators fail to recognize that the *causes* behind the symptoms outlined above are not obvious. It is certainly possible that a student may not participate in class because she is instead looking at a friend's photos or writing a message. But more troubling and less obvious causes of distraction or unwillingness to participate also exist. These problems seem largely unknown to faculty and administrators, even though they have substantial impact on classroom and social dynamics at academic institutions.[7] For example, a student who is *not* online during class may not be willing to participate in class because she fears her comments will be critiqued online.

Studies of cyber bullying among girls indicate that one form of cyber bullying involves being teased by peers for sharing opinions. Unlike the teasing that occurs in traditional academic communities, targeted communications in online communities have the potential to be more widely broadcast, to take place in groups rather than individual capacities, and to occur without monitoring by educators and administrators. Their spread and impact can be even broader, extending well beyond the confines of the traditional academic community. Fear of this particular form of cyber bullying—rather than actual in-class Internet use—may be the true cause of a student's silence. Other, similar causes abound.

It is easy for administrators, particularly those who are unfamiliar with social-networking websites, to be dismissive of how the effects of online harassment may impact the academic setting. Suicide, significant damage to professional and personal reputation, and the inability of instructors to function in their professional capacities are among the many outcomes of extreme cyber bullying.

Facebook groups most threaten academic environments when they are used to bully, defame, or engage in hate speech against students, administrators, and faculty. Recent reports of campus-related cyber bullying highlight the gravity of this problem. At Syracuse University, sixteen students joined a Facebook group solely devoted to criticizing an English doctoral student teaching a writing class. They engaged in crass and sexualized criticism of the instructor. One entry was described by a different instructor as "level[ing] a crude and personal accusation of possessing an infectious disease, which, though meant hyperbolically, crosses a . . . line.[8] At a Canadian University, a post written to a 200-student Facebook group ridiculed a business student and even acknowledged that "[w]e are pretty much ruining someone's life here."[9] Three hundred sixty students in the United Kingdom joined a Facebook group targeting a library worker at Kent University that included physical threats and speculation about his sexual orientation.[10] Students at a high school posted a false profile of a school principal with lewd language implying he was a pedophile who propositioned students. They also leveled attacks on his wife and child.[11]

Significant anecdotal evidence demonstrates that what occurs in online communities affects traditional academic communities. At an extreme, several student suicides have been attributed to cyber bullying.[12] A study conducted by researchers at the Yale School of Medicine found no direct links but indicated that there is a likely association between bullying and suicide.[13] Less dramatic cases illustrate that cyber bullying negatively impacts traditional academic communities. While no studies were found illustrating this point, anecdotal evidence abounds. For example, one postgraduate student who was a victim of cyber bullying reported that online harassment affected his ability to study.[14] Educators targeted by students online have filed suits pursuing claims for intentional infliction of emotional distress.

Cyber bullying is a small but pervasive negative aspect of a social network that produces many positive effects. It is likely, however, that less obvious but more widespread impacts of cyber bullying may harm classroom and academic dynamics. For example, the potential for online harassment may chill class participation. Some Facebook groups are specifically designed to target students who are active classroom participants.[15] Fear of becoming the target of such groups may cause many students to reduce their in-class participation. Studies exploring the link between online cyber bullying and in-class participation are both lacking and necessary. Classrooms and schools no longer exist as a closed, protected sphere with limited outside influence. The extent, detection, and addressing of concerns stemming from social-networking sites present unique problems. Each of these is exacerbated because those responsible for monitoring and enforcing social norms in traditional communities are functionally excluded from online communities.

Academic Response to Online Communities

Given the potential for social-networking tools to disrupt the academic environment, school administrators face a challenge. The first is recognizing the seriousness of cyber bullying. While some administrators have begun to mobilize in response, there exists a legal debate concerning the extent to which administrators may restrict or punish certain forms of online behavior—whether in class or off campus—that disrupt the integrity of the learning environment. Despite a lack of clear legal precedent, school administrators have adopted strategies to combat the negative effects of online communities on students and academic culture. Surveying administrative approaches designed to lessen inappropriate online behavior illustrates both the strengths and shortcomings of current strategies.

Many current strategies demonstrate the failure of administrators to understand the complex and widespread nature of online communities. Some academic institutions believe they have addressed the problems presented by Facebook by taking technological measures to regulate Internet use within the classroom. For example, some institutions allow only selective use of the Internet in the classroom. Modern technology enables administrators to implement Internet "kill switches" that allow selective access to various websites and course management systems, while temporarily banning all other access.[16] While a testament to increased sophistication in science and technology, students can circumvent these "kill switches" through open wireless (WiFi) networks that are not subject to such regulation.[17] Further, as information technology officials at the University of North Carolina-Chapel Hill found, these technological measures can be extremely time-consuming and costly.[18] And as the director of Computing Services at the University of Michigan Business School states, "There's nothing you can do to keep a student from getting on the Internet."[19] Limiting Internet use through selective website blocking presents cost and efficacy concerns.

Another, more radical approach is to ban Internet use altogether. The University of Chicago Law School has adopted this approach. Disconnecting in-class Internet availability reduces the symptoms of inattention and poor participation. Additionally, for the period of time that students are in the classroom, it limits them to a single community, in which the professor plays the central role. However, while this solves the immediate problem of distracting sub-communities within the classroom, it fails to recognize that Facebook dynamics outside of the classroom can still affect in-class dynamics. Banning Internet use entirely in classrooms may provide a partial answer. However, it would be an error to think that by doing so administrators have protected their students. Taking away in-class Internet use to prevent cyber bullying is like unplugging a television set to prevent violence on television: it fails to address the core concern.

Other institutions refrain from banning Internet use in the classroom on principle. They suggest that the benefits of Internet access in the classroom outweigh the potential for distraction and reputational concerns. The argument underpinning this hands-off approach—that students online will be driven by the same social norms as those in traditional settings—fails to capture the unmonitored nature of the Internet. Administrators have firmly established that they will step in if students begin to abuse one another in the classroom or even at the fraternity house. In contrast, most administrators have yet to establish that their school norms extend to the Internet.

While each in-class Internet policy has certain advantages, none fully addresses the extent to which Facebook use—in and out of the classroom—may affect the academic environment. More important, these approaches undercut the value of the Internet as a powerful learning tool. As one official at the University of Louisiana at Baton Rouge states, these solutions are tantamount to "throwing the baby out with the bathwater."[20] It is therefore necessary to evaluate new and more comprehensive approaches to controlling the impact of Facebook in academic settings.

One reason for abuses in online communities is that they do not have a metaphorical adult in the room. Some school officials address this problem by taking an active role in online communities. "Administrators within higher ed[ucation] are finding ways of embracing the technology, using it as a new medium for interacting with students while tackling these very problems rather than ignore them."[21] Administrators join websites like Facebook to monitor or engage with their students online.

Some administrators join online communities to monitor their students. For example, some school officials pose as students online by creating "dummy Facebook profiles."[22] Administrators use these Facebook profiles to "friend" students, so they can view their profile pages. Once they have access to a student's profile, administrators may view their photos, comments, and group memberships. This information may be used to warn or discipline students.[23] For example, "four Northern Kentucky students received University Code of Conduct violations based on pictures posted on Facebook that showed them drinking."[24] Monitoring students' online activities gives administrators information that would be less available if they relied only upon traditional sources.

Should administrators actively monitor students' online behavior? Opponents of monitoring cite privacy concerns, boundaries between school and other areas of life, and chilling of free speech. They suggest it is deceptive for administrators to pose as students, and costly to pay people to do so. Proponents of monitoring assert that schools have an obligation to protect academic communities from online abuses. At Brandeis University, administrators screen student Facebook profiles for campus-related employment.[25] Both academic and outside employers are increasingly using Facebook searches as part of the hiring process.

Other administrators are actively, publically participating in online communities rather than simply monitoring activity. School administrators urge faculty to become members of the Facebook community in order to temper student behavior online by injecting an authority figure into a previously unregulated community.[26] At Brown University, several high-ranking school administrators have Facebook accounts.[27] Participants include the associate dean for judicial affairs, associate vice president of campus life and dean for student life, a psychotherapist, and three members of the Department of Public Safety.[28] This approach addresses one of the fundamental challenges of Facebook by placing an authority figure into the setting. Embedding an authority figure to enforce rules of conduct and assert social norms makes online communities more analogous to traditional communities. One analogy is to the "mother," whose presence checks the behavior of members of the fraternity. However, there are roadblocks to such interactions. A faculty member or school administrator who fails to identify himself on Facebook might later be held to have violated a student's right to privacy. It is possible that student monitoring could fill this void, inasmuch as students surely expect fellow students to be present in the networking site.

Finally, school administrators have adopted punitive measures to mitigate the growing challenge that off-campus Facebook use presents for the academic environment. Increasing awareness of the potential ugliness of online social-networking communities has produced punitive responses to cyber bullying and other forms of inappropriate online student conduct. Students face suspension and expulsion for their actions, as well as potential criminal charges. At Syracuse University, four students were expelled from their writing class and placed under "disciplinary reprimand" for creating a Facebook group with vulgar comments about an instructor.[29] In reacting to the disciplinary measure, the students' primary concern was that the university failed to provide adequate notice that Facebook posts could lead to punishment. As one of the students implicated in the Syracuse scandal said, "The student body needs to be aware of the [the administration's] expectations and if Facebook is fair grounds for policing, they need to make us aware of it."[30] Without clear guidelines, harsh punishment will be controversial.[31] As an associate dean at the Newhouse School of Public Communications at Syracuse University argues, "If [the judicial office] wants to operate on a case-by-case basis, that doesn't seem like a standard process. . . . What can and cannot be said on the internet should be spelled out clearly."[32]

This need for *ex-ante* rule making is illustrated through one student's battle against the administration at Ryerson University; he was expelled for contributing to a Facebook group dedicated to peer discussion of physics homework. The student, who faces 147 violations of the code of conduct, argues, "If this kind of help is cheating, then so is tutoring and all the mentoring programs the university runs and the discussions we do in tutorials."[33] If a school chooses to punish students for their online communication, it must clearly delineate the boundaries of acceptable and prohibited interaction. In response to such criticisms, some administrators have clarified rules to reflect the claim that online behavior is subject to school regulations. By extension, online abuses fall under the purview of acceptable disciplinary action if the behavior disrupts the learning environment.[34]

Administrators and courts face difficult line-drawing questions. May schools discipline students who cyber bully from home? Is it the student's behavior or the school's reaction that disrupts a student body? As academic responses to cyber bullying become more robust, it will be necessary to address these concerns. The challenge Facebook presents to school administrators to monitor online communities highlights the shortcomings of current policies to combat the potential negative effects of online social-networking tools. Disallowing Internet use in the classroom may reduce the symptoms of Facebook use in the real-time classroom. However, this fails to address the extent to which online community dynamics impact traditional communities. Administrators seem unaware of the extent to which Facebook and other online-networking tools permeate the academic culture, and indeed form unmonitored social communities within the classroom. The primary approach to infusing online communities with the norms present in other areas of an institution is to introduce an authority figure into such communities. Regulating and normalizing online behavior is necessary to maintaining cohesive traditional academic environments. Doing so requires accountability for action and involvement by administration when abuses do occur.

Freedom of expression and privacy rights must be balanced against protecting students. One approach is for school administrators to use social-networking tools while continuing to respect student privacy as they would in traditional settings. For instance, the possibility of educating and encouraging students to self-monitor and report instances of cyber bullying can be an important first step in combating the most serious symptoms of Facebook. This would also address the second shortcoming of administrators' current approaches: the failure to understand how off-campus Facebook use affects in-class dynamics.

At present, many administrators fail to appreciate the pervasive nature and potentially harmful impact of Facebook on campus. A crucial first step in tackling this problem is for school officials to clearly amend academic codes of conduct regarding permissible behavior to include online networking both on and off campus. One legal expert argues, "Policies should inform students [and their parents] that disciplinary action may be taken against them when their off-campus speech causes a substantial disruption to the education environment or interferes with another student's rights."[35] This would be an important first step in notifying students that their actions, statements, use, and involvement with social-networking tools such as Facebook are subject to university policing and punitive standards. Clear policies alone may substantially chill online abuses and allow schools to sidestep the costs of dedicated monitoring of online communities. Extending the academic administrative reach to Facebook can inject the social norms of traditional academic communities into the online realm, which in turn will deter students from cyber bullying.

Administrators underestimate the detrimental impacts of social-networking groups on traditional academic communities. First, the negative impacts of inappropriate use of online-networking websites are real and serious. They include reputational damage, inability to function in academic settings, and links to suicide risks. Although similar to fraternity activity that has long been associated with campus life, the danger of cyber bullying lies in its ability to pervade many aspects of a target's life, while flying under the radar of campus administrators who may be reticent to block it. Second, what happens in online communities tangibly affects traditional communities, even if students are not online during class. The technology presented by these networking sites provides a forum for online communities. At present, many such communities are unmonitored by academic administrators, thus providing a haven for those who engage in hate speech or bullying behavior that would be blatantly unacceptable in traditional academic environments.

The responses by academic administrators to the challenges presented by online-networking sites reflect some progress in addressing the most serious concerns. However, much remains to be decided and enacted. First, courts, legislators, and administrators will need to define the role that academic institutions may play in regulating acts of bullying that do not physically occur on school grounds. Next, administrators must find a balance that simultaneously protects the norms of their institutions and protects the privacy and free speech of its students. Doing so without incurring tremendous monitoring costs is a challenge. Among current approaches, attempts to merely ban Internet use at school seem incomplete in addressing the widespread sense of community provided by online-networking sites. Attempts to actively monitor websites present privacy and cost concerns. Clearly defining standards formally through codes of conduct and informally through administrators' public engagement with the issue is a good foundation. Encouraging student monitoring of peers for truly egregious violations provides a backstop against extreme abuse.

Social-networking websites present new and largely unrecognized challenges to academic administrators who are unaware of the pervasiveness and potential for abuse within online communities. Understanding the severity of the problems that may arise, and surveying the available approaches, provides administrators with the information necessary to begin considering and addressing these concerns effectively.

PART III

Speech

CHAPTER 9

Cleaning Cyber-Cesspools:
Google and Free Speech

BRIAN LEITER

I shall use the term "cyber-cesspool" to refer to those places in cyberspace—chat rooms, websites, blogs, and often the comment sections of blogs[1]—which are devoted in whole or in part to demeaning, harassing, and humiliating individuals: in short, to violating their "dignity." Privacy is one component of dignity—thus its invasions represent an attack on dignity. But they are not the only such affront: implied threats of physical or sexual violence also violate dignity; so too non-defamatory lies and half-truths about someone's behavior and personality, so too especially demeaning and insulting language, so too tortious defamation and infliction of emotional distress. Cyber-cesspools are thus an amalgamation of what I will call "tortious harms" (harms giving rise to causes of action for torts such as defamation and infliction of emotional distress) and "dignitary harms," harms to individuals that are real enough to those affected and recognized by ordinary standards of decency, though not generally actionable.

The Internet is currently full of cyber-cesspools. For private individuals without substantial resources, current law provides almost no effective remedies for tortious harms, and none at all for dignitary harms. Dignitary harms are off-limits for legal remedy because U.S. constitutional law effectively subordinates the dignity of persons to a particular conception of liberty. Speech, however, causes real harms (dignitary and otherwise), so much so that the only reason to think government ought not protect against such harms is that government actors have too many obvious incentives to overreach in placing restrictions on speech.[2]

Since cyber-cesspools are in large part beyond the reach of regulation by the state in America because of constitutional protections, a number of commentators[3] have suggested enhancing private remedies by, for example, making intermediaries—those who host blogs or perhaps even service providers—liable for tortious harms on their sites. This would require repeal of Section 230 of the Communications Decency Act (47 U.S.C. §230), which provides that "No provider or user of an interactive computer service shall be treated as the publisher or speaker of any information provided by another information content provider." The effect of that simple provision has been to treat cyber-cesspools wholly differently from, for example, newspapers that decide to publish similar material. Whereas publishers of the latter are liable for the tortious letters or advertisements they publish, owners of cyber-cesspools are held legally unaccountable for even the most noxious material on their sites, even when put on notice as to its potentially tortious nature. But why should blogs, whose circulation sometimes dwarfs that of many newspapers, be insulated from liability for actionable material they permit on their site?[4] Although it is common for cyber libertarians to talk as if *all* speech is immune from legal regulation, even U.S. constitutional law permits the law to impose penalties for various kinds of "low-value" speech, such as defamation. So why should the law, via Section 230, treat cyberspace differently than the traditional media?

Defenders of Section 230 worry about what I shall refer to as "spillover effects": because website owners are more likely to err on the side of caution when facing legal liability, so the argument goes, if they do not have Section 230 immunity, they will be more likely to "censor" speech, including "valuable" speech. This is probably true, but it has a flip side: namely that insulation from liability via Section 230 will increase the prevalence of low-value speech, as well as speech that causes dignitary harms, as anyone familiar with cyberspace can attest. Why think the balance should be struck in one direction rather than the other? In all kinds of contexts— newspapers, classrooms, workplaces, and courtrooms—we restrict speech not only for the sake of legally protected interests but also for the sake of avoiding dignitary harms, no doubt at the cost of spillover effects. If no academic institution or newspaper would permit its classrooms or pages to turn into the analogue of cyber-cesspools, why should the law encourage that outcome in the virtual world?

The harm of speech in cyberspace is sufficiently serious that we should rethink the legal protections afforded cyber speech that causes dignitary harms. Thanks to Google (and similar search engines), cyber speech tends to be (1) permament, (2) divorced from context, and (3) available to anyone. If the law should not remedy this problem, it must be because the value of speech that inflicts dignitary harms or the value of the speech swept up in the spillover effects is such that legal regulation is not justified. As I argue below, it is not clear whether either case can be made.

Let us first begin, however, with some case studies. I will quote *verbatim*, because too often academic discussion of this topic whitewashes what is really going on in the cyber-cesspools. Those easily offended—even those not so easily offended—are duly warned.

A Tale of Two Cyber-Cesspools

In late 2004, I noticed that my blog[5] was getting hits from what purported to be a pre-law chat room called "AutoAdmit." I followed back some of the links, and so discovered a website that I have since described—generously, I might add—as a "cesspool of infantile morons, racists, and misogynistic freaks." Especially alarming was the fact that, while about half the "threads" in the chat room actually had something to do with law school or the practice of law—suggesting that there were actual law students utilizing this board—another half had as their primary purpose racist, misogynistic, and anti-Semitic abuse or simply vicious harassment, defamation, and implied threats against named individuals, usually other law students.

Oddly, there was no indication who was responsible for the AutoAdmit site, since it was devoid of contact information. In March 2005, after watching AutoAdmit for several months, I wrote a short note about AutoAdmit to Eugene Volokh, proprietor of a well-known right-wing law blog (prompted by a related post on his blog), knowing that many law students read his blog and thinking he might help "shame" the still-anonymous proprietors of the site into cleaning it up. To my surprise, Professor Volokh's posting about the site[6] led the "administrators" to "out" themselves the following day! Professor Volokh posted a response[7] signed by Anthony Ciolli, then a law student at the University of Pennsylvania, and Jarret Cohen, an insurance salesman in Allentown, Pennsylvania, defending the huge amount of racism, sexism, and anti-Semitism on the site on the grounds that,

> We are very strong believers in the freedom of expression and the market-place of ideas. This is why we allow off-topic discussion and almost never censor content, no matter how abhorrent it may be.

We shall return to the contention that "the freedom of expression and the marketplace of ideas" are in any way relevant to the existence of cyber-cesspools. In any case, now that Mr. Ciolli had outed himself, I made my own attempt to shame the proprietors of this cyber-cesspool into cleaning it up, since I had been collecting some interesting, shall we say, statistics on the site over the prior weeks. The day after the AutoAdmit proprietors outed themselves on the Volokh blog,[8] I posted some examples of "the freedom of expression and the marketplace of ideas" to which Mr. Ciolli and Mr. Cohen were so committed. I noted that there were hundreds of threads with the word "nigger" in the subject line, as well as hundreds about Jews, some benign, but the majority of the variety "Are Jews Smarter, or Just Craftier?" and "Did jew bitches give blowjobs in Auschwitz for the protein?" the latter of which introduces another feature of the site perhaps even more prevalent than the racism and anti-Semitism, its vulgar and abusive sexism. Of course, the racism, anti-Semitism, and sexism would not have been complete without abusive remarks about homosexual men, as in the hundreds of threads about "fags."

Similar searches today on what remains of the AutoAdmit site dwarf these numbers. Consider the site exactly three years later (March 11, 2008) and only *in the section of the site that calls itself "school related"*: there were not quite 200 threads here, of which *maybe* 10 percent were actually related to law school and the practice of law. Many were about current events, dozens of threads once again concerned "niggers," while the rest are well represented by such subject lines as "fantasizes about making you cry with the girth of my cock" and "i cum hard each time my cunt shits out a dead baby." All this disturbed, misogynistic adolescent "trash talk" was in the section of the AutoAdmit site that was supposed to be "school related"; if one were to add in the "off-topic" threads, the law school-related chat on this particular cyber-cesspool drops to perhaps 2 to 3 percent of the content.

In retrospect, the idea of shaming Mr. Ciolli and Mr. Cohen was naïve. I had assumed, falsely, that they had humane sensibilities and some minimal amount of prudence. The response of Mr. Ciolli, Mr. Cohen, and the anonymous posters on AutoAdmit to the exposure I gave their site was a torrent of defamation, criminal threats, and harassment directed at me. I contemplated legal redress, but in the end, it did not seem worthwhile given that the website was rather clearly a cyber-cesspool without any credibility in the real world against a quasi-public figure.[9]

Because I was the first adult to write about this cyber-cesspool, I started to receive emails from those who had suffered far worse assaults on their dignity at the hands of the site administered by Mr. Ciolli and Mr. Cohen. There was, for example, the woman at a top law school who was repeatedly subjected to threads demeaning her by name. Initially she was charged with being unqualified to study at her law school, but soon it turned into threads "reporting" her "gang bangs" and other sexual exploits. This woman, understandably, transferred to another law school. Who wants to study at a small school where classmates are cyber stalking you?

Soon, some of the anonymous misogynists posting on AutoAdmit descended on two women studying at Yale Law School. Among the contributions of these anonymous posters to the "marketplace of ideas" were statements like the following, all of which targeted the innocent women by name (I have substituted Doe I and Doe II for the actual names):

*"just don't FUCK her, she has herpes"
  *"I think I will sodomize her, repeatedly"
  *"clearly she deserves to be raped so that her little fantasy world can be shattered by real life"
  *"I wish to rape [Doe I] and [Doe II] in the ass"
  *"I'm doing cartwheels knowing this stupid Jew bitch is getting her self esteem raped" (this was posted in the context of multiple threads harassing Doe II)

This is but a small selection of the hundreds of postings devoted to defaming, harassing, and threatening or recommending criminal and sexual violence against the Does.

Mr. Ciolli and Mr. Cohen generally reacted with anger and derision to requests from the victims to remove the abusive and threatening threads; in some cases, they threatened to post the email of the complainant—which would, of course, subject them to further abuse and humiliation. In March 2007, the *Washington Post* ran a story about the harassment of the women on AutoAdmit.[10] Not long thereafter, the law firm where Mr. Ciolli had clerked the summer before rescinded its offer of permanent employment to him,[11] stating that "the content of the messages on the [AutoAdmit] board are 'antithetical' to the values of the firm and the 'principles of collegiality and respect that members of the legal profession should observe in their dealings with other lawyers.'" Referring to Mr. Ciolli and Mr. Cohen's defense of the AutoAdmit board on the Volokh blog, the managing partner of the firm wrote:

We expect any lawyer affiliated with our firm, when presented with the kind of language exhibited on the message board, to reject it and to disavow any affiliation with it. You, instead, facilitated the expression and publication of such language. . . .

The increased attention to the plight of the two Yale women, alas, brought a proliferation of new abusive threads directed at them on AutoAdmit. The female victims eventually sued. They were represented pro bono by one of the nation's leading firms and a leading cyber-law expert. After two years, a handful of the harassers had been identified, some settled, and much of the abusive content had been removed from Google. In short, it took legal representation costing, one surmises, hundreds of thousands of dollars already, to achieve some modest success against only a handful of anonymous misogynists on one cyber-cesspool.

Our second cyber-cesspool is less colorful, and the harm it inflicted trivial by comparison. Yet, by way of contrast, it will prove useful for our analysis.

I run a blog that is widely read by philosophers. An obscure, and quite right-wing, philosophy professor at a university in the American South wrote to me asking that I link to his own blog. I had not been in the habit of simply linking to other blogs on request, but I did look at his blog, and it seemed a bit peculiar and not very interesting. I did not link to it. The obscure philosophy professor—I will call him K.[12]—had been writing nice things about my blog, but when I failed to link to him after a couple of months, he became angry. He started attacking me on his blog: he wrote a hundred different items attacking me as a "disgrace," a "buffoon," a "nut," and the like. The attacks became rather vicious and personal. He began making up incidents and hurling wild accusations. He linked to a story about a left-leaning professor in a small Texas town whose home was vandalized and who received other kinds of threats of violence. He suggested that this should be a warning to me (I lived in Texas at the time). My dean reported this incitement to violence to the university system in which K. worked. He calmed down for a while, but then resumed his irrational attacks.

I finally responded on my blog, documenting K.'s history of vicious and irrational attacks on me and others. I did not realize at the time that K. was probably mentally ill, and that my response would cause him to crack. Not quite two months later, K. spent his Christmas day creating a separate blog devoted to insulting, defaming, harassing, and threatening me—*and* my wife, my children, my parents, and anyone who reminded him of me! He wrote several hundred posts to this effect over the next two years, declaring, more than once, that "By the time we're done with this sorry excuse for a human being, he'll be crying," and noting that my having responded at all to his attacks constituted "a terrible mistake, one that will haunt [Leiter] for the rest of his life. At 48 years of age and in great health, I expect to be around for another 25 to 30 years." This adult man, a tenured professor of philosophy, would often link to photographs of me in order to mock my appearance as "effeminate," also pointing out how "lucky" my children were that "President Bush protected them, for their father certainly wouldn't have." He also compared me to Stalin and Hitler, and denounced me as, variously, an "imbecile," a "monster," and a "cretin." He declared that he would humiliate me in front of not only my children, but my grandchildren![13] Soon I began to hear from other academics he had harassed. The whole display was sufficiently strange that my dean asked a psychiatrist to review the blog to try to shed some light on K.'s mental disturbance and whether he was dangerous.

Economists say, correctly, that the "barriers to entry" are low in cyber-space. They are thinking mainly of financial cost, but the barriers are "low" in a more significant way as well. Prior to cyberspace, if you wanted to reach more than your immediate circle of acquaintances, you usually had to have some kind of competence, education, status, intelligence, and ability: otherwise no one would listen to or publish you. Indeed, in the old days, you generally had to be moderately sane to get an audience! That is no more. The K.s of yesteryear were confined to writing letters, or ranting to their friends (if they had any), or handing out leaflets, or doing other things that involve personal contact, the kind of contact that would, in most instances, reveal the profound level of emotional disturbance afflicting the speaker. Now the K.s and the AutoAdmit sociopaths need only a computer in order to abuse their targets, and to do so in a way that permits their defamation and harassment to be visited and revisited again and again by countless people anywhere on the planet, visitors who are often deprived of almost all relevant information about the speaker or his targets.

Google Is Part of the Problem

This brings us to the final villain in our story of cyber-cesspools: Google, the dominant search engine in the market today. (I shall refer in what follows just to "Google," but the same points apply mutatis mutandis to other search engines.) For without Google, every K. and every chat-room sociopath stews in obscurity. It is Google that retrieves the rantings of a friendless madman typing away on his hate blog, or the anonymous smears directed at a female law student by a vicious misogynist in a chat room, and associates those rantings and smears with the victim's name for any Google user to find. How exactly Google decides what search results to return is shrouded in a bit of mystery, though they do reveal[14] using a "PageRank algorithm" that "considers the importance of each page that casts a vote [by linking], as votes from some pages are considered to have greater value, thus giving the linked page greater value" and a "hypertext-matching analysis," which looks at how a particular search term (e.g., "Brian Leiter") figures in a web page's content.

The idea that the "most relevant and reliable results" about a female student at Yale Law School consist of the anonymous rantings of misogynistic sociopaths would be amusing if real people were not involved. Why Google searches give such prominence to blogs and Internet chat rooms—which, as a class, may be among the least reliable sources of information in human history—is puzzling. As the historian and blogger Juan Cole delicately puts the point: Google does not necessarily "put[the most relevant and reliable results first," though it most certainly facilitates what Professor Cole aptly dubs "the Google smear": the discrediting of an opponent by abuse that has a high web profile and is indexed through Google.[15] When the AutoAdmit posters attacked the Does, they were attacking private individuals with hardly any Internet presence at all. But when posted on a highly trafficked site, AutoAdmit, with the names of the victims in the thread titles, the attacks very quickly became the top search results for anyone—a friend, a family member, a prospective employer, a new acquaintance—Googling their names. Google "smearing" someone like me, with a substantial Internet presence (in the form of blogs and university home pages) is a bit more challenging. K., however, had a cyber friend, another far-right racist blogger, also of dubious sanity. This blogger emailed his entire circle of far-right blogging friends to advertise K.'s hate blog, telling them in the process a series of bizarre falsehoods about me and concluding: "[P]lease blogroll the new blog so that it rises in Google's rankings, so that when people type 'Brian Leiter' into Google, the new blog comes up." His network of extremists obliged, and a new Google smear was briefly born.

What, if anything, should Google do about its clear complicity in the viability of cyber-cesspools? What, if anything, should the law do about it? Is the moral value of "free speech" an obstacle? To these issues we now turn.

The Value of "Free Speech"

All young children are advised at some point to remember that "Sticks and stones can break your bones, but names can never hurt you." Like many things told to young children, this isn't true. Indeed, on its face, the advice is a non sequitur: there are harms other than broken bones, and there is no reason at all to think that "names," that is, words, are not capable of causing them. To be sure, "names" do not break bones, but humans are creatures whose lives are suffused in meaning, and these meanings constitute their sense of self and large parts of their well-being. Words may not be the un-mediated cause of a fracture, but they can certainly cause humiliation, depression, debilitating anxiety, incapacitating self-doubt, and devastating fear about loss of safety, respect, and privacy. There are three standard rationales offered for permitting speech, even when it causes some harm: individual autonomy, democratic self-governance, and the discovery of the truth ("the marketplace of ideas"). I will assume that something like John Stuart Mill's "Harm Principle" should be a limitation on individual liberty, and that certain degrees of harm can override the value of speech. I will also assume (contra, perhaps, Mill) that "harms" can include psychological ones—such as dignitary harms to reputation and privacy interests, as well as tortious harms that our law does recognize.[16] Since no one contests the propriety of regulating tortious harms, I concentrate on speech that causes dignitary harms, as well as speech that is included in the spillover effects of more effective regulation of tortious harms through the abolition of Section 230 immunity for website owners. The question, in short, is what value the speech on cyber-cesspools can be said to have. If there is any legally significant difference between the virtual and actual worlds, it is that speech in the virtual world may be more likely to cause harms because of its ability to reach a wide audience stripped of relevant context thanks, in large part, to Google.

Notice, to start, that cyber-cesspools, at least insofar as they target private individuals, will get no help from considerations of democratic self-governance:[17] the viability of informed democratic decision making is not at stake when an anonymous poster on AutoAdmit reports that Jane Doe has herpes or that he would like to sodomize her forcibly. That means that if there is a reason not to regulate the kind of abusive speech that is the hallmark of cyber-cesspools it must come from the other two considerations: individual autonomy and/or the discovery of the truth ("the marketplace of ideas"). Let us consider the "marketplace of ideas" rationale first.

Mill believed that discovering the truth (or believing what is true *in the right kind of way*) contributes to overall utility, and that an unregulated "marketplace of ideas" was most likely to secure the discovery of truth (or believing what is true in the right kind of way). Mill's commitment to the so-called "marketplace" is based on three claims about truth and our knowledge of it. First, Mill thinks we are not justified in assuming that we are infallible: we may be wrong, and that is a reason to permit dissident opinions, which may well be true. Second, even to the extent our beliefs are partially true, we are more likely to appreciate the whole truth to the extent we are exposed to different beliefs that, themselves, may capture other parts of the truth. Third, and finally, even to the extent our present beliefs are *wholly* true, we are more likely to hold them *for the right kinds of reasons,* and thus more reliably, to the extent we must confront other opinions, even those that are false.

For this line of argument to justify a type of speech, the speech in question must be related to the truth or our knowledge of it, and discovering this kind of truth must actually help us maximize utility. Now one might wonder whether some of the purported "truths" that cyber-cesspools proffer—for example, the purported truth that Jane Doe has herpes—are actually truths that contribute to maximizing utility. But, from the utilitarian perspective, that is not even the right way of framing the question: for the real question is whether claims about Jane Doe's alleged herpes on Internet sites by anonymous individuals with unknown motives (it is even unknown whether they have any interest in the truth!) are likely to maximize utility. It would seem not unreasonable, I venture, to be, at most, agnostic about an affirmative answer to this question, especially once we factor in the likely harms in the event that the claim is false.

But Mill, it is important to recall, did not actually accept the thesis about our fallibility in its strongest form. For Mill held that there is no reason to have a "free market" of ideas and arguments in the case of mathematics (geometry in particular) since "there is nothing at all to be said on the wrong side of the question [in the case of geometry]. The peculiarity of the evidence of mathematical truths is that all of the argument is on one side."[18] This is all the more striking a posture in light of the fact that Mill is a radical empiricist, and so denies that there is any a priori knowledge: even logical and mathematical truths are a posteriori, vindicated by inductive generalizations based on past experience. On Mill's view, then, there simply would not be any epistemic case for making room for the expression of opinions on which there is no contrary point of view that could make any contribution to the truth. This point is particularly important to bear in mind when it comes to material on cyber-cesspools aimed at private individuals.

Permit me to take what I hope is not a very controversial position, namely, that there actually are *not* two sides to the question of whether Jane Doe ought to be forcibly sodomized. If there are any moral truths, surely all the epistemic bona fides are on just one side of this issue. In other words, the explicit and implied threats of sexual violence central to cyber-cesspools like AutoAdmit simply have no moral standing based on the "market-place of ideas": they are in the same boat, for any Millian, as a website de-voted to establishing that the square of the hypotenuse of a right triangle is equal to the product, rather than the sum, of the squares on the other two sides.

But what of dignitary harms more generally, and what of the spillover effects attendant upon a legal regime in which website owners face inter-mediary liability? Surely some speech that causes dignitary harms actu-ally *does* facilitate the discovery of the truth, and surely much of the speech that falls within the scope of spillover effects from more effective regula-tion of tortious harms in cyberspace would do so as well (and some of it might even affect democratic self-governance). If we are to be genuine utilitarians, we must weigh the competing utilities and disutilities of dif-ferent schemes of regulation of speech. I shall advance two claims: first, dignitary harms are much more harmful in the age of Google; and, sec-ond, spillover effects of more effective regulation of tortious harms in cyberspace will have little effect on the discovery of truth or democratic self-government.

The AutoAdmit sociopath no doubt had his analogue in an earlier era: call him the Luddite Sociopath. The Luddite Sociopath could indeed tell his friends and acquaintances that Jane Doe is a "slut" with herpes, but there is little reason to think the law ought to provide redress, except in extreme circumstances. The reasons are worth emphasizing. The Luddite Socio-path, in the first instance, reaches hardly anyone with his hateful message. We cannot control, and would not in any case want the law to control, the *thoughts* of others. People may think whatever they want, however false, foolish, disgusting, or demeaning. Even when the Luddite Sociopath ar-ticulates his thoughts, the impact is minimal: a small circle of acquain-tances, perhaps, hear it, and some of them, thanks to their familiarity with the Luddite Sociopath, may appropriately discount them. The harm to Jane Doe is still almost nonexistent: she is insulated both by the size of the audience *and* the availability to the audience of their *experience* with the Luddite Sociopath. Jane Doe may prefer, understandably, that no one think these thoughts or express them, but that is not a preference the law can satisfy.

Suppose, now, that the Luddite Sociopath is dissatisfied with his limited audience, and with the fact that his audience generally knows a fair bit about him—for example, his propensity to rant and rave, or his misogyny, or his inability to interact normally with other people, or his membership in fringe political groups, and the like. The Luddite Sociopath wants the *world at large* to "know" about Jane Doe, he wants to *harm* Jane Doe with his words. Our Luddite Sociopath needs an intermediary who can broadcast his words far beyond any audience he can reach, and who can detach his words, and their meaning, *from him* so that they are free-standing meanings that supply no context for interpretation that might defuse their force.[19] The Luddite Sociopath thus sends letters to the editors of newspapers, tries to place ads in magazines, and tries to weasel his way on to radio and cable television programs that will give him a potent forum for his message about Jane Doe.

But now, of course, the law steps in and places some obstacles in his path. For the law declares that any one of these intermediaries who picks up the Luddite Sociopath's "message" about Jane Doe can be liable for defamation and infliction of emotional distress. None of these intermediaries can say, "We did not say those nasty things, the Luddite Sociopath did!" Thus, the law gives every intermediary a significant incentive to be cautious, to investigate what the Luddite Sociopath says before broadcasting it, and to look into the Luddite Sociopath's background and motivations. Notice, too, that even in the absence of intermediary liability, most of the traditional media also give weight to dignitary harms in deciding what ought to be published about private persons.

In the age of blogs, Internet chat rooms, and Google, our formerly Luddite Sociopath has new intermediaries who have no current incentive to place *any* obstacles in his way. With the help of a chat room or blog, he can disseminate his message about Jane Doe to those who know nothing about him, and with the help of Google, the Sociopath's message can now be widely disseminated well beyond the blog or chat room to anyone with any interest in Jane Doe. Because the law, through Section 230, insulates the intermediaries from any liability, the law no longer puts any obstacles in the way of the Sociopath: no blog owner, or chat room administrator, or search engine operator, has any legal reason to make it harder for the Sociopath to express his thoughts about Jane Doe, to express them with no contextual information about the Sociopath or his target, and to do so in ways that are no longer ephemeral, but etched into the Internet's permanent memory, thanks to Google, for anyone, anywhere to discover. Both Tortious harms and dignitary harms are, in consequence, *more harmful* than ever before.

As Internet sources gradually displace or replicate the functions of other media, the reasons for thinking that they, unlike their old media counterparts, should be exempt from familiar forms of legal regulation will seem increasingly bizarre. Let us assume, then, that Section 230 will be repealed or significantly modified. Hopefully we shall then see the application of ordinary tort law not to Internet service providers, but to the intermediaries more proximate to the harmful words: for example, blog proprietors and chat room administrators/owners. The result would unquestionably be a significant reduction in the freedom with which individuals, especially anonymous individuals, are able to speak on the Internet. That effect would be enhanced if the law were also to provide remedies for some dignitary harms in cyberspace.

There would, however, be no reduction at all in the ability of individuals to speak freely, just in their ability to exercise that purported right to speak freely in cyberspace. It is important to emphasize *purported,* since, as with Ciolli and Cohen's defense of AutoAdmit, appeals to "free speech" are invoked on behalf of speech that in fact enjoys no special legal or moral standing (e.g., defamation of private individuals). Repeal of Section 230 together with causes of action for some dignitary harms will undoubtedly reduce, dramatically, the number of comments sections on blogs, since most blog proprietors fail to monitor the content on their sites. Why that would be a greater loss in cyberspace than it is in the traditional media, which do not permit nearly as much unregulated anonymous self-expression, is a question I have not seen addressed. Certainly anyone who has spent much time reading anonymous comments on blogs would not conclude that they are an especially notable repository of human wisdom, rational insight, or moral acuity. Indeed, if the entire Internet vanished tomorrow, we would still have all the traditional media and the traditional fora of communication: not just the so-called "mainstream media," but the alternative newspapers and presses, the foreign newspapers, the libraries, the scholarly periodicals, the satellite radio and the cable television, and on and on.

The issue, though, is not the Internet, but only certain sites on the Internet, like blogs and chat rooms, which are the primary loci of cyber-cesspools. The world is not obviously better because of these parts of the Internet, and in many ways it is obviously worse. Prior to blogs and chat rooms and Google, female law students were not subjected to campaigns of anonymous vicious harassment accessible to thousands of other students and lawyers around the country. Prior to blogs and chat rooms and Google, it was rather harder to irresponsibly invade privacy, circulate defamatory statements, or threaten sexual and criminal violence with seeming impunity. What *precisely* are the contributions to human knowledge and well-being that are attributable *solely* to these aspects of the Internet, that would have been impossible without its existence in its current unregulated form?[20] It is far from obvious that there are any, at least in otherwise democratic societies.

The preceding considerations leave us, it seems, with only one free speech argument for not regulating cyber-cesspools: namely, the value of permitting individuals to express themselves freely. But what exactly is *valuable* about such expressive freedom or autonomy? Consider the idea that the value of autonomy resides not in free choice per se but in choosing wisely or valuably.[21] If *autonomy* or *freedom* per se has value, then we should think it better that Hitler chooses *freely* to kill the Jews of Europe than that he does so because of a chemical imbalance in his brain. But most of us think the opposite: freedom of choice, exercised poorly, has even less value than the same action performed unfreely![22]

The line of thought I am criticizing here trades on an ambiguity about the "value" of an action: between, that is, its blameworthiness (which is increased when one *autonomously* chooses badly) and its utility for the agent. What is really at stake is the idea that an individual is better off when he can "express" himself than if he has to "bottle up" who he is, what he feels, and so on.

There may well be a type of *value* for the agent in his being able to express himself: Hitler feels better, one suspects, if given the opportunity to rant and rave about the Jews. But that fact leaves unanswered key questions. Is Hitler's "feeling better" a relevant criterion of utility? Can his "feeling better" be outweighed by the disutility to others? We should not conceive of utility in terms of preference-satisfaction alone, so that if Hitler's preference is to spew his venom about the Jews, then it creates utility to let him do so. Satisfying many kinds of preferences makes people worse off: the heroin addict's ability to satisfy his preference for more heroin does not add to his well-being

Even if self-expression has utility for the self that gets to express itself—however depraved or ignorant or foolish—we still need to weigh the utility of others. Let us assume the AutoAdmit sociopath gets utility, in the sense of preference-satisfaction, from his ability to express his desire to sodomize Jane Doe. It surely is not plausible that this utility outweighs the harm to Jane Doe of having that message broadcast, repeatedly and widely. But in that case, we no longer have a justification for permitting such speech.

I conclude that there is no clear reason to think that speech about private individuals on cyber-cesspools has any moral standing as free speech that should be protected, and there is no reason to think spillover effects of better regulation of cyber-cesspools will not be offset, many times over, by all the other avenues by which knowledge is shared and opinions expressed, both on the Internet and in the other media of communication. Legal defenses already exist against abuse of legal process, in the form of SLAPP (strategic lawsuit against public participation) suits against meritless defamation actions whose intent is to suppress protected speech. Yet the main prophylactic against such abuse is to restrict remedies against cyber-cesspools to "private" individuals, as understood in American libel law.[23] "Private" individuals, unlike public figures, are less likely to have the resources to mount frivolous assaults on cyber-cesspools and, by the same token, speech about them is less likely to implicate democratic values or truths that really maximize utility. This is, after all, the solution we have preferred in the rest of American law. The real question is why cyberspace should be treated *more protectively* when it comes to tortious harms and why it should not, in fact, be treated more restrictively when it comes to dignitary harms, given how much more harmful they are in cyberspace.

Regulating Google to Reduce Tortious and Dignitary Harms

What *ought* Google to do about its role in facilitating cyber-cesspools? Here are some simple steps an ethical search engine company might take in response to the harms caused by cyber-cesspools:

First, Google could set up a panel of neutral arbitrators who would evaluate claims by *private* individuals that Google is returning search results that might constitute tortious or dignitary harms. I would limit the right of appeal to *private* individuals precisely because speech about public figures is far more likely to implicate actual free speech values such as democratic self-governance. Google might impose a modest fee for this right of appeal, in order to reduce the number of frivolous complaints filed with the panel. But even a modest fee (say, $500) would be miniscule by comparison to the cost to victims of filing a legal action. The Google panel would receive and evaluate whatever materials the complainant deems relevant.

Second, the Google panel would have authority to provide several possible remedies in the event it concurs with the complainant that the material in question is more likely than not to constitute actionable material or a dignitary harm (the panel would apply something akin to a "preponderance of the evidence" standard). Possible remedies might include (1) delisting the material in question from the search engine results or demoting the results so that they turn up after the first page of results (the first page, or the "top five," being the only ones that most search engine users peruse); (2) awarding to the complainant, per a proposal of Frank Pasquale,[24] a "right of reply" in the form of an asterisk attached to the search result that links the searcher to the complainant's response; or (3) requiring the proprietor of the site on which the material in question appears to provide evidence to the Google panel that the material in question is neither actionable nor a dignitary harm; in the event the proprietor fails to do that, either one of the first two remedies would be available.

Imagine how this system would have worked in the case of the Auto-Admit Does. They are private individuals. They could have provided URLs to the offending postings at AutoAdmit, the majority of which, on their face, were actionable. For those not constituting per se libel or obvious inflictions of emotional distress, the Does might have needed to submit some additional information: for example, evidence of actual LSAT scores (which were alleged on AutoAdmit to be extremely low). The Google panel would have, presumably, awarded the delisting remedy, and the whole matter would likely have ended. The anonymous AutoAdmit sociopaths could rant and rave about the Does, but their ranting and raving would be far less likely to reach employers, friends, and relatives, and so would be far less harmful.

On this proposed voluntary scheme, it is less clear whether a quasi-public figure like me would be helped. The likelihood that highly critical speech about a public or quasi-public figure actually has some *value* is prima facie higher; one cannot craft legal rules around freak cases, like mentally ill individuals with delusional obsessions. By the same token, the ability of what is really actionable speech to do damage to a public or quasi-public figure is significantly less, precisely because there is so much other information available.

Google is unlikely to adopt this voluntary scheme, so the law will probably have to create incentives for Google to address its role in the proliferation of cyber-cesspools. The most promising analogue from existing law would make Google liable for its negligence in disseminating tortious material. (A more radical proposal would make Google liable for disseminating material constituting dignitary harms as well; I remain agnostic on whether that would be advisable.) To be sure, under existing law, neutral disseminators of even actionable material are rarely deemed liable, except in cases where they are aware of the tortious nature of the material, the harms are serious and highly probable, and the burdens on the disseminator to deflect the harm are not too great. The Dobbs torts treatise takes the view,[25] for example, that libraries are not likely to be held liable for maintaining on their shelves material that they know to be defamatory. Yet one of the state statutes Dobbs cites, Cal. Civ. Code §48.5, actually does impose liability on a radio broadcaster who fails to exercise "due care" in disseminating tortious material.[26] This is, I think, the right paradigm for the treatment of Google.

Here is the proposal: if Google is put on notice by a private party complainant that material returned in its searches is tortious, it has an obligation to evaluate the claim in accordance with something like the procedure sketched above; if it fails to evaluate the soundness of the claim, then it is liable for negligent dissemination of tortious material, and can be sued by the complainant. If it undertakes a fair review of the complainant's claim about the material, and deems it nonactionable, then it is not liable, unless the complainant can establish negligence in the review process. Google is, after all, a formidable defendant to sue, and one can imagine that will deter many private individuals. On the other hand, if Google, even after being put on notice, continues to disseminate actionable material, why should it not face liability? We already impose similar obligations on Internet intermediaries with respect to copyright infringement,[27] why not accord as much protection for private individuals from tortious harms (and maybe even dignitary ones)?

Conclusion

The rhetoric about "free speech" in cyberspace usually obscures more than it illuminates, even in scholarly discussions. Daniel Solove observes that, with respect to the regulation of speech on the Internet, "We are witnessing a clash between privacy and free speech, a conflict between two important values that are essential to our autonomy, self-development, freedom and democracy."[28] Yet when it comes to cyber-cesspools, most of these values are not implicated at all, except on the side of the victims. Only the incredible view that all expression, regardless of its subject or character, has value could sustain the idea that there is a significant clash here. James Grimmelman writes that "[R]emoving content from a search engine's index at the demand of a third party . . . is offensive to free-speech values."[29] His example is China's demand that search engines block users from finding information about the Falun Gong, a quasi-religious movement banned by the Chinese government. That might, indeed, implicate some free speech values—such as democratic self-governance and the discovery of the truth—but removing AutoAdmit content threatening sexual violence from a search engine implicates no free speech values I can discern. Mark Lemley—who represented pro bono the women suing AutoAdmit—claims that "The amazing diversity of the Internet, with its abundance of user-generated content, would be impossible" without some safe harbors for intermediaries from liability.[30] But is there really an amazing diversity of *valuable speech* in and around cyber-cesspools such that we should give them safe harbors? We do not protect safe harbors in the traditional media for "cesspool speech"; why is cyberspace different?

It would, of course, be a cost not worth bearing if measures like those described here chilled rough-and-tumble political debate and scathing social criticism. There is already too much faux civility in our public discourse, which permits charlatans and villains to claim the patina of legitimacy because no one dares, for fear of being rude, to call them out for what they are. We do not want to regulate speech, on the Internet or elsewhere, in a way that would make it impossible for a modern-day H. L. Mencken to excoriate his targets. But surely it is not hard to draw the line between a Menckensque scathing critique of public figures and calls to sexually assault female law students or to make someone "cry" and humiliate her in front of her children. Recognizing how little moral standing cyber-cesspools have as bastions of "valuable" speech about private individuals ought to encourage us to rethink Section 230 of the Communications Decency Act and rethink tort liability for search engines like Google. The Internet, and the real world, would both be better places if we did so.[31]

CHAPTER 10

Privacy, the First Amendment, and the Internet

GEOFFREY R. STONE

There is a lot of talk these days about the nasty nature of the discourse on the Internet. As the film critic David Denby notes in his recent book, *Snark,* there is a new "strain of nasty, knowing abuse spreading like pinkeye through the national conversation." Discussion threads on websites are often free-fire zones "of bilious, snarling, resentful, other-annihilating rage." The Internet, Denby observes, has allowed "a degeneration of invective" to "metastasize" through our culture, and once such material is there, "it's there forever, since it's easily Googled out of obscurity." The Internet "provides universal distribution of what had earlier reached a limited number of eyes and ears," and "the knowing group has been enlarged to an enormous audience that enjoys cruelty as a blood sport." The result, he predicts, will undermine the quality of public discourse and leave everyone "in a foul mood."[1]

To what extent may the government regulate such expression, consistent with the First Amendment? As the Supreme Court made clear in New York Times v. Sullivan, the First Amendment embodies "a profound national commitment" to the principle that public discourse "should be uninhibited, robust, and wide-open, and that it may well include vehement, caustic, and sometimes unpleasantly sharp" speech.[2] Indeed, the Court has declared that the freedom of speech may "best serve its high purpose when it induces a condition of unrest . . . or even stirs people to anger."[3] The Court has therefore long and consistently held that the First Amendment generally forbids restrictions of speech in public discourse on the ground that it is offensive, unsettling, insulting, demeaning, annoying, snarling, bilious, rude, abusive, or nasty. As the Court held some sixty years ago, free speech is generally protected unless, at the very least, it is "likely to produce a clear and present danger of a serious substantive evil."[4]

174

This does not mean that speech can *never* be regulated on the Internet. The Court has recognized that there are "certain well-defined and narrowly limited classes of speech"[5] that can be restricted even in the absence of a "clear and present danger of a serious substantive evil." These include, for example, false statements of fact that defame individuals, fighting words, threats, obscenity, commercial advertising, express incitement of unlawful conduct, and child pornography, all of which can be restricted in certain circumstances.[6] Moreover, such speech can be regulated on the Internet in the same way and to the same extent it can be regulated in any other setting. Thus, bloggers who make false and defamatory statements of fact or threaten others with violence can be punished for their speech just as they could if they conveyed such messages in a newspaper, a leaflet, or a public speech.

Indeed, as a general matter speech on the Internet should be no more or less protected than in any other venue. There are, of course, differences between the Internet and leafleting, in the same way that there are differences between newspapers, pamphlets, movies, radio, television, loudspeakers, and soapboxes. But, for the most part, the core First Amendment principles apply in the same manner, regardless of the means of communication.

It is sometimes said that the harm from speech on the Internet is potentially greater than the harm from speech in other media, because the potential audience is much larger, the speech remains indefinitely discoverable, and information can be easily located through search engines like Google. All of this is true. A false and defamatory statement can cause more harm to its victim if it is conveyed on the Internet than if it is communicated over a backyard fence or in a local newspaper, and this is certainly relevant in determining damages or punishment, if the speech is unprotected by the First Amendment. But none of this is relevant to whether the speech should be protected in the first place.

If speech is sufficiently valuable to merit First Amendment protection when it is spoken over a backyard fence or published in a local newspaper, then (at least presumptively) it is also sufficiently valuable to be protected when it is disseminated on the Internet. This is so because just as the harm caused by the speech may be magnified by the power of the Internet, so too is the value of the speech. As a general proposition, as speech reaches a larger audience, its cumulative value will increase in the same proportion as its cumulative harm. Thus, as a matter of first approximation, the fact that speech on the Internet can cause more harm than speech in a local newspaper is not a reason to accord it any less protection under the First Amendment. The balance between value and harm remains more or less constant.

In this essay, I focus on a category of expression whose status under the First Amendment is unclear—non-newsworthy invasions of privacy. As already noted, the general principles that govern such expression are not unique to the Internet. They apply without regard to whether the speech takes place on the Internet, in a newspaper, in a leaflet, or in any other form of public discourse.

General Principles

In what circumstances, if any, may the government penalize an individual for communicating "private" information about another person? The First Amendment forbids the government to abridge "the freedom of speech, or of the press." On its face, the First Amendment would seem to prohibit any effort of government to punish or censor an individual for communicating private information about another person. Any such penalty or censorship would seem literally to abridge "the freedom of speech, or of the press." This was essentially Justice Hugo Black's view of the First Amendment. The First Amendment says what it means and means what it says. The First Amendment is an absolute. The government "shall make no law abridging the freedom of speech, or of the press." End of discussion.[7]

This view of the First Amendment has not carried the day. The First Amendment cannot plausibly give individuals an unlimited right to say anything, at any time, in any place, in any manner. Justice Oliver Wendell Holmes made this point succinctly with his famous hypothetical of the false cry of fire in a crowded theatre.[8] To make sense of the First Amendment, we must define the "the freedom of speech, or of the press" that may not be "abridged."

Three inquiries have framed the Supreme Court's analysis of this inquiry. First, is the challenged law directed at the content of speech? If the law is neutral with respect to content, that is, if it restricts expression without regard to what is being said, then the Court generally balances the state interest against the speech interest to decide whether the restriction is constitutional. Under this approach, a law prohibiting all public speeches in public places is unconstitutional, whereas a law prohibiting the use of loudspeakers after midnight in residential neighborhoods is constitutional.[9] Insofar as the government penalizes an individual for communicating private information about other persons, the restriction is clearly directed at the content of the communication, so content-neutral analysis is irrelevant.

Second, if the restriction is directed at content, does it regulate only "low-value" speech? The Court has held that there are several categories of expression, such as false statements of fact, obscenity, commercial advertising, fighting words, express incitement of unlawful conduct, and threats, that do not appreciably further the central purposes of the First Amendment. If a challenged restriction is directed at low-value speech, the Court employs a form of balancing to determine whether the state interest is sufficiently weighty to justify the restriction. We will return to this doctrine shortly.

Third, if the law is directed at content, and the speech restricted is not of low First Amendment value, then the restriction ordinarily will be upheld only if it is necessary to prevent a clear and present danger of a very grave harm, such as a threat to the national security.[10] No one seriously argues that laws prohibiting the publication of non-newsworthy private information address a sufficiently grave harm to meet this standard. Thus, the central issue with respect to invasion of privacy is whether such expression is low-value speech.

Protecting Privacy at the Source

Before turning to the issue of defining a category of expression as low-value speech, however, it is important to note there are many ways in which the government can constitutionally protect individual privacy without directly forbidding the publication of "private" information. For example, in order to protect the interest in privacy, the government often restricts particularly intrusive means of gathering information about others, such as wiretapping, unauthorized mail opening, and burglary. Such laws protect privacy not by directly restricting expression, but by enabling people to shield actions, communications, and information they deem private from prying eyes and ears. Laws forbidding such invasions of privacy generally do not violate the First Amendment, because they are not only content-neutral, but are not even directed at speech. Rather, they have only an incidental effect on free expression. As a general proposition, the First Amendment does not give individuals a constitutional right to violate laws of general application merely because doing so would enable them to speak or to gather information more effectively. A reporter, for example, has no First Amendment right to break into a public official's home or to wiretap her phone calls in order to learn whether she has taken a bribe.[11]

An important twist on this method of protecting privacy is whether the government can constitutionally prohibit not only the wiretapping, burglary, or unauthorized mail opening, but also the publication of the unlawfully obtained information. A reporter who burgles a public official's home in order to obtain evidence that she has taken a bribe can clearly can be punished for the unlawful break-in, but can the reporter's newspaper also be punished for publishing the fact that the politician took a bribe? The argument for restricting the newspaper's speech in this situation is not that the publication itself violates the politician's right to privacy but that punishing the publication helps to deter the unlawful burglary.

The Supreme Court has wavered on this question. In some instances, the Court has held that the publication can be prohibited in order to reduce the incentive for the underlying illegality. For example, in the context of child pornography, which involves the depiction of actual sexual acts by real children, the Court has held not only that the government can punish the producer of child pornography for the underlying child sexual abuse, but that it can also punish those who knowingly exhibit or disseminate the images, both to eliminate the incentive for the underlying illegality and to protect the child from the continuing harm that would be caused by the ongoing distribution of the speech.[12]

In other situations, however, the Court has separated the punishment of the person who commits the underlying crime from the right of the press to disseminate the information. In Bartnicki v. Vopper, for example, the Court held that the government could not constitutionally punish a radio commentator for broadcasting an unlawfully wiretapped telephone conversation, where the information related to a matter of public concern. The Court left open the question whether the government could constitutionally have punished the commentator if the broadcast had involved only a matter of "domestic gossip of purely private concern."[13]

The law also protects individual privacy by recognizing and enforcing a broad range of confidential relationships. Some of these relationships are created by private contract, others by statute, regulation, or common law. For example, the law generally protects the confidentiality of client-lawyer, patient-doctor, penitent-priest, source-journalist, and inter-spousal communications, as well as the confidentiality of tax, financial, medical, educational, and psychiatric records.[14]

To the extent these relationships are created by private contract, the general understanding is that such contracts are binding even though one of the parties has agreed to contract away what otherwise would be a First Amendment right to disclose information. As the Supreme Court has observed, in the contractual context the "parties themselves determine the scope of their legal obligations, and any restrictions that may be placed on the publication of truthful information are self-imposed."[15] Thus, if X, a public official, tells Y, a friend, that he took a bribe, Y ordinarily is under no legal obligation not to disclose this information to others and cannot be held legally accountable for doing so. But if X reveals this information to Y, an author, as part of a contractual agreement in which Y promises not to disclose the information, then Y can be held liable for violating the contract. This is so because the law of contract, like laws against burglary and wiretapping, is not directed at speech and has only an incidental effect on free expression.[16]

When these relationships are created by statute, regulation, or common law, the analysis is more complex. For example, the law may prohibit employees of the Internal Revenue Service from disclosing the contents of individual tax returns or it may prohibit doctors and other medical personnel from revealing the contents of confidential medical records. Such laws are directed at speech, but because they govern the conduct of individuals in a special relationship with government—public employees or licensees—who have knowingly agreed to limit their First Amendment rights in order to gain access to confidential information, they are generally upheld as long as they serve a substantial government interest.[17]

In these situations, as in the wiretap and burglary situations, an issue can arise about whether the restriction on speech can be enforced not only against the party to the contract or the public employee or licensee, but also against third parties who obtain the information as a result of a breach of a confidential relationship. For example, suppose a doctor impermissibly discloses confidential medical information about his patient, a political candidate, to a reporter. As in the burglary and wiretap situation, the doctor could be held legally accountable for breaching the confidentiality requirement. But can the political candidate sue the reporter's newspaper for publishing the information?

In decisions like the Pentagon Papers case, the Court has held that even if a reporter gains access to confidential information through an unlawful leak, and even if the public employee who leaked the information can be punished for unlawfully disclosing it to the reporter, the government cannot constitutionally prohibit the publication of the information in order to deter the initial leak.[18] Thus, as in *Bartnicki*, if a newspaper published the information leaked by the doctor about the political candidate, it would be constitutionally protected if the information involved a matter of public concern (for example, if the medical condition was relevant to the candidate's fitness for office). As in the burglary and wiretap situations, however, it is unclear whether the publication would be protected if the information concerned only a matter of "domestic gossip of purely private concern" and the purpose of the restriction was to deter the underlying breach of confidence.[19]

Thus, the law protects privacy in a variety of ways. It enables individuals to be reasonably confident that certain places, activities, communications, and relationships, such as one's home, one's phone calls, one's bank records, and one's private communications with doctors and lawyers, will generally be protected against public exposure. The underlying assumption is that individuals who are truly concerned about the privacy of certain information or activities will have a reasonable, though imperfect, way to safeguard their privacy by controlling how, when, where, and to whom they reveal such information. In this way, they can control their privacy at its source.

Warren and Brandeis

This brings me back to the central question, which is whether the government can constitutionally penalize the publication of private information about an individual *in the absence of any underlying wrongdoing*. To get at this question, suppose a law student writes on a law-related blog that one of her professors is gay. In fact, the professor is gay. He has generally been discreet about this fact, however, preferring to keep it to himself. But he has had several lovers, and he has discussed his sexual orientation with close friends. One of the professor's former lovers told his cousin about his affair with the professor, and the cousin then told the student, who published the information on the blog.

The professor sues the student for invasion of privacy. In this case, the student learned the information without any underlying illegality. Neither the student nor anyone else in the story line engaged in an unlawful wiretap, rummaged through the professor's home or office, breached any contractual agreement with the professor, or did anything else unlawful or improper. Is the student liable to the professor for invasion of privacy?

Historically, Anglo-American law did not recognize a common law right of privacy that would cover this situation. It was traditionally assumed that people would guard—or not guard—their own privacy as they saw fit, and that they would assume certain risks, inherent in a free and open society. If they did certain things in public that were observed or if they chose to share certain information about themselves with others, they assumed the risk that the information might be disseminated to others. In this legal regime, those who wanted to preserve their privacy had to act carefully and with discretion. In what was predominantly a rural or small-town society, this was surely an imperfect protection of privacy. But, as with many risks in everyday life, the law generally assumed that individuals were responsible for their own choices and actions, including their decisions about how best and how much to safeguard their privacy.

The idea of a tort of invasion of privacy for the publication of non-newsworthy information was first advanced by Samuel Warren and Louis Brandeis in an 1890 law review article.[20] Warren and Brandeis's critique of the state of the media at the end of the nineteenth century is especially interesting, because it is strikingly similar to the contemporary critique of discourse on the Internet:[21]

> The press is overstepping in every direction the obvious bounds of propriety and of decency. Gossip is no longer the resource of the idle and of the vicious, but has become a trade, which is pursued with industry as well as effrontery. To satisfy a prurient taste the details of sexual relations are spread broadcast in the columns of the daily papers. To occupy the indolent, column upon column is filled with idle gossip. . . . In this, as in other branches of commerce, the supply creates the demand. Each crop of unseemly gossip, thus harvested, becomes the seed of more, and, in direct proportion to its circulation, results in the lowering of social standards and of morality. Even gossip apparently harmless, when widely and persistently circulated, is potent for evil. It both belittles and perverts. . . . Triviality destroys at once robustness of thought and delicacy of feeling.

To remedy this state of affairs, Warren and Brandeis proposed the recognition of a new tort, based on the "right to privacy," that would protect individuals from the "ruthless publicity" caused by the "discussion by the press" of their "private affairs."[22] The idea gradually took hold, and most states now recognize the tort, holding that an individual can be held liable for the public disclosure of even truthful facts about another if the information is "non-newsworthy" and the disclosure would be "highly offensive" to a reasonable person.[23]

The question is whether this tort can be squared with the First Amendment. Harry Kalven once suggested that the freedom of speech protected by the First Amendment is so broad and "overpowering as virtually to swallow the tort."[24] The Supreme Court has never directly addressed the question.[25] As already noted, the critical issue is whether such expression can appropriately be deemed "low-value" speech within the meaning of the First Amendment.

Low-Value Speech

The Supreme Court has never offered a clearly defined theory of low-value speech. The case law, however, suggests that several factors are relevant to the analysis. First, categories of low-value speech (for example, false statements of fact, threats, commercial advertising, fighting words, express incitement of unlawful conduct, and obscenity) do not primarily advance political discourse. Second, categories of low-value speech are not defined in terms of disfavored ideas or political viewpoints.[26] Third, categories of low-value speech usually have a strong noncognitive effect on the audience.[27] Fourth, categories of low-value speech have long been regulated without undue harm to the overall system of free expression.[28]

A defining characteristic of speech that is actionable as an invasion of privacy is that it is "non-newsworthy." In principle, this takes care of the first two criteria. That is, "non-newsworthy" information, by definition, presumably does not primarily advance political discourse and is not defined in terms of a disfavored idea or point of view.

The third and fourth criteria, however, are more problematic. Unlike, say, threats, fighting words, and obscenity, all of which arguably have a powerful noncognitive impact on the audience, non-newsworthy information does not have that characteristic.[29] Some other low-value categories, however, such as false statements of acts and commercial advertising, also do not share this characteristic, so its absence should not be taken to be dispositive.

The fourth criterion is critical. A long tradition of regulating a particular category of low-value expression creates a shared understanding of the contours and definition of the category and demonstrates from experience whether the category can be regulated without doing undue damage to First Amendment interests. Every recognized category of low-value speech has long been subject to legal regulation, and most classes of low-value speech were regulated at common law even before the adoption of the First Amendment.

The importance of this criterion makes considerable sense, for the recognition of novel categories of low-value speech poses serious constitutional dangers. The very concept of low-value speech is inherently problematic. As Thomas Emerson once observed, the doctrine inevitably involves courts in "value judgments concerned with the content of expression," a role that is awkward, at best, in light of "the basic theory of the First Amendment."[30] Placing great weight on experience and tradition in this context is therefore a reasonable way to capture the benefits of the low-value doctrine without inviting freewheeling judicial judgments about constitutional "value."[31] The Court has rightly been very reluctant to recognize new categories of low-value speech, and this reluctance has stood us in good stead.

There is no long-standing tradition of regulating the publication of non-newsworthy private information. Although the tort was first proposed in 1890 and has been adopted by most states, even now, 120 years later, there is no extensive case law defining the boundaries of the tort and no well-developed understanding of how to reconcile the tort with the First Amendment. For the most part, the tort has been enforced rarely and idiosyncratically. As Daniel Solove, a strong advocate of the privacy tort, has conceded, courts have "struggled when applying the newsworthiness test."[32] There is simply no track record to suggest that this category of expression can meaningfully be regulated without unduly impairing the freedom of speech more generally.

The central argument for treating this category of speech as low value is that it is said to be "non-newsworthy" and therefore does not meaningfully contribute to the sort of public discourse that the First Amendment was intended to promote. But the very concept of "non-newsworthy" is exceedingly slippery. Of course, it is easy to hypothesize specific examples of speech that most people would readily agree constitute non-newsworthy disclosures of private information, the publication of which would be highly offensive to reasonable people. Consider, for example, a nude photograph of an otherwise private individual that someone posts on the Internet for no reason other than to embarrass him. It is difficult to see how such an image, standing alone, could be deemed "newsworthy," or how it could be denied that the posting would be deemed highly offensive by reasonable people.

But identifying a few easy cases does not answer the vagueness concern, for it is just as easy to hypothesize a great many difficult cases. Consider a nude photograph of Sarah Palin. Suppose it reveals her sunbathing on a nude beach. Is that non-newsworthy? Suppose the nude photograph shows a professor naked in his backyard with a student.Or, to change the theme a bit, suppose the post reveals that a professor is gay. Is that non-newsworthy? What if the disclosure is part of an accusation that the professor favors gay students or discriminates against students who are Christian fundamentalists? Suppose a post on the Internet discloses that a student is gay. Is that non-newsworthy? What if the post is intended to inform other students about the student's sexual orientation? Is this "none of their business"? What if some students prefer not to socialize with homosexuals? Don't they have a right to make that choice?

Suppose the post reveals that a particular woman has had an abortion. Is that non-newsworthy? What if the woman is running for student body president? What if the woman is a babysitter and the information is posted on a website about prospective babysitters? Don't parents have a right not to hire as a baby-sitter for their children a woman who, in their view, has murdered her own child? Is such information newsworthy or non-newsworthy?

Or consider the identity of an alleged rape victim. Is there anything newsworthy about the publication of her name? Wouldn't the person accused of the alleged rape want the victim's name broadly disseminated so people with relevant knowledge about her might come forward with information that would help prove his innocence? Perhaps she has made false accusations against other people in the past or told other people a different story about what happened. Is her identity non-newsworthy?

My point is not to deny that there are some hard-core situations that would surely qualify as non-newsworthy publications, or that their dissemination would be highly offensive to reasonable people. It is, rather, that "non-newsworthiness" is an extraordinarily vague and open-ended concept. Other categories of low-value speech, like express incitement of unlawful conduct, threats, fighting words, commercial advertising, and false statements of fact, although inevitably vague at the margins, are much more easily defined and identified than "non-newsworthy" speech, which is highly context and value dependent. Even the doctrine of obscenity, which has vexed the judiciary for decades, is at least limited to a relatively narrow category of expression encompassing only the explicit and patently offensive depiction of certain clearly defined sexual acts. The concept of non-newsworthiness embodies no objective limitations. As Randall Bezanson has aptly observed, the "standards of taste or propriety" that are necessarily embedded in the idea of non-newsworthiness are "simply unascertainable on a societal level" because contemporary society is "too pluralistic and culturally diverse."[33]

Even Warren and Brandeis acknowledged that there would be serious "difficulties" in the articulation of their proposed tort. They conceded, for example, that "the propriety of publishing the very same facts may depend wholly upon the person" about whom they are published," and that "no fixed formula" can be designed to separate the newsworthy from the non-newsworthy. Indeed, they acknowledged that any effort to enforce the invasion of privacy tort would necessarily require a "rule of liability" that "must have in it an elasticity which shall take account of the varying circumstances of each case,—a necessity which unfortunately renders such a doctrine not only more difficult of application, but also . . . uncertain in its operation."[34]

Warren and Brandeis recognized these obstacles long before the Supreme Court had explored the challenges of creating a truly robust system of free expression, a system in which concerns about vagueness, over-breadth, discretion, and chilling effect have come to play a central role. Ambiguity in the law governing the freedom of speech was commonplace in 1890. Today, in light of our constitutional experience, the Court has rightly insisted on a degree of precision in First Amendment doctrine that renders implausible the idea of holding people legally accountable for *truthful* publications because some court or jury later finds them to be "non-newsworthy."

At this point, it might be useful for me to offer a brief aside on threats, both because they were much discussed, often rather casually, at the conference on which this volume is based, and also because the concept of a threat illustrates the necessity for a clear definition of low-value speech categories. A threat, for First Amendment purposes, is not a statement that is intended to frighten or intimidate another. For example, a statement by a doctor to a patient that if she does not quit smoking she will take years off her life is not a threat, even though it is intended to frighten and intimidate her into action she does not want to take. To constitute a threat, a statement must, among other things, clearly suggest that the harm will be brought about by the speaker or his confederates. Thus, the statement "I will kill you if you don't pay me what you owe me" is a threat. The statement "X deserves to die because he didn't pay me what he owes me" is not a threat under the First Amendment, because the speaker is not suggesting that he or his accomplices will kill X. The specificity of the definition of a threat is necessary to avoid ambiguity that would otherwise chill constitutionally protected expression.[35]

Similarly, incitement to commit unlawful conduct does not mean statements that might cause others to commit crimes or even statements that are intended to encourage others to commit crimes. The former would reach all sorts of criticism of the government (for example, speech criticizing the conduct of the war in Iraq might be thought to encourage terrorists); the latter would afford speakers who criticize the government inadequate protection against jurors who abhor their views and are therefore likely to find bad intent even when that intent was lacking. Thus, as Judge Learned Hand recognized more than eighty years ago, for speech to be punishable as incitement, it must *expressly* incite unlawful conduct. These examples underscore the fatal ambiguity of the "newsworthiness" concept.[36]

Private and Public Speech

Having said all this, I must acknowledge that there are elements of First Amendment doctrine in which the law distinguishes between public and private speech, and that this distinction is, in some instances, somewhat similar to the distinction between newsworthy and non-newsworthy expression. Does this save the invasion of privacy tort from extinction?

At the outset, it is necessary to separate two different public/private distinctions. Some speech is "private" in the sense that it is not part of public discourse. An example might be a conversation between two friends about a mutual acquaintance over a cup of coffee. Although the Court has not embraced any overarching First Amendment principle for dealing with such nonpublic speech, the general assumption seems to be that a libelous statement, or a threat, or a bribe, or an effort to persuade someone to commit a crime in such circumstances would not necessarily be tested by the same First Amendment standards that govern public discourse.[37] But this element of the public/private distinction is not relevant to speech on the Internet (except, perhaps, to private emails between two individuals), because blogs and most other forms of expression on the Internet are disseminated to a large audience and are therefore clearly on the "public" side of the line in terms of this aspect of the public/private distinction.[38]

The other variant of the public/private distinction is more relevant to the non-newsworthiness inquiry. In several areas of First Amendment law, the Court has held that speech will be protected from restriction if it concerns matters of public concern, even though similar speech might be regulated if it involves matters of only private concern. We have already noted one example of this phenomenon in the discussion of *Bartnicki,* in which the Court held that a radio commentator could not be held liable for broadcasting a tape recording of an unlawfully wiretapped telephone conversation, because the tape concerned a matter of public concern, while at the same time noting that the result might be different if the recording dealt only with "domestic gossip of purely private concern." Similarly, in libel law, the Court has indicated that false statements of fact about "matters of purely private concern" are entitled to less First Amendment protection than false statements on "matters of public concern."[39] And in the regulation of speech by public employees, the Court has held that the government has greater leeway to restrict public employee expression that disrupts government activities when the speech concerns only matters of personal interest, rather than matters of "political, social, or other concern to the community."[40]

Thus, although the Court has generally expressed grave "doubt" about "the wisdom of committing" to judges and jurors the task of distinguishing "on an ad hoc basis" between matters of public and private concern in the interpretation and application of the First Amendment,[41] it has, in at least some circumstances, recognized that such an inquiry may be necessary to strike the right balance between the freedom of speech and competing government interests. Put differently, inquiries into whether speech is relevant to matters of public concern have not been deemed so fundamentally incompatible with the basic premises of the First Amendment that they must be ruled out entirely. But it is important to note that the Court has authorized such inquiries only in very narrowly defined circumstances in which the expression at issue is already presumptively subject to regulation—even apart from the public/private distinction. In the *Bartnicki* situation, for example, the information was initially obtained unlawfully and would not have been available at all but for the underlying illegality. In the libel situation, the expression at issue consists of false statements of fact, which are already deemed low-value speech. In the public employee situation, the Court has long recognized that because the government has special interests "in promoting the efficiency of the public services it performs through its employees," it has much greater latitude in regulating speech that may interfere with those interests than in regulating public discourse generally.[42] Thus, in each of these situations, the protection of speech that is relevant to public debate can be seen as an exception to what would otherwise be a presumption of constitutionally permissible regulation.

In the invasion of privacy context, however, the *only* characteristic of the expression that purportedly justifies characterizing it as low-value speech subject to government regulation is its asserted non-newsworthiness. To put so much weight on so subjective, vague, and open-ended a concept goes beyond anything the Court has ever upheld in its First Amendment jurisprudence, and it is therefore no surprise that the Court has never put its imprimatur on this doctrine.

There is one other possible twist worth noting. There was much talk during the conference on which this volume is based about the tort of intentional infliction of emotional distress. Perhaps actions for invasion of privacy can be squared with the First Amendment when they also constitute intentional inflictions of emotional distress.[43] In the traditional invasion of privacy action, a defendant can be held liable if he published the information with reckless disregard for the offensiveness of the disclosure. Suppose, instead, the law limited such actions only to circumstances in which the defendant intended the publication to cause "severe emotional distress." This would cover the most egregious invasions of privacy. But is the tort of intentional infliction of emotional distress consistent with the First Amendment?

In Hustler Magazine v. Falwell,[44] the Supreme Court held that public figures may not recover for the tort of intentional infliction of emotional distress as a result of even "outrageous" publications that insult, degrade, or humiliate them, in the absence of proof of falsity. The Court explained that although a "bad motive may be deemed controlling for purposes of tort liability in other areas of the law," the "First Amendment prohibits such a result in the area of public debate." The Court added that, like the concept of non-newsworthiness, the concept of "outrageousness" in the realm "of political and social discourse has an inherent subjectiveness about it which would allow a jury to impose liability on the basis of the jurors' tastes." The Court therefore concluded that the "outrageousness" standard "runs afoul of our long-standing refusal to allow damages to be awarded because the speech in question may have an adverse emotional impact on the audience."[45]

Falwell dealt only with statements concerning public figures. It did not address the constitutionality of the intentional infliction of emotional distress tort in the context of private individuals. As with the invasion of privacy tort, however, the argument for enforcing the intentional infliction of emotional distress tort in the realm of public—as distinct from private—discourse seems thin. Historically, the common law did not recognize such a tort, in the absence of physical harm. There was great skepticism about such a tort because of the difficulties of proving mental injury, the risk of fictitious claims, and the fear of a flood of litigation over trivial matters. Although the Second Restatement of Torts recognized the tort in 1965, in the years since most courts have continued to take a decidedly negative approach to intentional infliction of emotional distress claims that involve statements in public discourse. As the New York Court of Appeals observed in 1993, it had rejected every such claim over the preceding quarter-century because in no case was the alleged conduct sufficiently "outrageous" to justify liability.[46] Viewed in this light, it seems unlikely that the tort of intentional infliction of emotional distress can be reconciled with the demands of the First Amendment, even as applied to private figures, as long as the speech is in the domain of public discourse.

The Interest in Privacy

Another difficulty with the invasion of privacy tort concerns the strength of the state interest. Even when speech is deemed of low First Amendment value, the Court generally insists that the state must have at least a substantial interest to justify regulating the expression. This is so both because even low-value speech usually has some First Amendment value and because any effort to regulate low-value speech usually has chilling effects on high-value speech.[47] Those problems are especially acute in the invasion of privacy context, because the very concept of non-newsworthiness is so elastic, subjective, fact dependent, and, in the words of Warren and Brandeis, "difficult of application."

Of course, it is easy to romanticize the interest in forbidding the publication of non-newsworthy information about individuals that causes them embarrassment and emotional distress. Warren and Brandeis waxed eloquent about the right "to be let alone," the right to "an inviolate personality," and the right to have one's "social and domestic relations be guarded from ruthless publicity."[48] Similarly, Paul Gewirtz has noted that privacy, in the sense of "the ability to control and to avoid the disclosure of certain matters about oneself," is "an important precondition for human flourishing."[49] Indeed, there are quite clearly legitimate reasons for being concerned with privacy in this sense. The ability of individuals to engage in private conduct without having it broadcast to the world, the capacity of individuals to make mistakes without being haunted by them forever, and the freedom to live one's life without having to answer publicly for every choice, are unquestionably legitimate personal and societal interests.[50]

But there is another side to the issue. As Richard Posner has observed, if as is often the case "what is revealed is something the individual has concealed for purposes of misrepresenting himself to others, the fact that disclosure is offensive to him and of limited interest to the public at large is no better reason for protecting his privacy than if a seller advanced such arguments for being allowed to continue to engage in false advertising of his goods."[51] In many situations, in other words, those who assert an interest in privacy can reasonably be seen as trying to deceive others about themselves. They would rather that other people believe that they are "better" than they are, that they not know that they once had an affair or an abortion, or cheated on a test, or have an embarrassing illness, or drink to excess, or strike their children, or sunbathe in the nude. There may be good reasons for wanting to keep such information private, but Posner is surely right that in many cases people invoke the right of privacy because they want to mislead others into thinking better of them than they would if they knew the truth. In such circumstances, they are engaged in a form of fraud, and we should be careful not to see that claim for more than it really is.[52]

There is at least a partial answer to Posner's insight, for in many cases people who learn negative things about others may exaggerate the significance of the fault and overreact in their judgment about the person. As Jeffrey Rosen has noted, "when intimate knowledge" is taken out of context, and "revealed to strangers, we are vulnerable to being misjudged on the basis of our most embarrassing, and therefore most memorable, tastes and preferences."[53] Moreover, as Daniel Solove argues, in at least some instances the "law protects against disclosures of private information because society believes that such information is not appropriate for making public judgments about people."[54]

Thus, the real trade-off may not be between truth and falsity, but between fair and unfair evaluations of individuals. We recognize this danger in other areas of the law. In the law of evidence, for example, we routinely make evidence of a party's bad character inadmissible, because we know that jurors tend to overvalue the importance of the evidence.[55] The invasion of privacy tort can be understood as an application of the same basic insight about human nature. But, at least in the realm of public discourse, for the government to deny people access to information because they may overvalue it reflects a form of paternalism that is directly incompatible with the basic assumptions of First Amendment theory.[56]

Defenders of the right of privacy in this context will argue further, however, that whether or not the invasion of privacy tort sometimes enables people to deceive others about themselves, the publication of non-newsworthy information serves no legitimate First Amendment purpose, and that the Constitution is therefore simply irrelevant to the social policy question of whether people should be able to know or not to know such information about others. In Edward Bloustein's words, there is no First Amendment right "to satisfy public curiosity and publish . . . gossip about private lives."[57] But this assumes a distinction between legitimate matters of public concern and "gossip about private lives" that is not so easily sustained. Not only, as we have seen, is the concept of "non-newsworthy" speech exceedingly vague and difficult of application, but it is not at all clear that, even if we "know it when we see it,"[58] such speech is in fact of low First Amendment value.

Eugene Volokh argues, for example, that speech about "daily life" is "worthy" of full First Amendment protection,[59] and Diane Zimmerman insists that contemporary society uses "knowledge about the private lives of individual members" to "preserve and enforce social norms." Indeed, by providing people with a rich way "to learn about social groups to which they do not belong, gossip increases intimacy and a sense of community among disparate groups and individuals." Speech that is seen by some as unfairly invading privacy constitutes "a basic form of information exchange that teaches about other lifestyles and attitudes, and through which community values are changed or reinforced." Indeed, "perceived in this way," such expression "contributes directly" to the First Amendment's "marketplace of ideas."[60]

Beyond all this, though, the practical reality is that changes in technology may have largely made moot the very idea of the tort of invasion of privacy.

In 1890, when Warren and Brandeis first promulgated the tort, the notion that the law could meaningfully distinguish between newsworthy and non-newsworthy publications and could effectively regulate those that were non-newsworthy seemed plausible, although difficult even then. Today, however, with the advent of the Internet, the very idea of attempting to regulate such invasions of privacy is beyond the reasonable capacity of the law. Perhaps the professional press that was the principal target of Warren and Brandeis's legal innovation could reasonably have been expected to conform their publications to professional and legal standards of newsworthiness. With a medium like the Internet, however, in which every individual can disseminate information to the world, the concept of the professional press is largely irrelevant. The private conversations that Warren and Brandeis would themselves have exempted from their tort now occur in a forum that instantly reaches everyone in the world with access to a computer.

This makes the legal enforcement of the concept of non-newsworthiness staggeringly problematic. Consider, for example, a student who posts accurately on a blog dealing with her school that a teacher recently had an abortion or had cheated in college or was seen in a gay bar. Within the confines of the school community, it would be difficult to argue that this is non-newsworthy information or that the student could be punished for revealing it to others. But with modern technology, this information will be available not only to those in the particular school community, at that time and place, but to all Internet users and forever. With the availability of search engines like Google, a person thinking of hiring the teacher twenty years later will be able with just a few keystrokes to find this information. This expands profoundly both the potential value and the potential harm of the initial posting. The main point of the hypothetical, however, is that one person's newsworthy information is another's invasion of privacy, and in the world of the Internet it is no longer possible to segregate audiences based on the immediate relevance of information to the community. We are all now part of a universal audience for everything and forever. This may be liberating or it may be unnerving and unwelcome, but in no event is it a state of affairs that can meaningfully be addressed by the invasion of privacy tort. That approach to the issue, which was problematic even in 1890, is no better than quaint today. It is an odd curiosity of an earlier and vastly simpler era.

A useful analogy is the law of obscenity. Through the 1950s and 1960s, the obscenity doctrine had a substantial impact (for better or worse) on the ability of individuals to gain access to sexually explicit expression. In 1973, the Supreme Court, concerned that such expression was becoming too readily available, and that it was increasingly exerting "a corrupting and debasing impact" on society, broadened the constitutional definition of obscenity.[61]

Despite this effort to use the law to control sexually explicit expression, technological change simply swamped the capacity of the law. With the coming of video rentals, cable television, and the Internet, sexually explicit material became more easily available on an unprecedented scale. This, in turn, affected (some would say corrupted) community standards of "decency" in the depiction of sex, and over time almost no sexually explicit material could be found to violate "contemporary community standards." The effort of government officials to prosecute the exhibition, distribution, or dissemination of obscene matter has effectively ended at the local, state, and federal levels. Put simply, the capacity of the law was overwhelmed by the forces of social and technological change. As a consequence, legal efforts have more recently been refocused on more specific problems posed by sexually explicit materials, problems that are both more serious and more plausibly subject to legal regulation, such as zoning and child pornography.[62]

Just as the law can no longer effectively deal with obscenity because of social and technological change, so too can it no longer effectively deal with non-newsworthy invasions of privacy. This is not to deny that there are situations in which invasions of privacy can be harmful to individuals or that, in an ideal world, we might have some way to prevent that harm. It is to say, though, that even if the First Amendment itself is not sufficient in principle to "swallow the tort," the combination of the First Amendment and social and technological change has, for all practical purposes, gobbled it up completely. To argue otherwise is simply to tilt at windmills.

Moreover, it is not clear that the importance Warren and Brandeis attached to this sort of privacy is relevant for the future. In the contemporary culture of Facebook, Friendster, and other social-networking websites, people increasingly seem to value transparency over informational privacy. In many ways, this may be a self-adjusting system. If one of the dangers of invasions of privacy by publication was the risk that people would seriously overvalue the importance of relatively minor instances of private misconduct that rarely came to light, the much greater visibility of human foibles in the modern era will likely lead people to learn how to put the mistakes of others in their larger context. In this sense, one might hope that the loss of privacy will result in greater tolerance and understanding, which itself might be a major triumph of the First Amendment.

The most realistic way to protect privacy today is at its source. By prohibiting highly intrusive methods of gaining information that people want to keep confidential it is still possible to enable individuals who truly care about their privacy to preserve it, if they act carefully and with discretion. But once information is out of the bottle, once we share it with others, once others know it, we can no longer hope to put it back. If that era ever existed, it is now the past.

CHAPTER 11

Foul Language:
Some Ruminations on
Cohen v. California

JOHN DEIGH

Great advances in technology sometimes directly increase the power of ordinary people. The invention of the telephone and that of the automobile are two obvious examples. The advance in information technology of the past twenty years is a third. Before the development of the Internet, only a small number of people commanded means of communication that could reach an audience larger than a few hundred. Now, however, anyone with access to a personal computer has the power to reach millions not only in his or her own country but around the world. The voices of ordinary people have thus gained a power to be heard that elites cannot ignore, and the benefits of this gain for democracy have been substantial.

At the same time, this gain carries significant costs. A great increase in the power of people's speech brings a corresponding increase in the harm that can be done to people when that power is abused. As a result, cases at law that forty or more years ago expanded freedom of speech in ways that did not then appear to create opportunities for serious harm, that did not, in particular, portend of abuse that could cause severe injury to a person's reputation or emotional stability, now have a different import. In view of this change, they invite renewed examination. One such case is Cohen v. California (USSC, 1971). This essay presents a set of reflections on the holding in this case.

Cohen extended the First Amendment's right of free speech to words that evince the speaker's emotions. The speaker in the case was one Paul Cohen. On April 26, 1968, he wore a jacket in a public place on the back of which were boldly inscribed the words "Fuck the Draft." The public place was a corridor in the Los Angeles County Courthouse, and the law of whose violation he was convicted was part of the California Penal Code. It prohibited offensive conduct that maliciously and willfully disturbs the peace or quiet of any neighborhood or person. On conviction, Cohen was sentenced to thirty days in prison. The California Appellate Court upheld the conviction, noting that women and children were present in the corridor when Cohen wore his jacket. The U.S. Supreme Court overturned the conviction.

The Court, in overturning the conviction, held that the First Amendment protects speech that expresses emotion per se, that is, regardless of whether the expression of the emotion is necessary to the speech's communicating the ideas and opinions it also expresses. The issue in the original case was whether Cohen in wearing his jacket had wrongfully caused a public harm, and the Supreme Court effectively removed this issue by giving First Amendment protection to Cohen's speech. But the Court's holding has broader implications. It gives similar protection to emotive speech that causes personal and private harms. Expletives, slurs, vulgarities, and other forms of speech that express contempt, disgust, animus, and the like toward someone or the members of some group can produce in their target considerable suffering and anxiety and at the same time make him or her the object of uninvited, demeaning attention and publicity. The latter, in particular, especially when it consists in ambushing the victim and forcing him or her into the glare of such humiliation and denigration, represents a gross violation of privacy. The government, then, if the holding in *Cohen* were applied to such speech, could not suppress it. Its victims could not look to the government for protection from these violations. And if they cannot, because of this holding, the case has an odd and unhappy result.

What makes the holding in *Cohen* odd is its mismatch with the leading philosophical defenses of the right to freedom of speech. None of these offers grounds for taking this right as guaranteeing freedom of emotional expression per se. None implies in its justification of a right to the freedom to express one's thoughts and ideas a justification of a corollary right to the freedom to express one's feelings and emotions. For this reason, one can question whether there is a sound basis for the Court's extending the First Amendment's protection of freedom of speech to include the emotive force of the speaker's words regardless of its importance to the thought those words convey. And while we might think there is a sound basis for protecting Cohen's speech in virtue of its being distinctively political speech—a possibility I will consider in the sequel—one can still question whether there is a sound basis for protecting the emotional force of a speaker's words generally, that is, regardless of whether they fall into a category of speech like political speech that ought to receive heightened protection from government interference. For this reason the opinion the Court delivered in support of its decision in *Cohen,* if taken as applying beyond distinctively political speech, seems problematic. And it may be problematic even if it is taken narrowly as applying only to distinctively political speech.

In questioning whether there is a sound basis for the holding, I do not mean to be questioning whether one can find support for it in past Supreme Court opinions regarding the First Amendment's protection of speech. Perhaps one can. What I question is whether one can find support for it in any of the leading philosophical defenses of the right to free speech. By a philosophical defense I understand a defense of a universal right of free speech, one that all men and women, either as individuals or as members of a people, have regardless of the particular state under whose rule they live. My interest, then, in the holding in *Cohen* does not extend to other Supreme Court decisions.[1] No other, as far as I know, speaks directly to the question of whether the First Amendment protects purely emotive speech. And if any others provide indirect support for the holding, then my misgivings about the latter may apply to them. I will not, however, be considering these broader issues.

Let me also state clearly at the outset that I am not questioning whether the right to free speech should include emotional speech. Obviously it has to. Some thoughts and ideas cannot be expressed except in words that convey emotion.[2] One cannot communicate deep personal loss except in language that expresses grief. One cannot protest cruel injustices except in language that expresses indignation. One cannot warn of coming dangers except in language that expresses alarm. Essential to Winston Churchill's famous warning of the dangers confronting Europe and America in the years immediately following World War II, for example, are words heavy with foreboding and threat. "An *iron curtain,*" Churchill declared, "has descended across the [European] Continent. Behind that line lie all the capitals of the ancient states of Central and Eastern Europe. . . . And all are subject in one form or another, not only to Soviet influence, but to a very high and in some cases increasing measure of control from Moscow. . . . In front of the *iron curtain* which lies across Europe are other causes of anxiety. . . . [I]n a great number of countries far from the Russian frontiers and throughout the world Communist fifth columns are established and work in complete unity and absolute obedience to the directions they receive from the Communist center. Except in the British Commonwealth and the United States where Communism is in its infancy, the Communist parties or fifth columns constitute a growing challenge and peril to Christian civilization. These are somber facts for anyone to have to recite on the morrow of a victory gained by so much splendid comradeship in arms and in the cause of freedom and democracy, but we should be most unwise not to face them squarely while time remains."[3] Plainly, it is impossible to separate Churchill's thought in this speech from the apprehension and unease that interpenetrates it. Plainly, it would have been impossible for Churchill to have delivered his warning to the West without using dark and chilling language, language designed to arouse fear.

What I am questioning is whether the right to free speech should include use of emotive language in speech when such language has no other point than to vent and arouse feeling. The word "fuck" in Cohen's speech is a clear example. It served to communicate Cohen's animus toward the draft and perhaps also to shock those who were unaccustomed to seeing the word so displayed. It did not convey any idea about the draft that would explain the appropriateness of animus toward it or contribute to the debates about its role in the conduct of a war that many people had come to regard as grossly immoral. Indeed, the idea the word most commonly expresses has no application in the linguistic context in which Cohen used it. You cannot, after all, engage in sexual congress with a legal institution. Its chief purpose, in Cohen's use of it, was to express virulently his contempt for the draft.

To be sure, "fuck" is now such a common epithet that it has lost the power to shock any but the most genteel soul. Indeed, the current range of its usage or that of its cognates is so great that in some cases one couldn't, without knowing the context of the utterance, tell what sort of emotion it expresses. It has taken over from "damn," it would seem, the function of expressing emotion generally or of infusing an exclamation with additional emotion. Accordingly, it may be placed in the class of pure exclamatory terms along with "ooh," "whoopee," and "yech."

It nonetheless continues to have, in many of its uses, the emotive force with which Cohen used it, and this places it in a different class of emotive terms. These are terms that function at once as common names and as mere expressions of emotion. They are mere expressions in that successfully applying the name does not make the emotion one expresses appropriate. Take

for example ethnic slurs like "wop" and "chink." Each is a name for someone who belongs to a specific ethnic group, and each expresses contempt
for people who belong to that group. Yet the contempt a person expresses
for his Italian neighbors by calling them "wops" is not appropriate by virtue of their being Italian. Consequently, because denying the truth of the
person's statement that his neighbors are wops is equivalent to denying
that they are Italian, refusal to share the person's contempt for them or to
think it appropriate does not imply that one denies the truth of what he
says. By contrast, if a person expresses contempt for his neighbors by calling
them "slobs" or "nitwits," then one's refusal to share his contempt or to think
it appropriate does imply that one denies the truth of what he says. For being
slovenly or foolish is a deficiency to which contempt is an appropriate response. "Slob" and "nitwit," though commonly used to express contempt, are
not mere expressions of the emotion. Similarly, Churchill achieves his aim of
eliciting fear through the use of such words as "peril," "somber," and "fifth
column." They express fear by virtue of the conditions they name; they are
not mere expressions of the emotion.[4]

It is clear, moreover, that the Supreme Court also saw the emotive force
of Cohen's language as, unlike that of Churchill's, separable from its cognitive content. Justice Harlan, writing for the Court's majority, set out, early
in his opinion, the distinction between the inscription on Cohen's jacket
and its meaning. There is no question, Harlan observed, that "the State . . .
lacks power to punish Cohen for the underlying content of the message
the inscription conveyed. At least so long as there is no showing of an intent to incite disobedience to or disruption of the draft, Cohen could not,
consistently with the First and Fourteenth Amendments, be punished for
asserting the evident position on the inutility or immorality of the draft his
jacket reflected."[5] The question, as Harlan saw it, is whether the state has
the power to punish Cohen for the linguistic manner in which he expressed
that position, for the words he chose to express it. And since the words
Cohen chose were not, in the context in which he used them, incendiary
or directed at particular individuals with the intention of provoking
them to violence, one precedent allowing the state to punish speech
because of the words its speaker used does not apply. Rather, as Harlan,
toward the end of his opinion, noted, Cohen chose his words for their
emotive force and not merely for their cognitive content, and such force
"may often be the more important element of the overall message sought
to be communicated."

While no one could quarrel with Harlan's point about words often being chosen more for their emotive force than their cognitive content, it does not follow from this point that such choices should always have the same immunity from government interference as choices of words for their cognitive content. When the two cannot be separated, of course, then the same immunity that a right to free speech secures for the ideas and thoughts that are expressed protects the emotive language with which they are expressed. But when the choice of words for their emotive force is superfluous to whatever ideas and thoughts they express, then the question of what justifies the same protection of that choice is genuine and pressing.

The reason is that people can, as I noted earlier, be seriously harmed by such words. The harm consists not only of the immediate pain they suffer and of its lingering in memory, but also of loss of ease and self-possession, which too can be lasting and debilitating. Part of the experience of being the object of another's contempt and animus is to feel naked and vulnerable, and this is especially true when the contempt and animus are arbitrary and leave one defenseless. People have a basic interest in social acceptance and the freedom from disparagement it entails. It is among the several interests that privacy and the respect it requires protect.[6] To be the target of slurs and expletives is, then, to suffer a violation of this interest and so the privacy that protects it when people, despite their differences and deviations from what is seen as normal, are respected.

In view of this harm, it is not obvious why protection of such verbal abuse should be upheld when it is not necessary for guaranteeing freedom to express one's ideas and opinions. And the difficulty in justifying such protection becomes even more apparent when we consider the major philosophical defenses of a right to free speech.

The classical defense in Anglo-American philosophy is John Stuart Mill's argument, in *On Liberty*, for protecting freedom of speech from societal interference. Mill makes his argument in chapter 2 of *On Liberty*. One cannot, however, fully comprehend the argument without taking into account what Mill says at the end of chapter 1 about the way it fits into the larger argument of his essay. The larger argument is his argument for "one very simple principle"—the harm principle.[7] This is the principle that the only purpose for which society can rightfully interfere with the liberty of any of its members, against that person's will, is to prevent him or her from harming others. It is the object of his essay, Mill writes, "to assert [this] principle."[8] Mill then describes the argument he will make in chapter 2 for protecting freedom of speech as offering, with respect to one division of his subject, grounds that he will in later chapters apply generally.[9] In other words, on Mill's own account, the reasons he advances in chapter 2 in support of the absolute liberty of speech are, when suitably generalized, the same reasons he adduces in support of the harm principle. Mill thus instructs us to read the argument of chapter 2 as a prelude to his general argument for the harm principle, and unless we read it as such, we will fail to understand how he conceives of speech as protected actions under that principle. Too often, however, chapter 2 is read as an independent argument. Too often it is taken as a simple utilitarian argument for protection of speech from societal interference and as such one that proceeds along a different line from the line on which Mill makes his general argument.[10]

Mill, to be sure, rests his case for the harm principle ultimately on considerations of utility. But as he says, these must be considerations of "utility in the largest sense, grounded on the permanent interests of man as a progressive being."[11] The promotion of utility is, consequently, for Mill a matter of advancing these interests, and as we learn in chapter 3 of *On Liberty*, their advancement requires securing for men and women liberty necessary for their self-development, the realization of their distinctively human capacities. Such liberty consists at a minimum in leaving each free, within the sphere of wholly self-regarding actions, to do as he or she chooses. Society, therefore, may interfere with only the actions of individuals that directly affect the interests of others, and only if such interference brings about more utility for humankind than leaving the actions unregulated. Thinking is plainly a wholly self-regarding activity, and accordingly the liberty of thought is a liberty whose immunity from societal interference Mill regards as necessary to advancing the permanent interests of humankind as a progressive species. And because the liberty of speech, Mill observes, is a cognate of the liberty of thought and impossible to separate from it, an argument for securing for people the freedom to think and form opinions for themselves requires an argument for securing for them freedom of speech. It too is necessary for individual self-development. Hence, Mill comes to treat speech as if it were a wholly self-regarding action and so to argue for its immunity from societal interference as he argues for the liberty of all actions that the harm principle protects.

To say this is to say that Mill treats speech as a wholly self-regarding action only insofar as it is an instrument for transmitting thought and opinion.

The qualification is essential. For Mill acknowledges that speech loses its immunity to being interfered with when it is delivered in circumstances in which it becomes "a positive instigation to some mischievous act."[12] So Mill is not arguing in chapter 2 for making speech as such immune from societal interference. Rather he is arguing for disabling society, government in particular, from interfering with speech when it interferes for the purpose of preventing the communication of ideas and opinions. Government, in other words, on the principle Mill defends, may not interfere with the transmission of ideas or opinions in order to stop them from being heard or read, though it may interfere with their transmission because of its manner or circumstances. Once one understands this as Mill's thesis, one can see why the argument of chapter 2 proceeds as it does.

The evil of government interference with speech, the harm it does to man's permanent interests as a progressive being, Mill argues, is that by suppressing particular ideas and opinions, it keeps people, both individually and collectively, from gaining knowledge or a sound understanding of the subject at hand. His argument proceeds by separating cases. First, the suppressed ideas and opinions may be true. However confident the government may be that they are false, it may nonetheless, because of human fallibility, be mistaken. And if the ideas and opinions it suppresses are true, their suppression deprives people of opportunities to overcome their ignorance and gain knowledge. It blocks them from exchanging error for truth. Second, even if the government is not mistaken and the ideas and opinions it suppresses are false, people, though they would not be kept from believing what is true, would still suffer a harm that is nearly as bad. For in this case they would be deprived of the opportunity of having their true ideas and opinions confronted with ones that oppose them, and in the absence of such opposition, their understanding of those ideas and opinions will eventually weaken to the point where they are held unreflectively and dogmatically. If not confronted with ideas and opinions opposed to their own, people will have little occasion to review the grounds that support their ideas. They will, in consequence, come to hold them with little understanding of those grounds. Their thought will become stagnant and shallow. In either case, then, Mill maintains, the government's suppression of ideas and opinions deprives people of knowledge and weakens their understanding. Consequently, it stunts the development of human intellect and moral sensibility.

It should be clear, even from this brief sketch of Mill's argument, that for Mill the point of protecting speech from government interference is to promote the interests of those who are its recipients. The evil of government censorship with which Mill is concerned is the harm it does to those who are deprived by the censorship of hearing or reading certain ideas.[13] Whatever harm the censorship does to the speaker qua speaker is not germane to the argument. Accordingly, we should understand Mill's defense of freedom of speech as an appeal to the interests of the audience and not to those of the speaker. And consequently Mill's defense could support our understanding the right to freedom of speech as protecting purely emotive speech only if government interference with such speech would harm the interests of the audience to which it appeals. Since it plainly does not, since interfering with purely emotive speech does not impede the mental development of men and women that Mill believed freedom of speech advanced, the defense offers no basis on which to justify the extension of the First Amendment right to free speech that the decision in *Cohen* brought about.

Mill's defense is a benchmark in being an appeal to interests of the recipients of speech that purely emotive speech does not advance. One finds the same feature in other major philosophical defenses of free speech. Hence, none of them supports the holding in *Cohen*. I will briefly describe two. They have been particularly influential in contemporary political theory. One is T. M. Scanlon's from his paper "A Theory of Freedom of Expression."[14] The other is Alexander Meiklejohn's, which appears in his book *Free Speech and Its Relation to Self-Government*.[15] I will describe Scanlon's defense in this section and Meiklejohn's in the next.

Scanlon, like Mill, argues for the right to free speech on the grounds of its value to individuals. Unlike Mill, however, he does not make considerations of utility the ultimate appeal. Instead, he makes a principle of respect for persons as rational, autonomous beings his ultimate appeal. Accordingly, Scanlon's defense is closer to Kantian ethics than the ethics of utilitarianism. In Kantian ethics, the fundamental principle forbids one from acting toward rational beings in ways that interfere with their freely exercising their rational powers, and Scanlon's principle, the principle he formulates and argues from, is in the spirit of this Kantian principle. On Scanlon's theory, what grounds the right is its facilitation of people's interest in having a government that respects their standing as rational, autonomous beings. Specifically, what grounds it is its making possible people's acceptance of limited government authority in the regulation of their speech consistently with their being treated respectfully as beings whose beliefs and choices are the products of the free exercise of reason. To be treated in this way, to be respected as a rational, autonomous being, while it does not mean that the government never, in the exercise of its authority, places limits on one's freedom to speak, does mean that the government may not impose such limits for the purpose of keeping one from doing harm to oneself that consists either in one's forming certain beliefs or in the consequences of one's determining that certain actions are worth doing. The right thus protects people from having their speech interfered with for this purpose.

As a preliminary to formulating his principle, Scanlon surveys some examples of speech whose legal prohibition is uncontroversial. One is speech whose pitch and volume are so great as to shatter glass. Since property damage is a harm that consists neither in the formation of some belief nor in being the result of concluding that some course of action is worth taking, the government's prohibiting such speech would be consistent with its respecting people as rational, autonomous beings. Having the potential to cause property damage could therefore be the basis for a justified legal limit on speech that could shatter glass. Other examples like speech that defames, speech essential to criminal conspiracies, and assaultive speech amounting to harassment have the same character. So too does speech that mischievously causes a panic, to recall Holmes's famous example of raising a false alarm in a crowded theater, though to see this, Scanlon notes, one must take acting in a panic as an automatism. Because the harm the speech, in each of these examples, causes does not consist in the formation of a belief or the result of one's having concluded that a certain action is worth doing, attempts by the government to prevent such harm are consistent with its respecting people as rational, autonomous beings. Accordingly, Scanlon uses these examples and a few others as guides to formulating the principle he takes to be the chief ground of the right to free speech.

The principle, on Scanlon's formulation of it, is one that excludes certain kinds of harm from the class of harms whose prevention can sometimes justify a legal prohibition on speech. Thus, on this principle, government is justified in enacting a prohibition on speech only if the prohibition is necessary to prevent harm and only if the harm it prevents does not consist in either the formation of a false belief or some harmful consequence of an action done as a result of one's having determined that it was worth doing. While, as Scanlon observes, the principle falls short of yielding a complete theory of freedom of speech, since it gives only necessary conditions for justifying legal prohibitions on speech, we can nonetheless see from this principle that the theory, at its core, takes as the grounds of the right to free speech the need to protect the interests of the recipients of speech in maintaining their standing as rational, autonomous beings when subject to external authority. Like Mill's defense, then, the interests to which the core of Scanlon's theory appeals to ground the right are those of the audience and not those of the speaker and, being interests in having the free exercise of their rational faculties respected, are not advanced by purely emotive speech. Though purely emotive speech can doubtlessly influence belief formation and practical judgment, because it does so by means other than direct engagement of its audience's rational faculties, interference with it is consistent with respecting people as rational, autonomous beings. Consequently, the core of Scanlon's theory too does not yield an understanding of the right on which it protects purely emotive speech.

Meiklejohn's defense of the right, in being an appeal to the value of free speech for people collectively as citizens of a democracy, differs from Mill's and Scanlon's. Meiklejohn makes his argument as part of an interpretation of the U.S. Constitution. The Constitution, he believes, organizes the government of the United States in accordance with the ideal of government by consent of the people. It is an ideal of self-government. To realize this ideal, Meiklejohn argues, the Constitution guarantees certain political rights including, in particular, the First Amendment's right to free speech. The right is necessary in a democracy, for it guarantees open debate among the people on the matters they decide through elections. Without such debate, people's votes would not reflect an informed and deliberative judgment and would therefore fail to be an expression of their collective will as determined by majority rule. Without such debate, elections in a democracy would not, in short, be exercises of self-government.

Meiklejohn presses his interpretive point by comparing the rights guaranteed by the First Amendment with those guaranteed by the due process clause of the Fifth Amendment. He characterizes the latter as personal rights, rights that protect the pursuit of private interests. As such they are subject to lawful abridgment, something that the language of the Fifth Amendment affirms. By contrast, the language of the First Amendment does not imply that the rights it guarantees may be lawfully abridged. To the contrary, regarding the right to free speech, the Amendment declares that Congress shall pass no law abridging this right. Meiklejohn infers from this difference that one must understand the First Amendment's right of free speech as a political rather than a personal right. The reason, he argues, for the Amendment's unqualified protection of free speech from abridgement by Congress is that unfettered speech is essential to the political system the Constitution defines. Self-government would not be possible if Congress could enact laws limiting people's freedom of speech. The basis for the right, then, on Meiklejohn's reading of the Constitution, is not the private interest in self-expression as an element of personal happiness but rather the public interest in full and open debate on the issues that the people decide.

While Meiklejohn develops his argument for the right to free speech through an interpretation of the Constitution, one can extract the argument from the interpretation and consider it separately. Hence, we do not need to be concerned with the merits of his interpretation. One can see the force of the argument, even if his interpretation is unsound. Crudely, the argument is that the right to free speech is necessary in a democracy, for democracy, as a form of self-government, depends on its citizens' making intelligent and informed decisions when they cast their votes. And to be well-informed and to use their knowledge intelligently in making these decisions citizens must be exposed to full and open debate on the issues their votes decide. The right guarantees that such debates can take place. Plainly, then, the right, on Meiklejohn's defense of it, is grounded on its serving the interests of the recipients of speech and not those of speakers. Meiklejohn himself makes this point when, taking the procedures of a town meeting as his model of self-government, he writes, "Now, in that method of political self-government, the point of ultimate interest is not the words of the speakers, but the minds of the hearers. . . . The welfare of the community requires that those who decide issues shall understand them. They must know what they are voting about. . . . As the self-governing community seeks, by the method of voting, to gain wisdom in action, it can find it only in the minds of its individual citizens. If they fail, it fails. That is why freedom of discussion for those minds may not be abridged."[16]

Meiklejohn's defense is, therefore, like Mill's and Scanlon's (at its core) in being a defense that appeals to the interests of the recipients of speech. At the same time, unlike the recipient interests to which Mill and Scanlon appeal, those to which Meiklejohn appeals are the interests the recipients of speech have as citizens of a democracy. Consequently, one cannot immediately infer that purely emotive speech does not serve those interests. The reason is that citizens of a democracy have not only an interest in hearing the full range of views on the issues that their votes decide but also an interest in knowing how strongly those views are held by their supporters. The depth of people's convictions about matters of public policy and how much people care about the outcomes of certain electoral decisions are often important considerations in deciding how one will vote. Thus, one can easily suppose that purely emotive speech serves this second interest, for one can easily suppose that such speech indicates the depth of the speaker's convictions and how much he cares about the matter on which he is speaking. Accordingly, it is easy to conclude that Meiklejohn's defense of the right to free speech supports taking the right as protecting purely emotive speech from government interference, though the protection applies only to purely emotive political speech.[17]

Yet this conclusion, though easy to draw, is mistaken. The expression of strong emotion in speech is not a reliable indicator of how deeply a speaker holds the view he is expressing or how greatly he cares about the outcomes of decisions on the issues on which he is speaking. He may care greatly, of course, but then again he may not. Consider, for instance, words spoken in anger when you have been provoked. Often, such words are instantly regretted. Someone provokes you, and you get angry. You retaliate with words that are meant to hurt, words you do not mean and wish to take back. Your words, in this case, are used as weapons. They are not expressions of views you deeply hold.[18] Or consider, as a second instance, angry words expressed by someone filled with unfocused hostility, someone with a chip on his shoulder, as we say. Hostility colors the attitudes and dispositions this person manifests in the way he conducts his life. Though largely unfocused, the hostility sometimes finds convenient outlets. On these occasions, it becomes focused. Plainly, though, the anger the person displays need not imply any deeply held views about matters he perceives the objects of his anger to have affronted. Nor does it imply that he cares greatly about such matters. His anger may of course indicate that there is something he cares greatly about, but one would have to uncover the source of the hostility that defines his personality to determine what that is. Cohen, after all, might have been such a person. Hence, one cannot infer from the message on his jacket that he greatly cared about ending the draft or that his view on the matter was deeply held. In particular, one cannot infer either proposition from the emotive charge that the word "fuck" gives to his message. His wearing a jacket with this message gives one no reason to believe his opposition to the draft was more strongly held than the opposition to war that others might have expressed by wearing jackets bearing messages that lacked such words, messages like "Peace Now" or "Make Love Not War," to take two popular slogans from that era.

Having seen, then, that the defenses of the right to free speech that appeal to the audience's interests do not support taking the right as protecting purely emotive speech, let us turn to defenses that appeal to the interests of speakers. Do any of them support taking the right as protecting purely emotive speech? Scanlon's wider theory of free speech makes such an appeal, though the appeal is limited to the right to freedom of political speech. Scanlon adds this appeal to his theory because the principle at the theory's core is insufficient for protecting speech from government interference in cases that the right has traditionally covered. One such case is government prohibition of marches on public streets because of the disruption to traffic, commercial trade, and daily life generally that such events would cause. In this case, the government would not be violating the core principle of Scanlon's theory, yet it could still be preventing speech that traditionally the right has protected. For example, a municipal government would be violating the right to free speech that the members of unpopular groups had if it prohibited marches by such groups on the grounds that their marches were more expensive to police than those, which it routinely permits, held by groups that enjoy broad public support. Hence, Scanlon sees the need to widen his theory so as to account for the traditional protection the right to free speech provides in this and similar examples. Accordingly, he appeals to the interests of speakers in participating in their country's political process as grounding this protection. "Access to means of expression is in many cases a necessary condition for participation in the political process of the country, and therefore something to which citizens have an independent right."[19]

Scanlon bases his appeal to the interests of speakers in participating in their country's political process on the high value of political speech in a democracy. Its value is such, Scanlon argues, as to give its protection priority over other values like public convenience. But since he could use Mill's or Meiklejohn's defense to explain why political speech has such value, its having such value does not necessarily derive from the interests of speakers in participating in the political process of their country. Scanlon's appeal to these interests is therefore unsupported in his theory. At bottom, he merely appeals to what he sees as an *intuitively* attractive basis for the right.

Undoubtedly, the right to participate in the political process of one's country is based at least partly on the interests people have in being able to protect their interests generally through participating in that process. The question, though, is whether the right comprises more than the right to vote and the political rights collateral to it, such as the rights to stand for elective office and to serve on juries. These rights guarantee that no citizen is denied the opportunity of having his interests taken into account in the political decisions that affect his life. But whether the right to participate in the political process of one's country includes more is still an open question. Scanlon thinks it does. Meiklejohn, by contrast, does not, or at least he does not think that it includes the right to make one's own case for promoting one's interests. Meiklehjohn thinks it is necessary that someone make that case, but that someone need not be the very person for whose interests the case is made. In a traditional town meeting, Meiklejohn observes, taking such meetings as the model of self-government, every view on the matter under discussion must be heard, but not every citizen present must be given the opportunity to speak. Citizens who would only repeat what the town council has already heard are routinely excluded from speaking. Such limits on debate are necessary for timely decision making and endurable meetings and are thus understood as consistent with each citizen's right to participate in the town's democratic processes.

Fortunately, we do not need to resolve this disagreement between Scanlon and Meiklejohn to move forward. We do not, that is, need to determine whether democratic decision making requires that each citizen be allowed to make his or her own case for his interests or only that the case be heard. There is a different, much older argument for taking the right to freedom of political speech to be based on the interests citizens have in participating in the political processes of their country. We can consider this argument instead. It appears in Plato's *Crito*. In the speech that the Laws of Athens deliver near the end of the dialogue, the Laws reprove Socrates for considering whether to escape his punishment and so disobey the Athenian assembly that lawfully convicted and sentenced him. The Laws insist on obedience from Socrates, though they do not declare that obedience to law is an unconditional requirement of citizenship. Rather they say that each citizen is required to obey the laws of the city if he has not persuaded the city of their injustice.[20]

Clearly, one implication of this statement is that because citizens are liable to sanctions for disobedience to law, because the city enforces its laws coercively, fairness requires that each citizen have the opportunity to argue against any law he opposes. No one, so the argument goes, whom the city, by virtue of the laws it enacts, places in jeopardy of loss of life, liberty, or property for noncompliance should be so placed without first having the opportunity to persuade his fellow citizens not to enact laws with which he disagrees. Fairness, in other words, requires that the city not impose burdens of obedience on its citizens without their having a voice in that imposition, and that voice must include speaking as well as voting. Hence, by invoking this principle of fairness, one can defend the right to free speech in a democracy on the grounds that each citizen has an interest in being able to persuade his fellow citizens to take his view on the issues they ultimately decide.[21] The defense, therefore, is one that appeals to the interests of speakers.

Let us now consider whether the right, on this defense, protects purely emotive speech. Whether it does depends on what counts as giving each citizen a fair opportunity to persuade his fellow citizens to take his view on the issues they ultimately decide. On one view, the opportunity that fairness requires is the opportunity to reason with one's fellow citizens about the issues being debated. Such persuasion excludes demagoguery. On this view, then, fairness is given narrow scope, so the right does not protect purely emotive speech. Alternatively, fairness may be given wide scope. Accordingly, the right is not limited in any way that unfairly puts some people at a disadvantage in their efforts to persuade their fellow citizens to take their view. In particular, the right does not disfavor inarticulate or poorly educated citizens, and arguably, to exclude purely emotive speech from its protection is liable to do just that.[22]

We can thus draw from the speech that the Laws of Athens make in the *Crito* a defense of the right to free speech on which the right protects purely emotive speech. The success of this defense, however, is still uncertain. For it depends on the scope of the requirement of fairness it invokes, and how one determines its scope is open to dispute. More important, though, is that the defense offers grounds for a right to free speech that covers only political speech. It is in this respect like Meiklejohn's defense. Consequently, the purely emotive speech that the right, on this defense, protects is purely emotive political speech. Cohen's speech would therefore be protected. But purely emotive speech that lies outside of the political sphere would not. The racist and homophobic chanting at soccer games, for instance, that were recently prosecuted in Britain under the Football Offences Act of 1991 would not be protected.[23] Nor would slurs and vulgarities on public message boards and in Internet chat rooms that are directed at private individuals. Vituperative language meant to express loathing and disdain for certain people and to expose them to denigration and scorn, though it no doubt serves the interests of speakers in expressing themselves as they wish, does not serve the interests of speakers as citizens of a democracy to which this defense appeals.

We need, finally, to consider whether there is a defense of the right to free speech that appeals to the interests of speakers outside of their interests as citizens of a democracy. Is there such a defense on which the right would be understood as protecting purely emotive speech? Ronald Dworkin has given one in his essay "Why Must Speech Be Free?"[24] It will be useful, in concluding our study, to see why Dworkin's defense and others like it are bound to fail.

Dworkin's argument turns on a distinction he makes between instrumental and constitutive justifications of the right to free speech. Instrumental justifications appeal to the "good effects" the right has for democracy, society, or all of humankind. Constitutive justifications appeal to an essential feature of a just political society: in such a society "government treat[s] all [the] adult members, except those who are incompetent, as responsible moral agents."[25] Dworkin thinks only constitutive justifications provide adequate support for taking the First Amendment right to free speech as protecting all speech. Instrumental justifications, he argues, are too "fragile" and "limited."[26] The essential feature to which constitutive justifications appeal entails, says Dworkin, two conditions on a political society's being just. First, the members must be free to make up their own minds about what to believe and what to take as a good reason for action. In this respect, constitutive justifications correspond to the principle at the core of Scanlon's theory. Second, the members must be free to express their opinions, convictions, social attitudes, and tastes. To be treated as responsible moral agents, they must have as much right "to contribute to the formation of the [society's] moral or aesthetic climate as they do to participate in politics."[27] Clearly, the first condition, being equivalent to the principle at the core of Scanlon's theory, does not support understanding the right to free speech as protecting purely emotive speech. It is the second condition that provides that support. Moreover, on the understanding it supports, the protection the right gives is not restricted to political speech.

This second condition, however, is bizarre. One might even say "Orwellian." To be a responsible moral agent is to be an agent who is morally responsible for his actions. And to be morally responsible for one's actions primarily means that one is rightly held accountable for them when one injures others or invades their rights. Accordingly, a politically just society treats competent adult human beings as responsible moral agents by holding them accountable for actions that injure others or invade others' rights.[28] It does not hold small children or incompetent adults accountable for such offenses, for neither are morally responsible agents. Society holds people accountable for their actions by making them liable to sanctions for the injuries and invasions that their actions cause. And this is true whether it is speech that causes the injury or invasion or some other kind of action. One is no less responsible for injury one causes by verbally abusing someone than for injury one causes by battering him. Dworkin's view, then, that a just society treats its members as morally responsible agents by granting them protection from government interference with their expressions of opinion, conviction, attitudes, and tastes is confused. It amounts to saying that a just society treats people as morally responsible agents by not holding them accountable for their actions even when those actions injure others or invade their rights.

Dworkin, to support his thesis that the right to free speech protects speech that expresses attitudes and tastes in matters beyond politics, appeals to the right to contribute to the formation of one's society's moral and aesthetic climate. But this right, if it exists, is surely too weak to provide any greater protection from government interference with speech than a general right to liberty like that recognized in the Fifth and Fourteenth Amendments.[29] The reason is clear. An action that seriously injures others or invades their rights does not gain protection from government interference merely by being an attempt to influence one's society's moral or aesthetic climate. Surely the government may prohibit setting off fireworks in residential neighborhoods, say, despite the contribution to the aesthetic climate that fireworks displays make. On any sensible view of a government's police powers, the injuries to innocent bystanders risked by letting amateurs set off fireworks in crowded neighborhoods make such prohibitions justifiable. Thus, while people are entitled to protection from their government's *arbitrarily* interfering with their efforts to change the aesthetic or moral climate by means other than speech, those efforts are surely open to government regulation when they risk harm to others.

And the same point applies when their efforts consist in purely emotive speech.

Dworkin's appeal to a right to contribute to the formation of one's society's moral and aesthetic values therefore fails to bring purely emotive speech within the scope of the right to free speech. Indeed, the appeal's implausibility suggests that Dworkin has discounted the injuries and invasions people can suffer when they become the objects of expressions of hatred and contempt. His view, then, may represent an all-too-common blindness to the issue such speech raises. To see it graphically, one need only consider the example described in several of the chapters in this volume of the two women law students who suffered severe emotional distress and egregious invasions of privacy as the result of being made, seemingly without cause, the targets of many vicious, misogynistic postings on a website whose owners allowed these anonymous postings to go on for weeks.[30]

In *Cohen*, Justice Blackmun, answering Harlan's majority opinion, wrote a dissent, which three other justices joined. Blackmun did not think Cohen's speech qualified as speech deserving First Amendment protection. At the same time, he did not think the California courts had given proper consideration to whether Cohen's behavior was sufficiently disruptive to warrant conviction for violating the part of the state's penal code prohibiting malicious disturbance of the peace. He argued for remanding the case back to the state court that had jurisdiction for reconsideration, especially in light of the California Supreme Court's subsequent clarification of this part of the penal code. Blackmun's dissent, I believe, is truer to the understanding of the right to free speech reflected in the leading philosophical defenses of that right.

PART IV

Privacy

CHAPTER **12**

Collective Privacy

LIOR JACOB STRAHILEVITZ

Collective action problems arise in privacy law where a single source of confidential information reveals something about multiple individuals, and these people disagree over whether the information should be disseminated. Such collective action problems are all around us. Perhaps the most familiar contemporary example is Facebook "tagging." Multitudes of Facebook users post photographs of themselves with relatives, friends, and acquaintances, and then provide a caption in which the other pictured individuals are tagged (i.e., named in metadata and on-screen). Depending on the privacy settings chosen by Facebook users, the photographs may then show up on the tagged individuals' Facebook pages as well as those individuals' friends' Facebook pages, and they often become a source of embarrassment.[1] For example, the newly nominated chief of MI6, the British central intelligence agency, was tagged in photos on his wife's Facebook page playing Frisbee and wearing short swimming trunks at the beach.[2] Also pictured were the spy chief's children, parents, and friends, in a series of snapshots that could be seen by any member of the general public. Members of Parliament fumed that the country had spent significant taxpayer money to protect the identity of Sir John Sawyers and his family, but these efforts had been compromised thanks to his spouse's Facebook activity (and subsequent tabloid coverage). Privacy has always been interdependent, but the dangers posed by its interdependence are magnified in the information age.

A recent case from the U.S. Court of Appeals for the Second Circuit starkly illustrates some of the thorny legal issues that can stem from privacy collective action problems. In Associated Press v. United States Department of Defense, the court tried to figure out what to do when a news organization requested the identities of detainees who alleged that they had been abused at Guantanamo Bay, Cuba. The government preferred to keep this list a secret. We know that some of the detainees wanted their identities publicized, and we can presume that other detainees (and their relatives) did not. The controversial question before the court was "what should result from this dissensus?"

This essay examines the issues raised by *Associated Press,* as well as another controversial case called Doe v. Quiring. In *Quiring,* South Dakota wanted to publicize on the Internet private information about a man who had been convicted of incest, but the victim of the crime asked the state not to publish such information, based on a reasonable belief that if her father were identified as an incest perpetrator it would be easy for the public to identify her as an incest victim.

In each case, the government got what it wanted. The Department of Defense (DOD) thwarted the Associated Press's (AP's) efforts to obtain the identities of even those Guantanamo detainees who wished to be identified. And South Dakota convinced the courts to let it identify Doe's father as an incest perpetrator, rather than a generic sex offender, as she had requested. I submit that the respective governments should have lost each case. Both pitted important privacy concerns against significant disclosure concerns, but the collective action problems were soluble via reliance on the express consent of the affected individuals.

The *Associated Press* court did not cite *Quiring,* and neither side in *Associated Press* even brought the prior case to the court's attention. That oversight is not surprising. The decisions of the South Dakota Supreme Court obviously do not bind the Second Circuit. Moreover, the former case raised a legal question concerning the Freedom of Information Act's interpretation and the latter case required the court to determine the meaning of South Dakota's Megan's Law statute. But the disconnect between the two opinions should disturb us still. The fragmentation of privacy law routinely results in conceptual incoherence. Given that the same sorts of privacy collective action problems arise in the context of the Freedom of Information Act and Megan's Law, to say nothing of the Fourth Amendment to the U.S. Constitution, privacy tort law, and other important privacy regimes, there is quite a lot to be gained from using a comparative lens to figure out how these sorts of problems ought to be solved. Considering privacy law holistically can improve the content of each of privacy law's parts. To that end, this essay both develops a framework for thinking about, and sometimes solving, recurring collective action problems in privacy law, and begins a larger scholarly project advocating the reunification of information privacy law.

Consent in Privacy Law

Although information privacy law is deeply and unnecessarily fragmented, there are a few blanket statements that can be made about the body of law. One of these is that if an individual validly consents to the widespread dissemination of her previously private information, the information at issue is no longer private. For example, if someone blogs about his medical condition or sexual hang-ups, he cannot complain when others freely discuss what he has voluntarily disclosed, even if he subsequently regrets his earlier statements. This rule is as applicable in the privacy tort setting as it is in the Fourth Amendment search and seizure context.[3]

Why should the unambiguous consent of the individual to the publication of previously private information prove decisive? The most attractive answer to this question stems from an intuition that the question of what sorts of information ought to be made public is a difficult one, and that the individual herself typically will be in a better position than the government to identify the circumstances under which disclosure is appropriate.[4] Although there are individuals who will disclose facts about themselves that make their friends and relatives wince or blush, the law expresses discomfort with paternalistic restrictions on what individuals might say. To be sure, some scholars have argued forcefully that privacy ought to protect individuals against their own wrongheaded or shortsighted decisions, but these arguments should not carry the day in most settings.[5] The law does create categories where people are deemed incapable of consent. The consent of children, intoxicated adults, and people with severe mental disabilities, for example, is not a decisive waiver of their privacy rights because we have reason to believe that in these contexts the state's agents will make better decisions about what information should remain private than the individuals whose information is at issue.

Setting aside special cases like the legal disabilities discussed above, the law's deference to individual consent is appropriate. Just as there are costs to protecting privacy too little, there will be costs from protecting privacy too much. Excessive privacy protection may chill speech in ways that conflict with important First Amendment values. Inordinately severe limitations on individuals' disclosure of information about themselves will hinder intimacy and the formation of friendships. Unduly strict limitations on the voluntary disclosure of information about one's self may exacerbate the problems of discrimination on the basis of immutable characteristics.[6] While there are certainly harms that can arise in the context of voluntary disclosures of information, and some contexts in which individual decisions about privacy may be optimal for them but not for society as a whole, "give people all the privacy they want, and no more" is likely the least problematic rule available to imperfect people and institutions.

Our consideration of consent so far has assumed a solitary actor with a choice about whether to reveal information about himself. Now suppose that multiple people possess a privacy interest in the same information. Whose consent should be required?

That was essentially the issue confronting the Supreme Court in Georgia v. Randolph.[7] In that case, Scott Randolph shared a home with his wife, Janet. The estranged couple was involved in a dispute over their child, and Janet called the police to their home. Shortly after their arrival, Janet told the police that her husband was a cocaine user and that there was drug paraphernalia in the house. The police requested permission to search the Randolph home. Janet immediately consented and Scott contemporaneously and unequivocally refused consent. The police searched the dwelling, found a drinking straw with cocaine on it in Scott's bedroom, and indicted Scott for possession of cocaine. He moved to suppress the evidence. The Supreme Court held that "a warrantless search of a shared dwelling for evidence over the express refusal of consent by a physically present resident cannot be justified as reasonable as to him on the basis of consent given to the police by another resident."[8]

In the process of invalidating the search, the Court admitted that it was creating a fine line between permissible and impermissible police conduct. An earlier Supreme Court decision, Rodriguez v. Illinois,[9] had held that the consent of an apparent cotenant was sufficient to authorize the search, even when the consent of another tenant, who was asleep inside the apartment, was neither solicited nor obtained. In explaining the divergent results, the Court was attuned to the practicalities of police searching and the burdens that the Fourth Amendment might place on law enforcement:

> For the very reason that *Rodriguez* held it would be unjustifiably impractical to require the police to take affirmative steps to confirm the actual authority of a consenting individual whose authority was apparent, we

think it would needlessly limit the capacity of the police to respond to ostensibly legitimate opportunities in the field if we were to hold that reasonableness required the police to take affirmative steps to find a potentially objecting co-tenant before acting on the permission they had already received.[10]

Pragmatic considerations, not first principles, would resolve this problem of consent, at least in the majority's view. The justices in the majority wanted to require unanimous consent where the lack of such unanimity was easy to discern by the police. The *Randolph* dissenters, however, favored a bright-line rule for these cases: the decision to cohabit meant assuming the risk that one cotenant would waive the other's Fourth Amendment privacy rights.[11] The dissenters arrived at this conclusion because they feared the majority's path would yield indeterminate rules across a range of outcomes: for example, what if a supermajority of cotenants consented to a search? As Chief Justice Roberts wrote, "the possible scenarios are limitless, and slight variations in the fact pattern yield vastly different expectations. . . . Such shifting expectations are not a promising foundation on which to ground a constitutional rule."[12]

Strikingly, none of the justices advocated a straightforward and obvious alternative approach: in the event of a conflict, Janet could authorize a search of her quasi-private spaces in the home (e.g., her bedroom, her closet) but she could not authorize a search of Scott's bedroom, where the incriminating evidence was found. Such an approach, which we will call *constructive partition,* resolves a collective privacy problem by fragmenting the collective resource into interests controlled by discrete individuals. The partition might provide imperfect protection when privacy interests are inextricably comingled: Scott could have revealing photographs of Janet in his bedroom, but he might have them in his office at work too, and she would have no legal standing to prevent the police from finding them there.

Perhaps this intuitive constructive partition solution did not appeal to the justices because as a formal matter, Janet and Scott were cotenants who shared ownership of every square inch of the home itself. But informal arrangements and expectations often inform reasonable expectations of privacy. Just as Scott might have been surprised and dismayed had Janet searched through the drawers of his bedroom desk over his objections, he might have had a legitimate expectation that the police would not do so without his consent.

The Freedom of Information Act's Privacy Exceptionalism

In 1966, Congress enacted the Freedom of Information Act (FOIA) to help make available to the citizenry information about the performance of its government. The act, with certain exceptions, enables citizens to request information that federal agencies possess so that they can learn "what their government is up to."[13] Given that federal agencies have a great deal of sensitive information about individuals, Congress exempted from disclosure information whose dissemination "would constitute a clearly unwarranted invasion of personal privacy."[14] Another FOIA provision specifically exempted from disclosure "records or information compiled for law enforcement purposes, but only to the extent that the production of such law enforcement records or information . . . could reasonably be expected to constitute an unwarranted invasion of personal privacy."[15]

FOIA's reference to an "unwarranted invasion of personal privacy" in the statutory language might have indicated congressional intent to have the statute's privacy provisions piggyback on the substantive protections offered by privacy tort law. Several state courts seeking to understand the scope of "personal privacy" under their state freedom of information acts have so held.[16] Nevertheless, the Supreme Court was quick to take FOIA privacy law in a different direction. In its landmark United States Department of Justice v. Reporters Committee for Freedom of the Press case, the Court noted that the disclosure of a compilation of rap sheet information culled from public records could reasonably be expected to constitute an "unwarranted invasion of personal privacy" under FOIA even though a private actor who compiled such information would be immune from liability under tort law and the First Amendment. In a footnote, the Court stated: "The question of the statutory meaning of privacy under the FOIA is, of course, not the same as the question whether a tort action might lie for invasion of privacy or the question whether an individual's interest in privacy is protected by the Constitution."[17]

This "convenient" bit of dicta prompted a sensible reaction of "Why not?" from one commentator, who observed that in the same year the Supreme Court was holding that FOIA's privacy provisions prevented the government from disclosing the rap sheet of an ex-con defense contractor who had close dealings with a corrupt congressman, a Florida statute prohibiting the publication of a rape victim's identity was deemed unconstitutional on First Amendment grounds.[18] The criminal background of the contractor in *Reporters Committee* was certainly of greater interest to the public than the identity of a private figure rape victim in Florida Star v. B. J. F., as evidenced by the Florida newspaper's admission that it had only published the rape victim's identity via an accidental breach of its own policies.

Although an act-omission distinction perhaps explains why privacy prevailed in *Reporters Committee* but not in *Florida Star,* the distinction should not prove decisive. The Supreme Court has held that state laws imposing defamation liability on newspapers implicate the First Amendment by raising the costs of news reporting in ways that will reduce the flow of information to the public.[19] By the same token, the government's refusal to share information it had already aggregated with CBS news reporters pursuing an important story rendered it less likely that newsworthy information would be shared with the public.

A second significant way in which FOIA privacy law has deviated from privacy tort law is its protection of familial privacy rights. The common law rule is quite clear with respect to privacy tort causes of action: dead men have no privacy rights.[20] In contrast to almost all other tort claims, any cause of action for tortious invasion of privacy dies along with the would-be plaintiff. Under FOIA, however, the Supreme Court has expanded the scope of privacy protections. In its recent National Archives and Records Administration v. Favish case, the Court held that the death of Vince Foster did not mean that there was no longer a "personal privacy" interest in images of his dead body, taken after Foster shot himself in a public park. The Court noted that for the purposes of privacy law, his relatives possessed a strong privacy interest in those images, both on dignitary grounds, and because the disclosure of the photographs in response to a FOIA request might subject Foster's next of kin to harassment or the risk of unwilling exposure to the images.[21]

The *Favish* opinion is ambiguous on the question of whether familial privacy interests arise only upon the death of the person whose private facts are at issue. One can read the opinion as a narrow holding that next of kin have privacy interests in images of their deceased relative. Alternatively, one can read the opinion to suggest that relatives would have a personal privacy interest in information that concerns a loved one during their relative's life. Some lower court opinions since *Favish* have hinted that familial privacy interests may arise for the purposes of FOIA even while the individuals whose information is at issue remain alive.[22]

There are other areas in which FOIA privacy deviates from tort privacy, but these two differences—the tendency of FOIA cases to protect privacy interests forcefully and speech interests weakly, and FOIA's recognition of posthumous familial privacy interests—are the nub of the legal problem in a case like *Associated Press*.

In late 2004 and early 2005, the AP was investigating the treatment of detainees at the military detention facility at Guantanamo Bay. Pursuant to that investigation, the AP made a series of FOIA requests for information concerning the identities of Guantanamo inmates who had alleged mistreatment. The DOD provided the AP with responses to the FOIA request that redacted the names of all Guantanamo detainees.[23]

The DOD probably had little inherent concern for the personal privacy of the Guantanamo detainees. Its real motivation for withholding the information likely stemmed from political considerations. Of course, a public relations calculus provides no statutory basis for resisting FOIA requests. As the litigation progressed, the personal privacy of the detainees and their relatives would provide the only colorable legal basis for the government's refusal to provide the AP with the information it was seeking. But even if the government's invocation of FOIA's privacy exception was entirely pretextual, it does not follow that the AP should have won the case. In enacting the statute and its enumerated justifications for resisting a FOIA request, Congress likely anticipated that personal privacy interests would be most fully vindicated if the executive branch could invoke those interests in cases where they really explained the government's reluctance to disclose documents (e.g., private information concerning federal employees), as well as instances in which the invoked privacy interest was a fig leaf (e.g., the privacy rights of suspected terrorists). The statute enables only the government, and not the individuals whose privacy is at issue, to resist a FOIA request. Congress therefore might have wanted the personal privacy interests of even those groups disfavored by the executive to be protected by FOIA, and the law's structure gave the DOD strong incentives to think hard about the privacy implications of the AP's request.

With one important exception, discussed below, the district court ruled against the department on all the contested issues. The court observed that many of the detainees whose identities were redacted had "participated in hunger strikes to protest alleged abuse," three had collaborated to produce a 115-page report alleging mistreatment, and others had sought to publicize their mistreatment via their attorneys.[24] To the district court, these episodes suggested that the detainees "have not hesitated to reveal their identities." The court went further, reasoning that "most people in such a situation— especially individuals detained incommunicado without many procedural safeguards—would want their plights, and identities, publicized."[25]

The government won in the lower court with respect to only one disclosure request, which involved a letter written by the wife of a detainee to her husband. The husband had reluctantly disclosed the letter to the Administrative Review Board in an effort to secure his release. Evidently, the letter was used to buttress the detainee's assertions that he held strongly negative attitudes toward the Taliban. The district court concluded that notwithstanding the husband's disclosure of this letter, she retained a reasonable expectation of privacy in its contents, enabling the government to redact her identity in light of the dangers she might face from pro-Taliban extremists.

The court of appeals reversed. The court characterized the detainees' interest in disclosure as "somewhat speculative" in light of the "limited number of detainees who have opted to come forward."[26] It offered a conflicting intuition that the disclosure of the detainees' names "could certainly subject them to embarrassment and humiliation." Of course, in an instance where some of the detainees wanted their identities disclosed and others did not, an obvious constructive partition solution is available: permit the government to disclose the identities of those detainees who are willing to opt in to disclosure. Sadiq Reza has advocated precisely such an approach.[27]

Reza's approach to the case has genuine appeal, though it is not without drawbacks: a rule tailored to individual inmates will be more cumbersome and costly for agencies to administer. In *Randolph* terms, some of the detainees may be asleep in another room, not objecting loudly at the vestibule. While this concern is mitigated in the case of detainees who are in federal custody, the costs of determining whether the inmates' relatives and other correspondents consent to the release of information would be quite high. The same is true for former inmates. Moreover, individuals in custody might feel pressured to withhold consent to disclosure based on a desire to win favors from their captors. These difficult issues were briefed and argued by the government and the AP. The government's argument was particularly forceful in light of the Supreme Court's previous support for applying categorical rules that forestall individuated inquiries in FOIA privacy contexts. For example, in the aforementioned *Reporters Committee* case, the

Court held that rap sheets were per se immune from disclosure in response to FOIA requests, rejecting a standard tailored to the nature of the request and the particularities of the person whose information was being sought.

The Second Circuit responded to these serious arguments with make-believe. The court began auspiciously enough, observing that the "first question to ask in determining whether [FOIA] Exemption 7(C) applies is whether there is any privacy interest in the information sought." This sentence was immediately followed by a footnote, which is where things went south quickly. It reads as follows:

> In *Reporters Committee*, the Supreme Court held, "as a categorical matter that a third party's request for law enforcement records or information about a private citizen can reasonably be expected to invade that citizen's privacy." The Court reasoned that "categorical decisions may be appropriate and individual circumstances disregarded when a case fits into a genus in which the balance characteristically tips in one direction." DOD argues that the privacy interests at stake here are readily assessed on a categorical basis. The AP counters that individualized consideration of those interests is appropriate. We are cognizant of the Supreme Court's holding in *Reporters Committee*. However, because our disposition of this appeal would be the same regardless of how we considered the privacy interest accommodated in Exemptions 7 and 6 for those persons whose information may be disclosed here, we do not need to decide whether we must analyze them categorically or individually.[28]

This paragraph is deeply wrong. Recall that the Second Circuit held that the government could withhold the identities of all the detainees under FOIA's privacy exemptions, while conceding that some of the detainees wished to make their identities public. In light of those two facts, there was no intellectually coherent way for the court to dodge the question of whether FOIA's privacy protections should be analyzed categorically or individually with respect to detainees. A categorical approach necessarily would result in complete disclosure or nondisclosure, whereas an individuated approach—constructive partition of the list of detainees—necessarily would result in partial disclosure. By ruling in favor of complete nondisclosure, the court had to embrace a categorical basis for deciding the issue, its protests to the contrary notwithstanding.

As the court saw it, the fact that some detainees wanted their identities disclosed was irrelevant. Moreover, under the court's holding, and its categorical-though-ostensibly-not-categorical approach, the objections of one privacy-seeking detainee would trump the desires of scores of other publicity-seeking detainees.

Such a unanimity rule creates problems akin to the "tragedy of the anticommons" that Michael Heller has identified in property and intellectual property. Heller famously noted the contrast between post-Soviet Russia's thriving commercial kiosks and its empty storefronts. The storefronts were empty because opening a shop there required permit approvals from countless bureaucrats and other stakeholders, but an entrepreneur needed only to buy off a couple of local government officials and the neighborhood mafia to start up a new sidewalk kiosk.[29] As this tragedy plays out, a resource does not get used efficiently because every individual is legally entitled to block an efficient use, and none of the other interested parties have the authority to "green light" the socially desirable use of a communal good. The same dynamic played out in *Associated Press,* with the names of the detainees as the valuable resource that nobody got to use.

In a better-reasoned section of the *Associated Press* opinion, the court noted that it was not oblivious to the danger that an anticommons problem might arise as a result of its FOIA privacy ruling. The court noted that it did "not mean to suggest that detainees should be prevented in any way from coming forward publicly with allegations of mistreatment or abuse at the hands of DOD in Guantanamo; this opinion does not empower the government to prevent such public disclosure by the detainees themselves based on this recognized privacy interest."[30] Of course, as Reza noted, the detainees were long deprived of access to counsel, contact with relatives, and opportunities to bring their plight to the attention of the outside world.[31] But since the Supreme Court's decisions in Boumediene v. Bush, Hamdan v. Rumsfeld, and Rasul v. Bush, the legal rights available to Guantanamo detainees have increased substantially, and there are stronger reasons to believe that FOIA might not be the only mechanism for the public to learn the identities of those who would wish to have that information made public.[32]

If one supposes that detainees with an interest in publicizing their identities now have alternative channels to communicate with the public, then the question arises as to whether there is any additional public interest served by FOIA disclosure. Three arguments spring to mind. First, the difference in mechanisms for disseminating identities implicates an opt-in versus opt-out issue. As a large literature on privacy already demonstrates, defaults are quite sticky.[33] Protecting the privacy of only consumers who opt in to heightened privacy protections will result in a much lower level of privacy rights than a regime that requires consumers to opt out of heightened protection. Presumably, the FOIA privacy regime that Reza has in mind would require detainees to opt in to privacy or eliminate any default option and force detainees to choose privacy or publicity, with the result being that the press (and public) will have access to a more complete picture of the identities and characteristics of the Guantanamo detainees.

Second, in any coercive setting, let alone Gitmo, there is a significant danger that detainees will feel pressured to conform their privacy preferences to the views perceived to be more welcome among their captors. A system of aggregating information about detainees where the press, rather than the inmates themselves, must take the first step toward publicizing identities could give inmates greater freedom to make choices that reflect their autonomous preferences. Of course, a system of compelled disclosure would fare better on this score, in that inmates would have no choice but to publicize their identities, and thus they could not be subjected to retaliation or pressure from their captors stemming from that publication. This argument, combined with an empirical hunch that most inmates would want their identities revealed, provides the most plausible case for affirming the district court's judgment. But if the Second Circuit's conflicting empirical intuitions were closer to the mark, then a forced choice regime in response to FOIA requests might best balance the competing expressive, monitoring, and privacy interests.

Third, permitting information concerning the identities of detainees to be disclosed in response to a FOIA request, rather than via the affirmative actions of the detainees themselves, may provide aggregation benefits to the media, facilitating the efficient transmission of information to the public. A FOIA response typically has the advantage of containing an aggregated list that is disclosed at one time. By contrast, voluntary disclosures by detainees themselves may trickle out over time, and information dissemination may occur via a multitude of mediums. There are reasons to favor simultaneous and aggregated disclosures. Sometimes a pattern regarding the detainees, which may reveal aspects of government policy, is not evident unless a large data set can be analyzed. The sum of the whole may reveal more than the sum of the parts. Moreover, although journalists can and do aggregate information that has been disclosed in a disaggregated form, doing so is a costly enterprise. As the costs of aggregating information increase, the probability that the media will incur these costs (and report on a particular story) decline. If the media can free-ride on the aggregation work that the government is peculiarly well suited to conduct, the press can pass the savings on to the public.

The Second Circuit dismissed the benefits of facilitating news reporting by the AP, observing that the only benefit they could see from disclosing some of the requested information was providing "AP with leads for investigating the detainees' claims."[34] To the court, this sort of interest did not square with the purpose of FOIA: "inform[ing] the citizens about 'what the government is up to.'" Absent direct evidence of government misconduct, the court saw no justification for denying the government's request for redaction. Bizarrely, the court did not consider allegations that the government may have tortured detainees at Guantanamo to be potential government misconduct.[35] The court instead focused on the absence of evidence to show, say, that the DOD had responded to allegations of abuse in a discriminatory manner, treating people differently based on their religion or national origin.

The court's analysis misconceives the nature of FOIA. FOIA requests are not exclusively a tool of "gotcha journalism." They can be used by the press to document good or bad government performance. If a citizen hopes to use FOIA to show that a government program is well designed and well managed, this motivation does not excuse the government's burden of disclosing information in response to the request. The *Favish* court was properly skeptical of Mr. Favish's request for photographs of Vince Foster's dead body in light of the fact that five separate and independent investigations into his death had all concluded that Foster's death was a suicide, not the result of a nefarious government conspiracy and cover-up. The treatment of detainees at Guantanamo was, at the time of the AP's request, subject to much greater uncertainty and debate.

In short, there are good reasons to believe that the public interest is well served by requiring the government to produce aggregated information about individuals even in a context where those same individuals can reveal duplicative information about themselves through voluntary actions. These concerns become particularly pronounced in settings where these individuals are incarcerated.

Recall that the district court in *Associated Press* also wrestled with the issue of whether detainees' family members had a FOIA privacy interest in administrative board review documents that identified these relatives. The district court concluded that redaction of the relatives' names was warranted where a detainee professed disdain for the Taliban but redaction was not warranted where a detainee's attitudes toward the Taliban were harder to discern, and the potential threat to his relatives from retaliation was therefore more speculative. The appellate court viewed disclosure as inappropriate in both instances—family members' identities and addresses might be the sort of information "that a person would ordinarily not wish to make known about himself or herself" and disclosure would not help "reveal what the government is up to."[36]

Note that under a broad reading of *Favish*, the consent of the detainees to have their names disclosed would not be decisive. The disclosure of detainees' identities quite plausibly could expose their relatives to violent retaliation even if the names and addresses of the relatives were unknown to the government. Disclosing the identities of the detainees themselves would enable extremists with local knowledge to identify and target detainees' relatives living abroad. It is therefore plausible to read Supreme Court case law as conferring upon the government a broad right to block the disclosure of private information based upon the privacy interests of someone other than the individuals whose information is at issue. Under such an approach, the fragmentation of privacy interests provides the government with a broad excuse to withhold data. If even one third party might object to the disclosure of the information, redaction would be permissible. Constructive partition stops being practical when so many people might assert an interest in the private information.

The anticommons tragedy of empty stores and vibrant kiosks has arisen in various settings in which the nonconsent of one of a number of stakeholders can prevent a socially desirable outcome. For example, even where an individual has issued unambiguous advance directives that his organs be used for transplantation upon his demise, hospital administrators commonly refuse to harvest organs if even one of the decedent's next of kin objects to such a procedure.[37] The social harm from a privacy anticommons would be too much privacy. This result seems relatively harmless compared with analogues like too many transplantable organs going to waste or too little innovation in biomedicine. But recall that the reasons why we defer to an individual's choices about what to make public largely underscore the dangers of excessive privacy protections. Privacy competes with other important values, like expressive interests, the need for robust public debate, and nondiscrimination imperatives. In the FOIA context, letting the government withhold information from credible journalistic entities like the AP necessarily deprived the public of information concerning a controversy that would become the subject of significant political debate. Privacy may be an important enough reason to keep this information out of the public's hands, but if privacy interests become too fragmented, public discourse will suffer.

This basic issue—what to do if an individual would like to disclose information about himself that necessarily implicates the privacy of a third party—is not a new one in privacy law. The leading precedent is Haynes v. Alfred A. Knopf.[38] Judge Posner, writing for the Seventh Circuit, astutely noted that if Ruby Daniels, a Chicagoan who was part of the Great Migration and endured an unhappy marriage as well as other tribulations, could not disclose private facts about her ex-husband, then she could not tell her own story: if the defendant "cannot tell the story of Ruby Daniels without waivers from every person who she thinks did her wrong, he cannot write this book."[39]

Judge Posner's analysis does not deny the significant privacy harm that can come from the publication of a kiss-and-tell memoir. Rather, it recognizes that if two participants in an interaction have conflicting views about its private or public nature, the views of each party deserve significant weight. In cases where there was an explicit or implicit meeting of the minds regarding the permissibility of subsequent disclosure, the law ought to enforce that bargain. But in the absence of such an understanding, the public's right to be informed about matters of legitimate public concern should tip the balance against liability for publication. Extreme cases, such as those involving the dissemination of a surreptitiously recorded videotape depicting consensual sex by one of the participants, are easy: the privacy harm to the nonconsenter is grave and the public's interest in the material is likely not weighty. Setting aside these sorts of cases, the public's interest in reading plus the consenter's interest in speaking typically will trump the objector's interest in not being written about.

Having said that, Posner's analysis in the *Haynes* case is not completely satisfying. He wonders whether a biographer needs to get the permission of anyone who is portrayed negatively in a book, but that is not the issue. Biographies rarely disclose intimate and highly offensive details about a very large number of people. The collective action problems presented in cases like *Haynes* are therefore not tragedies of the anticommons, in that no individual can block an entire story from being told. Assuming away broad familial privacy rights, at most one person could block a portion of a story being told in a particularly detailed way. Nevertheless, privacy tort law typically sidesteps the collective action dilemma by giving each potential speaker a rather strong right to disclose sensitive information about her own intimate associations.

Whose Privacy Counts?—Doe v. Quiring

The most wrenching cases implicating collective privacy interests arise in settings where constructive partition is impossible. *Quiring*,[40] a fascinating South Dakota Supreme Court opinion, surprisingly has been ignored by privacy scholars and barely cited in the case law.[41] *Quiring* concerned a challenge to the state's sex offender registry, brought by the daughter of an offender convicted of violating the state's law criminalizing incest. Under South Dakota's Megan's Law, the sex offender's photograph and address were published on the Internet, along with information specifying that he had been convicted of the crime of "incest." The plaintiff in the case continued to live at the same address as her father after his release from prison. South Dakota therefore cannot publicize his precise crime on Megan's Law without calling attention to her victimization. It can do what Doe asked, which is to identify her father as a generic sex offender, rather than an incest perpetrator.

The facts of *Quiring* potentially present two sorts of privacy conflicts of interest. First, the state likely deemed the perpetrator's privacy rights as substantially reduced by virtue of his having committed a serious crime. Courts sometimes refer to criminals as having "waived" their privacy rights in the process of violating the law, with the effects of such a waiver closely resembling those of consent.[42] Indeed, courts conceptualize a waiver as a form of implicit consent. Second, although we do not know whether Doe's father wished to have his crime classified as a generic sex offense, it is plausible that unlike his daughter he would have preferred the more specific designation. The available empirical research suggests that incest perpetrators are less likely to recidivate than sex offenders whose crimes have victimized strangers.[43] Similarly, among "child molesters, those most likely to sexually recidivate are those who offended against unrelated boy victims, followed by those who offended against unrelated girl victims and, finally, incest offenders."[44] We do not know whether the public generally understands that incest perpetrators present a lower recidivism risk than rapists or other sex offenders who target strangers. If the public does understand this, it might explain why notwithstanding the incest taboo, a sex offender would prefer an incest perpetrator designation to a less precise description. Being designated as an incest perpetrator might have subjected Doe's father to less harassment, suspicion, and surveillance than being described as a more threatening generic sex offender.

The plaintiff challenged the law on statutory grounds—basing her argument on a provision in the Megan's Law statute providing that "any identifying information regarding of the victim of the crime" was to remain confidential. The plaintiff also raised constitutional arguments at trial, but chose not to pursue them on appeal. Nevertheless, South Dakota's Supreme Court improperly held that the constitutional arguments would have been unmeritorious had they been pursued.[45] Turning to the statutory arguments before it, the court upheld the law by a three-to-two vote. The justices in the majority concluded that the designation of the victim's father as an incest perpetrator did not constitute "identifying information regarding the victim" because the plaintiff was one of a number of possible victims who were related to the perpetrator:

> [A] victim could be any one of a number of less than 21-year-old relatives of the offender. Under these circumstances, we believe that the mere listing of the offender and type of offense is not the disclosure of the "identifying information" that the Legislature intended to prohibit. It could not have been the Legislature's intent because, if carried to its logical conclusion, Applicant's position would prohibit the public disclosure of *any* detail of any offense. We do not think the Legislature intended such an absurd construction.[46]

The majority in *Quiring*, like the dissent in *Randolph*, uses the specter of a privacy anticommons to diminish the privacy interest of a party with an overwhelming interest in nondisclosure. The daughter is a cotenant adamantly withholding her consent at the front door, but the court does not want to differentiate her from the babysitter who works in the apartment one night every few weeks. In the process, the majority creates a kind of tragedy of the *commons*—the daughter's private information is disclosed excessively, because neither she nor anyone else is given the right to exercise control over the fact of her victimization.

The *Quiring* dissenters, by contrast, noted that the "size of the class of incest victims is limited to family members. The number of family members under the age of twenty-one is even smaller and, in some cases, may include only a couple of children. Publicly identifying the crime as 'incest' significantly increases the risk of providing 'identifying information of the victim' and may bring opprobrium on family members who were not victims."[47] The dissenters are perhaps understandably blind to the possibility that some family members may *want* to have their kinsman accurately identified as an incest perpetrator, perhaps for the same reason that the district court judge in *Associated Press* couldn't imagine why any abused Guantanamo detainee wouldn't want to be identified. The dispute between the majority and the dissenters boils down to a disagreement over whose privacy interests count. To the majority, nothing less than a categorical identification of "Jane Doe, incest victim" implicates the statute's confidentiality provision. The dissenters viewed the language more probabilistically, and also more realistically, given the ease with which data mining could be used to determine Jane Doe's real identity.[48]

The *Quiring* dissent also gets the better of the policy argument that informs the interpretation of the statutory text. Given that recidivism rates for incest perpetrators seem to be relatively low, and assuming that incest perpetrators are likely to recidivate against relatives, and that rapists of strangers are likely to recidivate against strangers, the blurring of incest perpetrators and generic sex offenders might make it harder for the public to take appropriate precautions. But the number of incest perpetrators seems sufficiently small to justify categorical blurring here. In Minnehaha County, where the plaintiff lived, there were a total of six sex offenders who had been convicted of incest. Although the number of sex offenders living in the county at the time of the lawsuit is unknown, there were 474 total registered sex offenders living in the county in June 2009.[49] If incest perpetrators comprise less than 2 percent of sex offenders, then the harm resulting from lumping them in with other sex offenders is unlikely to be great.

Conclusion

The results in both *Associated Press* and *Quiring* seem intuitively troubling, and an examination of the cases and their contexts reveals a neutral basis for questioning both opinions. A more satisfying resolution would ameliorate *Associated Press's* tragedy of the privacy anticommons and *Quiring's* tragedy of the commons by restoring "consent" to the central position it occupies in the rest of privacy law. Namely, the state should be proscribed from identifying someone as an "incest perpetrator" without the consent of the victim, and the government should be unable to withhold the identities of any detainee absent a showing that *either* that particular detainee or a majority of all detainees prefer anonymity.

How should we choose between those decision rules? Privileging individual consent is most appropriate where individuals did not choose to join the group in question. In the case of voluntary associations, there is a much stronger case for subjecting the individual to the preferences of the majority, as we do with corporations, homeowner's associations, student organizations, and university faculties. Such a rule facilitates coordinated action while encouraging people to choose their associates wisely. Doe did not elect to become an incest victim, so her individual consent should be required regardless of how other members of her nuclear family feel. Even if eleven siblings wanted their father designated as an incest perpetrator, and Doe was the lone hold-out, the court might appropriately embrace the *Associated Press* remedy of no disclosure without unanimous consent because Doe didn't choose her siblings. Applying voluntariness to the facts of *Associated Press,* some of the Guantanamo detainees chose to join the Taliban or Al Qaeda, but none of them chose to be abused, so deciding whether individual consent or majority assent is necessary becomes more difficult there. The costs of constructively partitioning the list of abused detainees will likely be determinative.

It is comforting to remember that collective action problems arise in many areas of law. Property law governs jointly owned resources, and typically requires unanimity where one owner's views conflict with those of her co-owners. In corporate law, by contrast, majority shareholders typically prevail over the minority. Privacy rules modeled on property law—where the consent of all affected parties is required—are most appropriate where courts are rather stingy in determining what "counts" as a privacy interest. As courts increasingly recognize familial privacy interests or encounter data sets that implicate the privacy interests of many individuals, either majoritarian decision making or constructive partition will become necessary to prevent tragedies of the privacy anticommons.

The dissemination of sensitive information concerning an individual often affects particular third parties by inferentially revealing information about them. In cases where these third parties are relatively few in number, and absent reason to doubt whether they can consent or withhold their consent effectively, it is tempting to say that the law should strive to treat these third parties as well as it treats the individuals whose privacy is more obviously at stake. This aspiration, however, has the potential to swallow up much of the Freedom of Information Act's disclosure requirements, with attendant losses to speech and transparency interests. As such, where a large number of people each have a low-stake interest in the dissemination of information concerning a particular individual and constructive partition is impractical, it is appropriate for the law to require only the consent of the obviously and primarily interested individual. Such an approach heads off a potential tragedy of the privacy anticommons, while recognizing the legitimate interdependency of information privacy interests. In short, recognizing the multiplicity of interdependent privacy interests should not make us unwilling to prioritize among those interests. There is, after all, sound logic behind our intuitions that the detainee's desire to publicize his captivity and mistreatment should prevail over the wishes of his publicity-shy relatives, and the incest victim's privacy preferences must matter more than the perpetrator's.

CHAPTER 13

Privacy on Social Networks:
Norms, Markets, and Natural Monopoly

Ruben Rodrigues

Introduction

Social-networking sites are the newest phenomenon to take the Internet by storm. Sites like MySpace, Facebook, and Twitter have created robust platforms for perpetual communication of all sorts of information: favorite foods and movies, contact information, where you're going, who you're with, and so on. Never before has so much information, traditionally private by nature, been so widely shared. The concerns for privacy in this new era are obvious: Who controls all this data? Who has access to it? What limits are imposed on its aggregation? Currently, competition between various websites provides strong incentives to protect user privacy. The market for social-networking sites, however, might not support such competition for much longer. We could very well be seeing the rise of a single dominant player who is capable of exercising monopoly power. Such a monopolist would not respond to pressure from competitors to protect the privacy of entrenched users. To effectively protect privacy interests in this market, the law must intervene.

Many commentators have discussed the implications this new communication medium poses for user privacy. In his book, *The Future of Reputation,* Daniel Solove portrays a world where once-fleeting harms to reputation, such as saying something incoherent, dumb, or offensive when under pressure, can be forever memorialized on the servers of YouTube. Not only is it permanently archived; but embarrassing, shameful, and intrusive information is also just a Google search away. In a bygone era, one could overcome reputational harms by finding a new social circle, moving to a new location in severe cases, or by simply waiting for time to pass and for people

237

to forget. Those would all seem futile efforts in an online world. The ability to simply move to a new town to avoid shame, or to hope that as time passes people forget, the hope of a "second chance," is gone.

The situations Solove and others in this book worry about are truly disconcerting. However, it is important to note that they often involve a degree of involuntariness on the part of the individual whose privacy is invaded. In fact, these situations might not really pose *privacy* issues in and of themselves. Rather, they often involve statements that are complete fabrications that are more properly the focus of a defamation or libel action.

The focus of this essay is social-network websites, where users often maintain *control* over their own information, even when it is pervasively shared. Users of these sites generally have the ability to control both who they are "friends" with and the manner in which information is shared. They also retain control over what others can say about them on their "profile" page by deleting undesirable comments. This degree of control prevents many of the harms associated with online slander. Furthermore, anonymous postings and accounts are rare in the context of social networks, and companies like Facebook actively purge accounts they suspect of being fake or anonymous.

The lack of anonymity on social networks allows privacy-enhancing social norms to develop. Society relies on these norms, in addition to legal regimes and liability rules, to influence individual conduct in other realms of life. Thus it only makes sense that such norms will have some effect on the Internet as well. Legal rules are usually left to dissuade particularly egregious conduct when social norms fail. Social norms can often be more effective than legal rules at inducing conforming behavior. For example, fines exist for littering; however, the glare you receive from someone who catches you throwing trash on the ground is more likely to create a disincentive to litter than is a $50 fine that is rarely enforced.

Similarly, the power of individual reputation and online social norms can go a long way toward preventing the abuse of personal information among users of social-networking sites. Any given user is generally just as vulnerable to abuse as any other. Any incentive I might have to abuse your information, or to post derogatory statements about you, is countered by the disincentive that you could conceivably do the same to me. In fact, the disincentives might often outweigh the incentives. Posting derogatory information could very well lead to a massive backlash by friends of the original target.

Still, there *are* privacy concerns with social networks. To the extent that a user's control over his or her network, profile, and personal information is an effective means for protecting user privacy, we must ask what the driving force behind user-friendly privacy-enhancing control mechanisms is. In the context of social-networking sites, market competition plays a large role in promoting user control and shaping privacy policies. Market competition also protects users from the possibility that a social-network provider may itself abuse private user information. Social-networking sites have responded rather quickly to consumer demands for greater privacy protection. These controls, however, can be effective only within the context of robust competition in the market for social networks.

The Market for Social Networking

We can break down the market for social networking into two main classes. First there are the *general*, all-purpose, social networks that act as substitutes for each other. Then there are the *niche* sites that do not act as substitutes, but rather can be used in concert with one another or as add-ons to general sites.

The general sites are the ones this essay is most concerned with. These sites provide a variety of user services such as the ability to have a general profile page accessible to others that can contain contact information, a narrative, pictures, lists of friends or connections, and various "status" updates revealing current information about one's activities. Most general sites provide further features such as the ability to add third-party "applications" to a profile, and the ability to use a profile in concert with niche sites (which are described further below). All general sites provide much of the same functionality, the core element of which is an online network of friends with no particular thematic connection. As such, the general sites act as substitutes for each other, and users will rarely actively use more than one. The distinction between actively using and simply "having an account" on a social-networking site is an important one. Over time many people create multiple accounts on multiple networks, even though they only consistently use a single network and account. The reasons for this are varied: some may simply want to guarantee that their desired user names are not taken, while others may be motivated to occasionally see what other networks are like.

Currently, large players among general social-networking sites are Facebook, MySpace, Orkut (Google's social-networking site), and Windows

Live Spaces (Microsoft's new social-networking site). Other general social-networking sites include early entrants like Friendster, whose popularity has diminished substantially. MySpace poses an interesting example of a general "all-purpose" social-networking site. It invested heavily in providing "niche" social-networking services to musicians and bands, and has developed a robust music-interested social network. This aspect of MySpace may more appropriately be regarded as a niche site. However, for the purposes of this essay, it is difficult to separate out this aspect of the network from the larger, general MySpace network.

Sites that should be described as "niche" are those that provide social-networking functions, but do not serve as substitutes to a general all-purpose site. They include LinkedIn, Twitter, and Flickr. LinkedIn provides users with a professional-minded social network focused on résumé building, recommendations, references, and business networking. Facebook allows users to link directly to their LinkedIn profile from within a Facebook page; the niche service is thus easy to use in concert with the general site.

Meanwhile, Twitter provides users with a "micro-blogging" service that allows users to share short 140-character statements with each other. The most common use of Twitter is through cell phones and PDA devices. Facebook also allows interoperability with Twitter, allowing users to make their Twitter feed and Facebook "status" one and the same. Flickr is a social network built around the concept of photo sharing and commenting on shared photos. The general social-networking sites provide some of the same functionality, but Flickr provides additional features, such as enhanced photo-search capabilities and a community specifically interested in photography.

The initial reaction to so much sharing of information on the Internet is often to assume that everything posted on these sites is no longer private. In one sense, things posted on social networks really do cease to be "private," but at the same time it's not completely "public." While it is true that users disclose a vast amount of information, they conduct this disclosure in a very limited fashion. The information becomes "public" in the sense that it is no longer under the exclusive control of the individual, but at the same time it is not public vis-à-vis the entire world. Users retain a good deal of discretion in determining who has access to what information. For example, on Facebook, users have the ability to limit profile visibility to certain networks of friends, and users can control the display of individual messages, "wall posts," and "photo tags" that refer to them. The social network itself generally retains access and certain rights to use this information, but even this is a form of limited, trusted, disclosure.

The use of social networks, and thus the sharing of all this information, is completely voluntary. No one requires that anyone sign up for a MySpace page. Even if you do, you need not use much of the privacy-deteriorating functionality it offers. However, online social networking has become a powerful trend. As social-networking sites become more popular, it may become harder or even impractical for individuals to avoid them.

A legal regime that addresses privacy concerns on social networks should not limit the ability of individuals to willingly give up traditionally private information. After all, the popularity of sites like MySpace and Facebook means that social-networking sites provide a service that users actually value. In fact, these sites can be extremely efficient modes of communications. But in a world where so much private information lies in the hands of others, how does the law protect individuals from abuse? As we will see, the law has an important role in protecting competition, the current force driving privacy protections across the market for general social-networking sites.

Competition in the Social-Networking Market

Social-networking sites compete with each other for users. While this might not always be apparent since no one pays money directly to Facebook or MySpace to use their services, social-networking sites engage in non-price competition over features, add-ons, and most importantly: privacy. The privacy aspect of social-network competition is multifaceted, and can come in the form of *privacy policies, privacy practices, privacy controls,* or *data security.*

Privacy policies reflect the contractual relationship between users and the social-networking site, often included within a site's "Terms of Service." The privacy policy will often also define the extent to which a social-networking site can use private information for the purpose of generating revenue through targeted advertising. Facebook has recently added documents entitled the "Facebook Principles" and "Statement of Rights and Responsibilities" to its website, which should also be considered in defining the site's overall privacy policy.

Privacy practices refer to a social network's actual practices in implementing its privacy policies. The way a site actually implements its privacy policies may differ substantially from what a policy says on its face. For example, are enough resources committed to redressing users' complaints under the terms of service? There may be situations where privacy policies are very friendly to the privacy interests of users, but are poorly applied in practice. Disallowing anonymous user accounts would be another example of a privacy-enhancing practice.

Privacy controls refer to the features social-networking sites make available that enable users to control how much, and what sorts of, information they post on the network. Examples of privacy controls include the manner in which users can limit profile page visibility, the degree to which access is limited to various "networks," the ability to delete, edit, or otherwise control comments and pictures linked to the user's profile, and a plethora of other features tailored to giving a user more control over his private information and online persona.

Data security refers to how diligent a social-networking site is at protecting users' data from external attacks by hackers or internal breaches, such as a leak. Data security breaches are widely discussed in the media when retailers suffer a breach of consumer credit card data, and social-networking sites are susceptible to similar compromises.

In the past few years, privacy, including all these facets thereof, has been increasingly recognized as an attribute of non-price competition, both within the market for social networking and beyond it. Social-networking sites, such as Facebook, have acknowledged that they compete on privacy. Many users have cited privacy as a major reason for switching from MySpace to Facebook. In addition, Facebook has quickly acted to address consumer privacy demands when faced with user backlashes over various privacy-hostile policies. Examples include the backlash against the release of Facebook Beacon, and the rush of users to change their privacy settings after Facebook announced it was going to make profiles searchable on Google. Consumers of social-networking sites care about privacy, and so far Facebook has reacted to meet consumer demands in the privacy space.

The Federal Trade Commission (FTC) also recognized privacy as a valuable form of non-price competition when faced with the merger of two large providers of online targeted advertising services, Google and Doubleclick. The FTC recognized "the possibility that [the] transaction could adversely affect non-price attributes of competition, such as consumer privacy."[1] The FTC ultimately held that the merger could proceed, since both entities operated in sufficiently different markets, and concluded that "the parties do not significantly affect each other's prices, nor non-price product attributes, such as consumer privacy protections or service quality."

While a typical user rarely considers his or her relationship to a social-networking site as commercial in nature, the transaction between user and site is essentially economic. Users contribute private information, in the form of profile content, communications with others, and consent to behavioral tracking, and in return receive useful services such as access to the network, communication tools, photo sharing, data storage, and a variety of other applications.

The market is two-sided. That is, the social-networking site has two separate, but interrelated, groups of consumers (see Figure 13.1). The first consists of the users who contribute private information, contacts, and behavior for analysis. The second contains the advertisers to whom Facebook sells advertising services. The users engage in non-price bargaining over privacy policies and user services, while the exchange between advertisers and the social-networking site is an area of traditional price competition.

Assuming competition in the market for social networking is an effective means for protecting user privacy, instances where the market ceases to operate effectively should be ripe for legal intervention in order to protect the bargaining relationship between the user and a social-network provider. A dominant social-network provider, who may very well be a natural

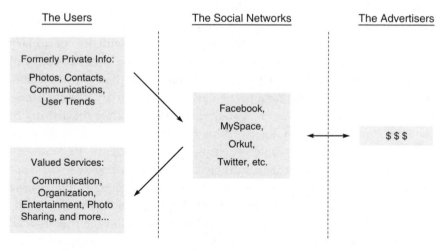

Figure 13.1 The Two-Sided Market for Social Networking.

monopolist, may leverage its monopoly power to provide less-than-desired levels of user privacy protection than would exist under competition.

A social-networking site could also exercise its monopoly power by charging users a price for services. However, it is more likely that it will simply forego investing in privacy protection since its core revenue model is focused on advertising revenue. A successful site enjoys advertising revenue and has little need to spend on privacy protections and other features that users might pay for in a competitive market. Monopoly power aside, it may also be difficult to charge for services consumers expect to receive without (direct) charge.

Social Networks and Natural Monopoly

The social-networking market exhibits *network effects* that make it susceptible to a natural monopoly. A network effect, also called a "network externality," occurs when one user of a good or service directly affects the value that some other user places on the same good or service. A canonical example is the telephone network. The value a particular user receives from a telephone network is directly dependent on how many other users he or she can access through the network. This effectively creates a positive feedback loop. In the end, and holding price aside, it is socially optimal to have a single, all-inclusive, telephone network as opposed to separate, competing, non-interoperable networks.

A natural monopoly in the market for social-networking sites would absolutely negate the ability of robust competition to effectively provide incentives that balance the privacy interests of users with the pecuniary goals of the social-networking site. The value of joining a particular social network derives directly from the ability to connect to all of one's "friends." As such, the more people on a particular social network, the more inherent value that network has. This self-reinforcing principle means that in the long run, a single social-networking site may prevail as all users flock to the site with the most "value" in terms of total number of users.

Social-networking sites are also subject to high *switching costs* that deter entry by new competing sites by making it hard for users of preexisting sites to switch. There may, however, be ways to overcome these costs, as this essay suggests. Users place a great deal of information on the initial social network of their choice. They post profiles, they form "connections," they develop communication routines, they keep track of contacts, and they host photos. After a period of participation, users become *entrenched*. The more information posted on a particular social-networking site, the greater a disincentive for that user to switch to a different site.

Some might perceive the costs of entry into the market for social networking as low. Anyone can cheaply start a website and purchase a domain name. In many ways, that is what Facebook did when it began as a small student-run site at Harvard and then grew to compete with MySpace. However, the costs of entry in the market are more complex than this simplistic model suggests. The costs lie not in creating the website, but in attracting and developing a critical mass of users and growing the overall network. The costs are thus very high when one considers established competitors with preexisting networks, especially if those competitors themselves develop tools and strategies to lock in users and keep switching costs high.

A natural monopolist in the market for social networking can extract monopoly rents on user privacy. A monopolist would have little incentive to respond to the demands of entrenched users concerned about privacy. A monopolist could also erode past privacy practices in exchange for greater income by directly reselling personal information and contact information, despite the interests of its entrenched users. While egregious violations may lead users to switch sites, or abandon social networking altogether, they will do so only once the costs to their privacy outweigh the benefits received from the site. Thus, the natural monopolist will simply engage in monopoly pricing (in regard to the bargaining that goes on between user and social-networking site) and charge "monopoly rents" on user privacy. Ultimately the social-networking site can engage in suboptimal pricing: users pay a lot more in terms of sacrifices to privacy in exchange for social-networking services than they would in a competitive market.

Given the two-sided nature of the social-networking market, this scenario could result even in light of robust price competition between the social-networking monopolist and other sources of targeted advertising. There are many providers of online targeted advertising, including email services (GMail and Hotmail), content distributors (YouTube), online retailers (Amazon), and direct advertisers (Google/Doubleclick). Social-networking sites are but one source of such targeted advertising. A monopolist in the market for social networking could compete strongly with these other players in the market for targeted advertising, while continuing to extract monopoly rents on the privacy of its users.

To put all of this in the context of a real-world scenario, let us look at the development of MySpace and Facebook. MySpace was once the globally dominant social-networking site, but Facebook has since dramatically encroached on MySpace's market share. In June 2008, Facebook had eighty million[2] users in comparison to MySpace's 100 million.[3] MySpace's lead has continued to erode throughout 2008 and 2009. As of September 2008, MySpace grew by six million users to 106 million;[4] while Facebook grew by forty million to achieve 120 million total users by October 2008, and then 200 million in March 2009.[5] Facebook surpassed MySpace to become the number one trafficked social-networking site in the world in 2008, and the fourth most trafficked website overall.[6] However, not all estimates of user traffic have Facebook ahead of MySpace.[7] But Facebook is plainly growing, and might well become the dominant social-networking site.

If social networking is a natural monopoly, why has there been competition between Facebook and MySpace? There are a number of possible explanations. MySpace was dominant only in the early phase of the development of social-networking sites. It is common to see competition in the early stages of a networked industry. There were once competing standards in the construction of railroad gauges and in the distribution of electricity on a national grid. More recently, there was competition between the HD-DVD and Blu-ray standards, with Blu-ray eventually dominating the market. It is possible that market segmentation within MySpace allowed Facebook to gain traction as it developed tools that users found more attractive. The early stage of development in the market also meant that users would be less entrenched than one might see now that the market has matured.

Possible Roles for the Law

There are numerous roles for the law in attempting to counteract the negative effects of a natural monopolist, many of which have been tried in other networked industries. The entirely digital nature of the social-network industry provides an interesting change from older forms of networked industries, and makes options that were impractical with older networks, such as telephones, optimal in the present case.

Standard options for countering the effects of natural monopoly include a command-and-control style regulatory regime or a mandated standard. Both are undesirable in the context of social-networking sites. A better route to keeping a social-networking monopolist in check would be to simply focus on keeping switching costs low and barring anticompetitive conduct through either an existing or a new antitrust law.

First, let's look at the possibility of mandating a regulatory regime with specific privacy protections. The Interstate Commerce Commission was one such command-and-control regime in the era of railroad monopolies. Of all the options for protecting privacy in light of a social-networking monopolist, this is the most undesirable. A natural monopolist would be able to charge monopoly "rates" in a number of areas besides privacy that would also require regulation, such as providing a suboptimal level of new user features. Dictating legal rules for each extremely technical area of concern would be highly inefficient, if not impossible.

Furthermore, a government-mandated privacy policy would likely provide either too great or too little protection. It would be difficult for regulators to gauge what sorts of information users are willing to give up, and what they would like to retain control over. The inability of government to accurately predict consumer demands is consistent with the history of command-and-control regulation in the face of a natural monopolist. For example, the 1996 Telecom Act was an attempt to make the telephone network more competitive, but the period following its passage was replete with litigation over the appropriate rates to charge competitors. A regulator is not in a good position to weigh the costs and benefits of various options and develop an efficient solution. Worst of all, in the context of user privacy, the value of private information is highly subjective. Different users like to protect or share their information to varying degrees, preferences that would be impossible for a regulator to fully accommodate.

A regulator might also have difficulty staying aware of the constant innovation in the market for social networking. New features are constantly added to social-networking sites, and a regulatory body would need to constantly adjust regulations to these changes.

Industry standards are often suggested as effective means for promoting interoperability among social-networking sites and thus, ideally, a mechanism for reducing switching costs and maintaining a competitive environment. Some have proposed the formation of a standard for social-networking profiles, and Facebook and Google have both signed on to the DataPortability project at Dataportability.org. Google (Orkut) and MySpace have also embraced the OpenSocial API as a standard for promoting interoperability, while Facebook retains its own proprietary systems. A standard could allow users to easily port information, contacts, and move from one social-networking site to another. However, for a standard to effectively lower switching costs, it must be accepted by all market participants, including the probable monopolist, and cover *all* aspects of the social network that help entrench users. Given the natural incentive to lock in users, the only way to achieve across-the-board adoption of a comprehensive standard is to impose a government mandate. This option, much like a regulatory regime, is also undesirable.

A mandated standard would likely hamper innovation, as social-networking sites would be discouraged from creating features that do not comply with the standard. To the extent sites would be allowed to develop features *beyond* the standard, it would lose its value in reducing switching costs. Users would be entrenched by the additional add-on features that they cannot port elsewhere via the standard. A mandated standard would also provide too much protection (discouraging innovation) or too little (allowing innovation, but not effectively reducing switching costs). Meanwhile, a voluntary standard would be ineffective since a social-networking monopolist could opt out, design around it, or create new entrenching features beyond the standard's scope.

A better option than a regulatory regime or mandated standard is one that focuses on keeping switching costs low and prohibiting anticompetitive conduct. This sort of regime would ensure that users are allowed to easily port content and contacts from one social-networking site to another, and prohibit sites from imposing artificial barriers to competition.

Competitors have a natural incentive to create scripts and programs that help entrenched users port information from one social-networking site to a competing one. A regime focused on banning anticompetitive behavior need only ensure that the use of such programs is explicitly allowed, and that social-networking sites are not allowed to block programs like these in order to deter competition. Niche sites in particular are well positioned to expand into the general social-network market if they see an opportunity to do so, and could act as an effective threat of entry, deterring a social-networking monopolist from extracting monopoly rents on user privacy.

Some social-networking sites are already embracing low-switching cost regimes, though generally in areas where websites do not act as direct competitors. For example, LinkedIn gives users the ability to search their Google-provided Gmail account for contacts to import onto LinkedIn. Users simply provide LinkedIn their Gmail login information and LinkedIn logs on to Google and acquires a list of possible contacts that LinkedIn users can then choose to add. Google does not block such services, and the model used here (turning over one's password to a trusted social-networking site) has been replicated on many websites.

A general social-networking site, even a monopolistic one, has many valid reasons to block third-party programs, either to protect its own network or in the interests of its users. Social-networking sites can be prone to spam attacks, involving attempts to either directly spam individuals through the network, or gather email addresses for later spamming efforts. Other malicious programs could come in the form of viruses or denial of service attacks designed to overrun the network and bring the system to a crawl.

Some cases may require a difficult determination as to whether a third-party program is a valid attempt to lower switching costs by a legitimate competitor or a malicious attack by a spammer. Blocking the latter should be considered legitimate, while blocking by the former is likely an anticompetitive refusal to deal. The situation between Plaxo and Facebook (described below) may be one such case. Litigation might be necessary to determine the appropriate line between legitimate and anticompetitive blocking in these cases. Some might oppose such litigation as wasteful, but it is a common approach in our legal system when difficult questions of line-drawing arise. Meanwhile, the majority of situations will pose a clear determination that blocking third-party applications by legitimate competitors is an anticompetitive practice. A site such as Facebook could hardly argue that reputable sites like MySpace, Orkut, or LinkedIn are malicious spammers. One could argue that by allowing interconnections of this sort, competitors would be emboldened to begin spamming, or attempt to bring down the monopolistic social-networking site through malicious code. However, such behavior is already prohibited by federal law, and an illicit attempt to bring down a competitor could itself be considered anticompetitive.

Blocking programs developed by competitors is just one way a potential monopolist might try to leverage the network effects of this market and thus artificially raise switching costs in an anticompetitive manner. Other avenues include asserting competitively questionable claims under contract law, while even daring to claim an extreme concern for the privacy interests of users. This could occur through anticompetitive application of a particular social-networking site's terms of service. For example, some sites block users who attempted to use unauthorized programs, while some terms of service prohibit users from sharing their login information with third parties.

In blocking users, and in prohibiting the sharing of login information, Facebook has repeatedly cited the privacy interests of its users as a justification. This could be considered a "false" privacy rationale to the extent a social network uses it to justify the blocking of programs or the banishment of users in ways that raise switching costs to the detriment of competition. Some have pointed out that lowering transaction costs might actually *degrade* privacy.[8] The argument is as follows: users who join a website consent to being connected to each other on a site such as Facebook, but they do not necessarily consent to the prospect of their friends' turning around and redistributing all their information to someone else. Therefore, when someone turns over a friend's user information to a third party, that person violates the friend's privacy interests. This has generally been Facebook's privacy argument. This view fits well with what Professor Lior Strahilevitz calls a "A Social Networks Theory of Privacy," the notion that just because someone has consented to disclosing information to a select group of people, does not mean the individual has consented to broader, public disclosure.[9] Although initially compelling, the argument as applied in this context is flawed, especially when weighed against the competing pro-privacy goal of lowering switching costs and fostering competition and effective threat of entry.

For one thing, it is common practice on many websites to allow users to share their login information in order to port contacts. Google's GMail service arguably contains much more private information about someone than does a Facebook account, yet people share their logins all the time in order to share and import GMail contacts to other services. There has also been no backlash against the use of third-party "Applications" on Facebook, even though use of such applications transmits a great deal of information to third parties without a user's explicit consent. Thus, we should be skeptical of the notion that users feel betrayed by friends who distribute information to third parties in a reasonable manner. Perhaps users have not consented to having their information publicly broadcast to the world (as Strahilevitz's "A Social Networks Theory of Privacy" would suggest), but they likely *have* consented to their friend's use of information to export contacts to Outlook, for example.

Second, Facebook's concerns here fly directly in the face of typical privacy norms. When deciding with whom to share information in everyday fashion, people generally rely on trust with others as a safeguard from abuse of that information. We do not typically feel an affront to privacy if someone passes on the fact that he or she is our friend. Similarly, we generally do not feel harmed if a trusted friend invites us to join a social network, such as LinkedIn, after the friend has imported contacts to the social-networking website via GMail.

Third, Facebook's justifications are directly contrary to its own practices. Facebook allows a growing number of "applications," developed by third parties, to exist on its site. Many of these applications have access to various user and friend information, and the use of such information is consented to only by the friend who adds the application. Facebook has also allowed users to port their contacts and information directly to Microsoft's Windows Live Spaces service, which would presumably pose the same privacy concerns.

In addition to blocking programs or using contracts, a potential monopolist may use questionable claims of intellectual property law to raise the costs of switching or directly attack a competitor. The Supreme Court in Lotus Dev. Corp. v. Borland Int'l, Inc. held that user interfaces in software programs may not be copyrighted, specifically citing the competitive concerns regarding the enforcement of intellectual property rights in user interfaces.[10] Similarly, user interfaces and layouts on social-networking sites should not be subject to copyright (though unique graphical elements may continue to be protected). Facebook recently filed a copyright suit against a German rival, studiVZ. While this site may very well have copied protected elements of Facebook's site (the two sites do, in fact, have a striking resemblance), competitive concerns should be weighed in the analysis as they were in *Lotus*.

With this description of the various ways a natural monopolist might anticompetitively raise switching costs or deter competition, let us look at some more things Facebook has done that could be considered anticompetitive and thus detrimental to privacy. Facebook recently made a questionable move in banning the use of Google's "Friend Connect" application. Friend Connect would go through a user's Facebook profile and port the profile and any contacts the user desired to Google.[11] This is precisely the sort of application designed with an eye toward lowering the switching costs involved in moving from one network to another.

Facebook cited user privacy concerns as a reason for denying access to Google's service. However, Facebook allows many other add-on programs that similarly degrade user privacy by allowing third-party access to user information (via Facebook's "Applications" interface). Facebook may have legitimate claims that a certain application might free-ride on its service, but anticompetitive concerns should be considered in evaluating the legitimacy of Facebook's actions, especially given that Google has its own competing social-networking service, Orkut.

Facebook took similar action against another competitor, Plaxo. Plaxo developed a script that users could use to port profile information and contacts over to its own site and into Microsoft Outlook.[12] Plaxo admittedly has a reputation as a source of unsolicited email, however, the program in question seems to have been narrowly tailored to a legitimate purpose. While Facebook may have justifiably blocked Plaxo, and some have applauded Facebook's blocking of Plaxo's scripts as pro-privacy,[13] anticompetitive concerns should at least be factored into evaluating the appropriateness of Facebook's behavior.

Curiously, Facebook has been much more willing to hand over user-contact information to its business partner, Microsoft, for use in expanding its Windows Live Messenger service.[14] It is unclear how the privacy interests of users are substantially different in this circumstance from those in situations with Google or Plaxo.

To support its claim of being more open and "interoperable," Facebook has created "Facebook Connect." This tool enables any *approved* website to interact with Facebook, by allowing Facebook users to log on to a variety of websites using their Facebook account. Rather than lowering switching costs, however, Facebook Connect actually exacerbates the network effects of Facebook's underlying social network. It makes Facebook an Internet-wide *platform* from which to conduct a large variety of transactions over the Internet, whether logging on to shop at Amazon.com or to chat via instant messaging services like Meebo.

Unlike data-porting tools such as the ones offered by LinkedIn to port contacts from Gmail to LinkedIn, Facebook Connect does not allow a third party wholesale access to a user's information and connections. Rather, Facebook Connect acts as an authentication tool for a variety of services. The difference is important; rather than allow users to share their username and password with third parties, Facebook requires the user to log in to *its* service *first*. The chat-consolidation program Meebo provides a telling example.

Meebo is an instant messaging service that allows a variety of instant messaging clients to communicate through a single interface. The interface accomodates Google's GTalk, Yahoo Messenger, MSN Messaging, AOL's

AIM, and most recently, Facebook. Rather than a user simply entering his or her username and password as with all the other services, and thus giving Meebo wholesale access to the user's account, the Facebook implementation requires the user to log in to Facebook first. Facebook is banning the practice of sharing login information in its terms of service with users as well. The effect is that while Facebook allows interoperability, in that users can use other sites, it ultimately has control over which sites can be used and what information those other sites obtain about a user.

Meebo originally implemented the addition of Facebook in the same way it implemented the incorporation of MySpace, Google, MSN, AOL, and Yahoo; it simply required that users give their passwords and usernames. However, Facebook quickly blocked Meebo and cited the privacy concerns of users as a justification, a rationale that we have already debunked. So what *could* be a justification for Facebook's blocking of Meebo? It is most likely that rather than protecting privacy, Facebook's goal is to increase the costs associated with porting information to a new network, since such portability is not possible through an authentication interface such as Facebook Connect. Requiring that users log in to Facebook first acts to raise the transaction costs of using other social-networking sites. Thus, Facebook Connect actually increases switching costs by deepening the entrenchment of users in the Facebook network and by making Facebook a platform for all sorts of tasks on the Internet.

The fact that Facebook can require another site to use its own authentication tool, rather than allow the site to simply use passwords and usernames (as Google and AIM allow on Meebo), might mean that Facebook is already starting to leverage its monopoly power. Otherwise, one would observe other sites' imposing such authentication measures rather than allowing simple sign-ons.

Facebook recently announced addendums to its terms of service that it calls the "Facebook Principles"[15] and "Statement of Rights and Responsibilities,"[16] which users were allowed to vote on in an "election." The new statement of rights and responsibilities explicitly prohibits users from sharing their login information with third parties. Statement 4.6 states that the user, "will not share your password, let anyone else access your account," while statement 3.2 states that users, "will not collect users' information, or otherwise access Facebook, using automated means (such as harvesting bots, robots, spiders, or scrapers) without our permission."[17] These provisions further inflame the competitive concerns at issue in the Meebo example.

Not only does Facebook block Meebo, but it additionally places a threat on its own users not to share their logins with others, a proven method of effectively porting content from one site to another.

Given the underlying competitive concerns, statements 4.6 and 3.2 can be viewed as diametrically opposed to the more loosely worded pleasant-sounding Facebook "principle" regarding the free flow of information, which states that "People should have the freedom to access all of the information made available to them by others. People should also have practical tools that make it easy, quick, and efficient to share and access this information."[18] It's clear that Facebook does not desire to allow full sharing of information under this principle, or else it would not place such tight restrictions on the sharing of login information with third parties. Perhaps those drafting the principles forgot to condition the words "share" and "access" with the phrase "only within the Facebook network."

All of these anticompetitive concerns have recently come to bear on a lawsuit Facebook filed in early 2009 against Power.com. Power.com is an aggregator of social-networking sites, and it engages in the practice of providing tools to users of social-networking sites, like Facebook and MySpace, that allow them to port content among social networks. These tools are, much like those advocated in this essay, means of keeping switching costs low and minimizing barriers to entry. While the case is still in its infancy, Facebook's complaint alleges questionable claims of copyright and trademark infringement, as well as competitively suspect claims arising out of violations of Facebook's terms of service. In particular, the complaint focuses extensively on Power.com's violation of Facebook's policy against sharing user names and passwords, and Power.com's refusal to cooperate with Facebook Connect as an alternative. Facebook's complaint against Power.com also alleges claims with fewer implications for competition, such as those arising out of the CAN-SPAM Act and misrepresentation. Going forward we should be skeptical of claims by Facebook that threaten competition; courts should weigh heavily the anticompetitive consequences of granting such relief.

Facebook is not a democracy. One common refrain by Facebook users in response to suggestions that Facebook might not have their best privacy interests in mind is that Facebook itself is an empowering tool that allows for user organization and the ability to "petition" Facebook for the redress of grievances through tools like Facebook "groups." This is, in fact, what happened in response to the Facebook Beacon controversy and the push back on changes to Facebook's terms of service. In those situations, Facebook users formed groups and signed online petitions in order to press Facebook for changes. Facebook users, of course, play no role in electing Facebook management, and have no effective check on what Facebook does other than their ability, as consumers, to stop using the service. All these successful online petition campaigns occurred with competition from firms like MySpace and Orkut lurking in the background, even as Facebook continued to increase its share of the market. Petitions may have some effect on a social-networking monopolist, to the extent that a site wants to avoid negative publicity, but in the end the profitable alternative will be the path Facebook takes.

The illusion of Facebook as a form of participatory democracy was further exacerbated with Facebook's recent "election" involving changes to its terms of service. Users were asked to vote on whether to approve a new set of "governing" documents for the site, the Facebook Principles and Statement of Rights and Responsibilities. Very few participated in the voting process. Brilliant marketing aside, it is clear that Facebook is a company, not a democracy. That is how Chris Cox, Facebook's co-founder, put it in an interview with the *New York Times* in March 2009: "It's not a democracy," he said. "We are here to build an Internet medium for communicating and we think we have enough perspective to do that and be caretakers of that vision."[19]

Facebook may already be leveraging its market power to the detriment of user privacy. In December 2009, Facebook announced drastic changes to default user-privacy settings. Facebook took away user control over pictures, contact information, and friend lists and made such information publicly available. It also increased the amount of information available to developers, without the consent of users. Not only do these changes fly in the face of the pro-privacy arguments Facebook has used to justify the blocking of competitors, but it reflects a revolutionary departure from it's original privacy-enhancing business model focused on attracting new users through enhanced user privacy and control. Mark Zuckerberg, Facebook's founder and CEO, has justified these changes by arguing that "social norms" have developed whereby users no longer value online privacy.[20] While more information sharing might be a general trend, it is doubtful that Facebook users, who vastly outnumber users of services like Twitter, would prefer giving up control over their information. Zuckerberg could have structured this change in such a way that people could opt in to more sharing if they wished, rather than make these changes defaults that cannot be opted out from. It may very well be that Facebook has decided to start exploiting the fruits of anticompetitive practices and network effects to the detriment of user privacy, and if that is the case, it may be time for the law to intervene.

Conclusion

Competition among social-networking site operators creates powerful market incentives for protecting user privacy. To the extent that one social-networking site develops monopoly power, and succeeds in raising switching costs and mooting the threat of entry, we can expect such a monopolistic site to engage in suboptimal levels of privacy protection. Because of the two-sided market for social networking, this may be the case even in the face of robust competition for targeted advertising. In order to avoid the loss to society and user privacy that would result, the law should act to ensure switching costs are low and should prohibit the sort of anticompetitive behavior that has been discussed.

While new pro-competitive regulations might be justified, we should not refrain from applying our existing antitrust laws in ways that reflect the important role non-price competition plays in the realm of privacy protection in our modern, networked world. Our laws should adapt to our shifting technological landscape, and protecting privacy via robust competition should become an even greater concern as more and more of our daily life occurs online.

NOTES

CONTRIBUTORS

INDEX

Notes

1. Speech, Privacy, and Reputation on the Internet

1. Danielle Citron, *Cyber Civil Rights*, 89 B.U. L. Rev. 61, 71–72 (2009).
2. John Dewey, *Experience and Nature* 167 (1925) (Jo Ann Boydston ed. 1987).
3. John Hechinger, *College Applicants, Beware: Your Facebook Page Is Showing*, Wall St. J., Sept. 18, 2008, available at http://online.wsj.com/article/SB122170459104151023.html.
4. Id.
5. Id.
6. Quoted in Daniel J. Solove & Paul M. Schwartz, *Information Privacy Law* 761 (3rd ed. 2009).
7. For example, see Simson Garfinkel, *Database Nation: The Death of Privacy in the 21st Century* (2001); Charles Sykes, *The End of Privacy* (1999); Reg Whitaker, *The End of Privacy* (2000).
8. Neil M. Richards & Daniel J. Solove, *Privacy's Other Path: Recovering the Law of Confidentiality*, 96 Geo. L. J. 123 (2007).
9. David Brin, *The Transparent Society* 8–9 (1998).
10. Pavesich v. New England Life Ins. Co., 50 S. E. 68, 70 (Ga. 1905).
11. 47 U.S.C. §230(c)(1).
12. Daniel J. Solove, *The Future of Reputation: Gossip, Rumor, and Privacy on the Internet* 153–160 (2007). Available as an e-book online at http://futureofreputation.com.
13. Id.
14. http://www.juicycampus.com.
15. Jessica Bennett, *What You Don't Know Can Hurt You*, Newsweek, Dec. 17, 2007, http://www.newsweek.com/id/74322.
16. http://www.juicycampus.com/posts/faq.
17. Id.
18. Id.
19. Drake Bennett, *Time for a Muzzle*, Boston Globe, Feb. 15, 2009.
20. Id.

21. 17 U.S.C. §512.

22. *Id.*

23. Amber Taylor, *Partial Book Review: The Future of Reputation,* Prettier than Napoleon, Nov. 18, 2007, http://bamber.blogspot.com/2007/11/partial-book -review-future-of.html.

24. Rebecca Tushnet, *Solove's Future of Reputation,* 43(B)log, Dec. 13, 2007, http:// tushnet.blogspot.com/2007/12/soloves-future-of-reputation.html.

25. Solove, *Future of Reputation.*

26. Lior Strahilevitz makes a compelling argument that social network theory should be used to determine when information exposed to a number of people should still be considered to be private. *See* Lior Jacob Strahilevitz, *A Social Networks Theory of Privacy,* 72 U. Chi. L. Rev. 919 (2005). I agree that social network theory has many useful insights for addressing this issue.

27. *See* Taylor, *Partial Book Review.*

2. Civil Rights in Our Information Age

1. This essay is drawn from my article "Cyber Civil Rights," *Boston University Law Review* 89 (2009): 61–125.

2. "Blog Death Threats Spark Debate," *BBC News,* March 27, 2007, news.bbc.co.uk (accessed May 18, 2009).

3. Secretary of Dep't of Housing and Urban Dev. v. Wilson, 2000 WL 988268 (HUD ALJ July 19, 2000).

4. Azy Barak, "Sexual Harassment on the Internet," *Social Science Computer Review* 23 (2005): 77–92, 81.

5. Plaintiffs' Memorandum of Law in Support of Opposition to John Doe 21's Motion to Quash Plaintiff's Subpoena, DOE I and DOE II v. 39 Individuals Whose True Names Are Unknown, Case No. 3:07-CV-00909, pp. 1, 6 (D. Conn. filed on Mar. 17, 2008).

6. Posting of Jill to Feministe, "What Do We Do About Online Harassment?" www.feministe.us/blog (Aug. 9, 2007, 22:26) (accessed May 18, 2009).

7. Posting of Aletha to Free Soil Party Blog, "Silenced!" freesoil.org/wordpress (Sept. 18, 2007, 1:41 EST) (accessed May 18, 2009).

8. Posting of Alyssaroyse to Blogher, "Rape and Death and Batman, OH MY!" www.blogher.com (Aug. 3, 2008, 11:42) (accessed May 19, 2009).

9. Posting of La Chola to La Alma de Fuego, "Here's What I'm Wondering," brownfemipower.com (Apr. 13, 2007, 11:15 EST) (accessed May 19, 2009).

10. Askthisblackwoman, http://askthisblackwoman.com/2007/10/01/death-threat .aspx (Oct. 1, 2007, 15:20 EST).

11. Roger Brown, *Social Psychology: The Second Edition* (New York: Free Press, 1986).

12. Tom Postmes and Russell Spears, "Deindividuation and Antinormative Behavior: A Meta-Analysis," *Psychological Bulletin* 123 (1998): 238–259.

13. Philip G. Zimbardo, *The Lucifer Effect: Understanding How Good People Turn Evil* (New York: Random House, 2007).

14. David R. Mandel, "Evil and the Instigation of Collective Violence," *Analyses of Social Issues and Public Policy* 2 (2002): 101–108.

15. Robert J. Kaczorowski, *The Politics of Judicial Interpretation: The Federal Courts, Department of Justice, and Civil Rights, 1866–1876* (New York: Fordham University Press, 2005), 66.

16. 47 U.S.C.A. §223(a)(1)(C) (West 2008).

17. Ohio Rev. Code Ann. §2903.211(A)(2) (LexisNexis Supp. 2009).

18. Restatement (Second) of Torts §652D (1977).

19. Martha C. Nussbaum, "Objectification and Internet Misogyny" (see Chapter 4 below).

20. 18 U.S.C. §245(b)(2)(C) (2006).

21. United States v. Syring, 522 F. Supp. 2d 125 (D.D.C. 2007).

22. Partners Against Hate, *Investigating Hate Crimes on the Internet: Technical Assistance Brief* (2003), 5.

23. Ibid.; 28 U.S.C. §994 (2006).

24. 42 U.S.C. §1981 (2000).

25. Vietnamese Fishermen's Ass'n v. Knights of the Ku Klux Klan, 518 F. Supp. 993 (S.D. Tex. 1981).

26. 42 U.S.C. §2000e–6 (2000) (covering gender, race, national origin, color, and religion discrimination); United States v. Original Knights of the Ku Klux Klan, 250 F. Supp. 330, 349 (E.D. La. 1965); see Katzenbach v. McClung, 379 U.S. 294 (1964); Heart of Atlanta Motel, Inc. v. United States, 379 U.S. 241 (1964).

27. Original Knights of the Klan, 349.

28. 42 U.S.C. §1985(3) (2000).

29. 18 U.S.C. §241 (2006).

30. United States v. Cruikshank, 92 U.S. 542 (1876).

31. Griffin v. Breckenridge, 403 U.S. 88 (1971).

32. Bray v. Alexandria Women's Health Clinic, 506 U.S. 263 (1993).

33. Chaplinsky v. New Hampshire, 315 U.S. 568 (1942).

34. Ibid.

35. Varian Med. Sys., Inc. v. Delfino, 6 Cal. Rptr. 3d 325 (Ct. App. 2003), rev'd on other grounds, 106 P.3d 958 (Cal. 2005).

36. 508 U.S. 476 (1993).

37. 505 U.S. 377, 380 (1992).

38. Owen M. Fiss, *The Irony of Free Speech* (Cambridge, Mass.: Harvard University Press, 2006).

39. Cass R. Sunstein, *Democracy and the Problem of Free Speech* (New York: Free Press, 1993).

40. Jack M. Balkin, "Digital Speech and Democratic Culture: A Theory of Freedom of Expression for the Information Society," *New York University Law Review* 79 (2004): 1–58.

41. Diane L. Zimmerman, "Requiem for a Heavyweight: A Farewell to Warren and Brandeis's Privacy Tort," *Cornell Law Review* 68 (1983): 291–367.

42. Abrams v. United States, 250 U.S. 616, 624 (1919) (Holmes, J., dissenting).
43. Robert Post, "Reconciling Theory and Doctrine in First Amendment Jurisprudence," *California Law Review* 88 (2000): 2353–2374.
44. Daniel J. Solove, *The Future of Reputation: Gossip, Rumor, and Privacy on the Internet* (New Haven, Conn.: Yale University Press, 2007).
45. 47 U.S.C. §230 (2000).
46. Solove, *Future of Reputation,* 159.

3. The Internet's Anonymity Problem

1. I use this word because it appears to be the most common on Internet sites I have investigated.
2. Inasmuch as the provider is often an intermediary between author and audience, and because my own earlier work on anonymity emphasized the role of an intermediary in raising the benefit-cost ratio of anonymity, I will use that term here. See Saul Levmore, "The Anonymity Tool," 144 *University of Pennsylvania Law Review* 144 (1996): 2191–2236.
3. In Heller v. Bianco 111 Cal.App. 2d 424 (1952), there was indeed liability for tavern owners who maintained a bathroom, the wall of which contained defamatory material, because knowledge of the existence of the material could be inferred and opportunity to remove the material had passed. A modern judge is more likely to care about the workplace than the washroom, where generations of users have probably come to discount what is written. Thus, Judge Easterbrook, in Tacket v. General Motors Corp., 836 F.2d 1042 (7th Cir. 1987), suggests that readers discount what they read on bathroom stalls, and also that tavern owners would find it costly to paint and repaint bathroom walls.
4. Some speakers would find it difficult to maintain anonymity in a visual medium. Note, however, that handbills appeal to advertisers but not juvenilists.
5. The principle of least cost avoider is embodied in the legal distinction made between "secondary publishers," such as bookstores, and "primary publishers," including broadcasters, on whom legal responsibility is more readily fixed.
6. The soapbox orator is subject to constitutionally permissible time, place, and manner requirements. Similarly, a student's suspension for calling his school's assistant principal a "dick" was upheld because the utterance was insubordinate and not about a political issue or a matter of public concern. Posthumus v. Board of Educ. of Moan Shores School, 380 F.Supp. 2d 891 (2005).
7. 47 U.S.C. §230(c)(1).
8. Such popular games as *World of Warcraft* and *SecondLife* appear to support a substantial infrastructure in order to ward off offensive speakers. In the case of *SecondLife,* anonymity is an important element of the game, which offers the opportunity to experience "life," or at least interactions with other players, as a very different person. An uncontrolled game would disintegrate, much as AOL "chat rooms" lost value; a costly central bureaucracy is required.

9. In my own experience with class discussion boards, I have found that identifiability is associated with higher-quality discussion and civility, but also fewer questions. Anonymity can encourage free-riding rather than studious behavior. Discussion board anonymity seems no better than encouraging students to arrive at one's office hours incognito.

10. http://en.wikipedia.org/wiki/Wikipedia:Sock_puppetry.

11. Amazon.com is another site that is able to incorporate the work of many reviewers without falling to juvenile contributors. As compared to Wikipedia, Amazon might be expected to attract less-devoted volunteers, because of its for-profit character; on the other hand, these volunteers provide book reviews and indications of approval, rather than serious research and editing. Both sites use software, or "bots," which delete material containing specified offensive words, but they must also invest in the labor necessary to monitor and delete offensive material and other noise. Other Internet forums have chosen to eliminate interactive comments or anonymity.

12. The comments on these student evaluations can on occasion be quite mean, but in my extensive encounters with them they are rarely crude. Why then was JuicyCampus so much less constructive? One possibility is that evaluative comments are written "for" the instructor, and this brings out munificence rather than offense. Another is that students respond generously to the authoritative status of course evaluations. Perhaps the inability to pile on, or simply to write in reaction to the comments of others, checks juvenile communication.

13. See, for example, Lawrence Lessig, "The Law of the Horse: What Cyber Law Might Teach," *Harvard Law Review* 113 (1999–2000): 501–546; Lawrence Lessig, "Law Regulating Code Regulating Law," *Loyola University of Chicago Law Journal* 35 (2003–2004): 1–14.

14. These arguments play parts in Jack L. Goldsmith, "Against Cyberanarchy," 65 *University of Chicago Law Review* 65 (1998): 1199–1250; Jack L. Goldsmith and Alan O. Sykes, "The Internet and the Dormant Commerce Clause," *Yale Law Journal* 110 (2000–2001): 785–828; Cass R. Sunstein, *Republic.com 2.0* (Princeton University Press, 2007).

15. The notice-and-takedown approach is familiar to students of copyright law. Under the Digital Millennium Copyright Act, there is a safe harbor for online service providers against copyright liability if they adhere to and qualify for certain prescribed safe harbor guidelines and promptly block access to allegedly infringing material (or remove such material from their systems) if they receive notification claiming infringement from a copyright holder or the copyright holder's agent. The act also provides for subpoenas to providers to compel disclosure of their users' identities.

16. Cohen v. California, 403 U.S. 15 (1971) (First Amendment prohibits the state from making the public display of a four-letter word a criminal offense without a more compelling justification than the general disturbance of the peace). Texas v. Johnson, 491 U.S. 397 (1989) (striking down forty-eight state

statutes criminalizing the desecration of an American flag); United States v. Eichman, 496 U.S. 310 (1990) (striking down the federal Flag Protection Act on First Amendment grounds). The Flag Protection Act was passed with the knowledge that most Americans opposed flag burning and favored legal intervention. See S. Rep. 101–152. Polls taken shortly after the *Johnson* decision showed that 65 to 78 percent of respondents disagreed with the holding of the case.

4. Objectification and Internet Misogyny

1. Nietzsche, *Genealogy of Morals*, I.15.
2. Nussbaum, "Objectification," *Philosophy and Public Affairs* 24 (1995), 249–291, reprinted in Nussbaum, *Sex and Social Justice* (New York: Oxford University Press, 1999), 213–239.
3. I draw on my *Hiding from Humanity* (Princeton, N.J.: Princeton University Press, 2004).
4. What follows is a brief summary of the argument in Nussbaum, "Objectification."
5. I continue to refer to the argument I presented in "Objectification."
6. Rae Langton, *Sexual Solipsism* (Oxford: Oxford University Press, 2008).
7. I present these three conditions as Langton gave them ("one treats . . . ," etc.); consequently they don't match the formulations in my own list.
8. Langton, *Sexual Solipsism*, 228–229.
9. See Langton, *Sexual Solipsism*, 231–232.
10. See Erving Goffman, *Stigma* (New York: Simon and Schuster, 1963).
11. http://www.feministe.us/blog/archives/2006/01/04/a-follow-up/. I am grateful to Brian Leiter for this reference.
12. R. Jay Wallace, "Ressentiment, Value, and Self-Vindication: Making Sense of Nietzsche's Slave Revolt," in *Nietzsche and Morality,* eds. Brian Leiter and Neil Sinhababu (Oxford: Clarendon Press, 2007), 110–137.
13. AutoAdmit also features racial objectification. As in the gender-based form: by shaming members of a subordinate group, the objectifier gains power for himself.
14. See Goffman. Empirical work supporting the analysis given here is documented in *Hiding.*
15. See Nancy Chodorow, *The Reproduction of Mothering* (Berkeley and Los Angeles: University of California Press, 1978); Marilyn Friedman, "Autonomy and Social Relationships: Rethinking the Feminist Critique," in Diana Meyers, ed. *Feminists Rethink the Self* (Boulder, Colo.: Westview 1997), 40–61.
16. Kindlon and Thompson, *Raising Cain: Protecting the Emotional Life of Boys* (New York: Ballantine, 1999), chap. 4.
17. Ibid., 75.
18. Ibid., 17.
19. Ibid., 3–10.

20. Ibid., 208–209.
21. Ibid., 210.
22. Ibid., 205. Of course girls masturbate too, but the fantasy of total control over the partner is far less likely to be involved. Indeed, surrender of control is a staple of erotic fiction aimed at women.
23. Ibid., 216.
24. Andrea Dworkin, *Woman Hating* (New York: Dutton, 1974).

5. Believing False Rumors

1. I draw here on David Hirshleifer, The Blind Leading the Blind: Social Influence, Fads, and Informational Cascades, in Mariano Tommasi and Kathryn Ierulli, eds., *The New Economics of Human Behavior* 188, 193–195 (Cambridge: Cambridge University Press, 1995), and on the discussion in Cass R. Sunstein, *Why Societies Need Dissent* 55–73 (Cambridge, Mass.: Harvard University Press, 2003).
2. See Matthew J. Salganik et al., Experimental Study of Inequality and Unpredictability in an Artificial Cultural Market, *Science* 311 (2006)
3. Id.
4. See Fabio Lorenzi-Cioldi and Alain Clémence, Group Processes and the Construction of Social Representations, in Michael A. Hogg and R. Scott Tindale, eds., *Blackwell Handbook of Group Psychology: Group Processes* 311, 315–317 (Oxford: Blackwell Publishing, 2001).
5. See Allport and Postman, *The Psychology of Rumor*, 35 (New York: Holt, 1947) .
6. See Roger Brown, *Social Psychology: The Second Edition* (New York: Free Press, 1986).
7. See J. A. F. Stoner, A Comparison of Individual and Group Decision Involving Risk (unpublished master's thesis, Massachusetts Institute of Technology, 1961).
8. See Lawrence Hong, Risky Shift and Cautious Shift: Some Direct Evidence on the Culture Value Theory, 41 *Social Psych* 342 (1978).
9. See id.
10. Serge Moscovici and Marisa Zavalloni, The Group as a Polarizer of Attitudes, *J. Personality & Soc. Psychol.* 12, 125–135 (1969).
11. Id.; Brown, *Social Psychology*, 210–212.
12. See Hong, Risky Shift.
13. John C. Turner, Michael A. Hogg, Penelope J. Oakes, Stephen D. Reicher, and Margaret S. Wetherell, *Rediscovering the Social Group: A Self-Categorization Theory* (New York: Basil Blackwell, 1987): 142–170.
14. Id., at 153.
15. Id.
16. Paul Cromwell, Alan Marks, James N. Olson, and D'Aunn Wester Avary, Group Effects on Decision-Making by Burglars, 69 *Psychol.* Rep. 579, 586 (1991).

17. See Norris Johnson, James G. Stemler, and Deborah Hunter, Crowd Behavior as "Risk Shift": A Laboratory Experiment, 40 *Sociometry* 183 (1977).

18. Id., at 186.

19. See E. Allan Lind, Laura Kray, and Leigh Thompson, The Social Construction of Injustice: Fairness Judgments in Response to Own and Others' Unfair Treatment by Authorities, 75 *Organizational Behavior and Human Decision Processes* 1 (1998).

20. Id., at 16.

21. Terry Ann Knopf, *Rumors, Race and Riots*, (New Brunswick: Transaction Publishers, 2006) offers examples in the domain of racial conflict

22. See Brown, *Social Psychology*, 200–245.

23. See Robert Baron, Sieg Hoppe, Chuan Feng Kao, Bethany Brunsman, Barbara Linneweh, and Diane Rogers, Social Corroboration and Opinion Extremity, 32 *J. Experimental Soc. Psych.* 537 (1996).

24. See Mark Kelman, Yuval Rottenstrich, and Amos Tversky, Context-Dependence in Legal Decision Making, 25 *J. Legal Stud.* 287–288 (1996).

25. Baron, Social Corroboration.

26. See Tolga Koker and Carlos Yordan, Microfoundations of Terrorism: Exit, Sincere Voice, and Self-Subversion in Terrorist Networks (unpublished manuscript, 2009).

27. Allport and Postman, *The Psychology of Rumor* at 182.

28. See Marc Sageman, *Leaderless Jihad* (Philadelphia: University of Pennsylvania Press, 2008).

29. Id., at 116.

30. Id.

31. See Joseph Henrich, Wulf Albers, Robert Boyd, Gerg Gigerenzer, Kevin A. McCabe, Axel Ockenfels and H. Peyton Young, Group Report: What Is the Role of Culture in Bounded Rationality? in Gerd Gigerenzer and Reinhard Selten, eds., *Bounded Rationality: The Adaptive Toolbox* 353–354, (Cambridge, Mass.: MIT Press, 2001), for an entertaining outline in connection with food choice decisions.

32. Edward Glaeser, Psychology and Paternalism, 73 U Chi L Rev 133 (2006).

33. Id. It has similarly been suggested that majorities are especially potent because people do not want to incur the wrath, or lose the favor, of large numbers of people, and that when minorities have influence it is because they produce genuine attitudinal change. See Baron, Social Corroboration, 82. The demonstrated fact that minorities influence privately held views on such contested issues as gay rights and abortion (see id., at 80) attests to the value of creating institutions that allow room for diverse voices.

34. For a catalogue, see http://www.chillingeffects.org/.

35. For discussion, see Cass R. Sunstein, *Infotopia* (New York: Oxford University Press, 2006).

36. See Daniel Solove, *The Future Of Reputation: Gossip, Rumor, and Privacy on the Internet* (New Haven: Yale University Press, 2007).

6. Reputation Regulation

1. David Brin, *The Transparent Society: Will Technology Force Us to Choose between Privacy and Freedom?* (Basic Books, 1999).

2. Daniel Solove, *The Digital Person* (N.Y.U. Press, 2004).

3. Darby Dickerson, Background Checks in the University Admissions Process: An Overview of Legal and Policy Considerations, 34 *J. College & Uni. Law* 419, 492, n. 514 (2008).

4. Robert Sprague, Googling Job Applicants: Incorporating Personal Information into Hiring Decisions, 23 *Labor Lawyer* 19 (2007); Thomas F. Holt Jr. & Mark D. Pomfret, Finding the Right Fit: The Latest Tool for Employers, 14 *Metro. Corp. Counsel* 29 (2006); Robert Sprague, Rethinking Information Privacy in an Age of Online Transparency, 25 *Hofstra Lab. & Emp. L. J.* 395 (2008).

5. Richard A. Paul & Lisa H. Chung, Brave New Cyberworld: The Employer's Legal Guide to the Interactive Internet, 24 *Lab. Law.* 109 (2008).

6. Jeana H. Frost & Michael P. Massagli, Social Uses of Personal Health Information within PatientsLikeMe, an Online Patient Community: What Can Happen When Patients Have Access to One Another's Data, 10 *J. of Med. Internet Research No.* 3 (2008), available at http://www.jmir.org/2008/3/e15#ref26.

7. Ian Ayres, *Super Crunchers* (Random House, 2008) (discussing data-driven decision making by "number crunchers" enabled by ever-faster computers); Stephen Baker, *The Numerati* (Houghton-Mifflin Harcourt, 2008) ("[S]ome 40 PhDs, from data miners and statisticians to anthropologists . . . comb through [IBM] workers' data").

8. Taylor, *The Politics of Recognition* (Princeton University Press, 2001) 25 ("The thesis is that our identity is partly shaped by recognition or its absence, often by the *mis*recognition of others . . .").

9. Martha Nussbaum, "Legal Weapon," *The Nation* (2006) (reviewing Catharine MacKinnon, "Are Women Human?") ("Inequality on the basis of sex is a pervasive reality of women's lives all over the world").

10. With personalized search, a search engine can use artificial intelligence and other methods to gradually "learn" what a user is most likely to want given his or her pattern of responses to past results. See James E. Pitkow, Hinrich Schütze, Todd Cass, Rob Cooley, Don Turnbull, Andy Edmonds, Eytan Adar & Thomas Breuel, Personalized Search, 45 *Communications of the ACM* 50 (2002) (discussing methods of personalizing search systems).

11. For a prescient examination of objectification resulting from reductionism here, see Julie Cohen, Examined Lives: Informational Privacy and the Subject as Object, *Stan. L. Rev.* 52 (2000) 1373.

12. ICRs are "dossiers on consumers that include information on character, reputation, personal characteristics, and mode of living. ICRs are compiled from personal interviews with persons who know the consumer." See Electronic Privacy Information Center, Fact Sheet on the Fair Credit Reporting Act, available at http://epic.org/privacy/fcra/.

13. Robert Ellis Smith, Ben Franklin's Website 317 (2000) (discussing routine invasions of privacy by CRA's; "countless reports included the fact that a prospective insured was living 'without benefit of wedlock' "; "unverified rumors of homosexuality" were common; the southern-based Retail Credit Co.'s "young, barely trained 'investigators' prepared reports for insurance companies that reported the drinking habits of consumers . . .").

14. *Id.*, at 316.

15. 15 U.S.C. §1681(a)(1)–(4).

16. 15 U.S.C. §1681(b).

17. 15 USCS 1681a(f).

18. 15 U.S.C. §1681o. This paragraph and the last summarize provisions from 15 U.S.C. §1681.

19. Jonathan Zittrain, *The Future of the Internet and How to Stop It* (Yale University Press, 2008), 227.

20. Viktor Mayer-Schonberger, *Delete: The Virtues of Forgetting in the Digital Age* (Princeton University Press, 2009).

21. Danielle Citron, Technological Due Process, *Washington L. Rev.* (2007).

22. Frank Pasquale, Rankings, Reductionism, and Responsibility, *Clev. St. L. Rev.* 54 (2006) 115; Frank Pasquale, Asterisk Revisited: Debating a Right of Reply on Search Results, 3 *Journal of Business & Technology Law* (2008) 61.

23. Kaimipono D. Wenger, Google Profiles and Online Self-Ownership, available at http://www.concurringopinions.com/archives/2009/04/google_profiles.html.

24. Nissenbaum assists us in understanding the use of the term "privacy" in the general sense as the "power to share information discriminately." Helen Nissenbaum, Privacy as Contextual Integrity, *Wash. L. Rev.* 79 (2004) 119, 121 (citing James Rachels, "Why Privacy is Important," in Ferdinand David Schoeman ed., *Philosophical Dimensions of Privacy: An Anthology* (1984) 290, 294).

25. *Act on the Protection of Privacy in Working Life* (759/2004).

26. For a discussion of the last area of law, see Paul M. Schwartz, Beyond Lessig's Code for Internet Privacy: Cyberspace Filters, Privacy Control, and Fair Information Practices, 2000 *Wis. L. Rev.* 743 (2000).

27. For an example of the limits of discrimination law, see Elizabeth Emens, Intimate Discrimination, 122 *Harv. L. Rev.* 1307 (2009) ("legal regulation targeting individual differentiation on these bases [in the intimate domain of sex and love] would be woefully misguided").

28. Ronald Moss, *When All Else Fails: Government as Ultimate Risk Manager* (Harvard University Press, 1999).

29. Richard Posner, *A Failure of Capitalism* (Harvard Univ. Press, 2009); Andrew Ross Sorkin, *Too Big to Fail* (Viking Adult, 2009).

30. J. Hoult Verkerke, Legal Regulation of Employment Reference Practices, 65 *U. Chi. L. Rev.* 115 (1998) ("Prospective employers and regulators confront three analytically distinct problems: falsely negative references, an inadequate supply of reference information, and falsely positive references").

31. *Id.*

32. Dennis D. Hirsch, Protecting the Inner Environment: What Privacy Regulation Can Learn from Environmental Law, 41 *Ga. L. Rev.* 1 (2006).

33. Tal Zarsky, Law and Online Social Networks, 18 Fordham Intell. Prop. Media & Ent. L.J. 741, 780 ("The state should take a proactive role in battling gaming practices transpiring in social networks and move to bring legal action against those engaging in these practices. In doing so, the state could rely on existing legal doctrines and laws, such as fraud, misrepresentation and various laws addressing unfair business practices").

34. Jon D. Michaels, All the President's Spies: Private-Public Intelligence Partnerships in the War on Terror, 96 *Cal. L. Rev.* 901 (2008) (describing in detail favors granted to FedEx and other companies for participation in fusion centers, which combine public and private data about individuals into unified dossiers upon request of homeland security officials); Jack Balkin, The National Surveillance State, 93 *Minn. L. Rev.* 1 (2008).

35. Lior Strahilevitz, Reputation Nation: Law in an Era of Ubiquitous Personal Information, 102 *NW. U. L. Rev.* 1667 (2008).

36. Liz Pulliam Weston, Eight Secret Scores That Lenders Keep, *MSN Money*, available at http://articles.moneycentral.msn.com/Banking/YourCreditRating/ 8SecretCreditScoresThatLendersKeep.aspx?page=all (describing "complex and largely secret scoring systems"); Liz Pulliam Weston, Your Credit Score, Your Money & What's at Stake (Updated Edition): How to Improve the 3-Digit Number that Shapes Your Financial Future (FT Press, 2009).

37. NAMIC Online, NAMIC's State Laws and Legislative Trends: State Laws Governing Insurance Scoring Practices 1 (2004), available at http:// www .namic.org/reports/credithistory/credithistory.asp.

38. Frank M. Fitzgerald, Comm'r, Office of Fin. and Ins. Serv., "The Use of Ins. Credit Scoring in Auto. and Home Owners Ins.: A Report to the Governor," the Legislature and the People of Mich. (2002), available at www.michigan .gov/documents/cis_ofis_credit_scoring_report_52885_7.pdf; Haw. Rev. Stat. §431:10C–207 (2005).

39. For example, see Birny Birnbaum, Insurer's Use of Credit Scoring for Homeowner's Insurance in Ohio: A Report to the Ohio Civil Rights Commission, 2 (Jan. 2003), available at http://www.cej-online.org/report_to_ohio_civil_ rights_commission.pdf.

40. Robert Berners, "Hospitals X-Ray Patient Credit Scores: More and More Are Buying Credit Data to See If the Sick Can Afford Treatment," Businessweek, (December 1, 2008) available at http://www.businessweek.com/magazine/ content/08_48/b4110080413532.htm?chan=magazine+channel_what %27s+next.

41. Jonathan Zittrain, The Future of the Internet and How to Stop It (Yale Univ. Press, 2008) 218.

42. Kevin Arrington, Rapleaf Tags, posting to the TechCrunch blog, available at http://www.techcrunch.com/tag/rapleaf/.

43. The next few paragraphs are based on the decision Browne v. Avvo, 525 F. Supp. 2d 1249 (W. D. Wa. 2007).

44. James Grimmelmann, The Structure of Search Engine Law, 90 Iowa L. Rev. 545 (2007).

45. See e.g. Suzuki Motor Corp. v. Consumers Union of United States, Inc., 330 F.3d 1110 (9th Cir. Cal. 2003).

46. See e.g. Complaint & Settlement Announcement, Washington State Medical Association v. Regence BlueShield (2006).

47. See e.g. Bose Corp. v. Consumers Union, 466 U.S. 485 (1984); David J. Grais and Kostas D. Katsiris, Not "The World's Shortest Editorials: Why the First Amendment Does Not Shield the Rating Agencies from Liability for Overrating CDO's, available at http://www.graisellsworth.com/Rating_Agencies.pdf.

48. See Surgistrategies, Lawsuit: Insurance Commission Physician Tiering Program Flawed, available at http://www.surgicenteronline.com/hotnews/insurance-commission-physician-tiering.html.

49. Id.

50. Id.

51. Physicians and Regence BlueShield Settle Lawsuit, Press Release, August 8, 2007.

52. Id.

53. Id.

54. Attorney General Cuomo Announces Doctor Ranking Agreement with GHI and HIP: Five Insurers in Three Weeks Adopt Model Created Together with National Medical and Consumer Groups, Press Release, November 20, 2007.

55. Molly McDonough, "Cuomo's Doctor-Ranking Model Gains Political Traction," ABA Journal (November 26, 2007) available at http://www.abajournal.com/news/article/cuomos_doctor_ranking_model_gains_political_traction/.

56. Email from Linda Lacewell, chair of the New York Attorney General's Health Care Task Force, to Frank Pasquale, October 27, 2008 ("CIGNA and other plans have agreed to disclose their methodologies to the public").

57. Chaplinsky v. New Hampshire, 315 U.S. 568, 572 (1942).

58. Robert Post, Recuperating First Amendment Doctrine, Stan. L. Rev. 47 (1995) 1249, 1250; Fredrick Schauer, The Boundaries of the First Amendment: A Preliminary Exploration of Constitutional Salience, Harv. L. Rev. 117 (2004) 1765, 1769.

59. Central Hudson Gas & Electric Co. v. Public Service Comm., 447 U.S. 557 at 561–563 (1980).

60. Id.; see also Metromedia v. City of San Diego, 453 U.S. 490 (1981). The regulation must be reasonably tailored to protect the asserted state interest.

61. Chaplinsky v. New Hampshire, 315 U.S. 568, 572 (1942); Nimmer for locus classicus; Eldred v. Ashcroft, 537 U.S. 186 (2003).

7. Youthful Indiscretion in an Internet Age

1. The rise and fall of a champion in Beijing, Associated Press, Aug. 11, 2008, at http://sports.espn.go.com/espn/wire?section=oly&id=3529287.
2. Richard Morgan, Revenge Porn, Details, Sept. 30, 2008, at http://men.style .com/details/blogs/details/2008/09/revenge-porn.html.
3. http://www.exgfpics.com/blog/ (accessed Nov. 13, 2008).
4. As these examples suggest, this essay focuses on truthful disclosures. For a discussion of false rumors, see Cass R. Sunstein, On Rumors: How Falsehoods Spread, Why We Believe Them, What Can Be Done (2009).
5. Mike Celizic, Her Teen Committed Suicide Over "Sexting," MSNBC.com, Mar. 6, 2009, at http://www.msnbc.msn.com/id/29546030/.
6. For a dissection of different interests often collected under the label "privacy," see Martha C. Nussbaum, Sex Equality, Liberty, and Privacy: A Comparative Approach to the Feminist Critique, in India's Living Constitution: Ideas, Practices, Controversies, eds. Z. Hasan, E. Sridharan, and R. Sudarshan (Delhi: Permanent Black, 2002) 242–283.
7. Doe v. Methodist Hosp., 690 N.E.2d 681, 692 (Ind. 1997).
8. See Jonathan Zittrain, The Future of the Internet 228 (2007) (proposing a right to declare "reputation bankruptcy").
9. Lawrence M. Friedman, Guarding Life's Dark Secrets (2007).
10. Fresh start, generally, in Bankruptcy Service §27:13 (2008).
11. Fred C. Zacharias, The Uses and Abuses of Convictions Set Aside Under the Federal Youth Corrections Act, 1981 Duke L. J. 477.
12. Department of Health Education, and Welfare, Secretary's Advisory Committee on Automated Personal Data Systems, Records, Computers and the Rights of Citizens (1973).
13. FCRA §605. The label "outdated" is used in FCRA §609 to characterize the information excluded by FCRA §605.
14. Melvin v. Reid, 112 Cal. App. 285, 292 (Cal. App. 1931).
15. Id.
16. Federal Trade Commission, Privacy Online: A Report to Congress, 42–43 (June 1998), at www.ftc.gov/reports/privacy3/index.htm.
17. Anita L. Allen, Minor Distractions: Children, Privacy and E-Commerce, 38 Hous. L. Rev. 751 (2001).
18. Friedman, Life's Dark Secrets, at 213.
19. 18 U.S.C. §§2252A, 2256 (criminalizing the visual depiction of explicit sexual conduct by persons under the age of eighteen years); United States v. Williams (2008).
20. 18 U.S.C. §2257.
21. A. H. v. State, 949 So.2d 234 (Fla.App. 1 Dist., 2007) ("16-year-old appellant, A. H., and her 17-year-old boyfriend, J. G. W., were charged as juveniles under the child pornography laws. The charges were based on digital photos A. H. and J. G. W. took on March 25, 2004, of themselves naked and engaged in sexual behavior").

22. See Beth A. Eck, Men Are Much Harder: Gendered Viewing of Nude Images, 17 Gender & Society 691, 692–693 (2003) ("The historical prevalence of female nude images cannot be denied").

23. The National Campaign to Prevent Teen and Unplanned Pregnancy, Sex and Text: Results from a Survey of Teens and Young Adults, at http://www .thenationalcampaign.org/sextech/PDF/SexTech_Summary.pdf (2008).

24. Lewis v. LeGrow, 258 Mich. App. 175 (Ct. App. 2003).

25. Wood v. Hustler Magazine, Inc., 736 F.2d 1084 (5th Cir. 1984); Douglass v. Hustler Magazine, Inc., 769 F.2d 1128 (7th Cir. 1986); Solano v. Playgirl, Inc., 292 F.3d 1078 (2002).

26. Restatement (2nd) of Torts §652D (1977).

27. Michaels v. Internet Entertainment Group, Inc., 5 F.Supp. 2d 823, 840 (1998).

28. Florida Star v. B.J.F., 491 U.S. 524, 527 n.2 (1989).

29. S. B. v. Saint James School, 959 So.2d 72, 79 (Ala. 2006).

30. Doe v. Friendfinder Network, Inc., 540 F.Supp. 2d 288, 302–303 (D.N.H. 2008).

31. Doe I v. Individuals, Whose True Names Are Unknown, 561 F.Supp. 2d 249 (D.Conn. 2008); see also Nathaniel Gleicher, Note, John Doe Subpoenas: Toward a Consistent Legal Standard, 118 Yale L. J. 320 (2008).

32. Anita L. Allen, Why Privacy Isn't Everything: Feminist Reflections on Personal Accountability (2003).

33. 491 U.S. 524 (1989).

34. Id., at 533.

35. 18 U.S.C. §2710.

36. Bartnicki v. Vopper, 532 U.S. 514, 533 (2001).

37. Allen, Privacy Isn't Everything, at 153.

38. Richard Posner, The Right to Privacy, 12 Ga. L. Rev. 393, 394 (1978).

39. Lior Jacob Strahilevitz, Reputation Nation: Law in an Era of Ubiquitous Personal Information, 102 Nw. U. L. Rev. 1667 (2008).

40. Posner, Right to Privacy, at 400.

41. Doe v. Methodist Hosp., 690 N.E.2d 681, 692 (Ind. 1997).

42. Saint James School, 81–83.

43. Lodge v. Shell Oil Co., 747 F.2d 16, 20 (1st Cir. 1984).

44. Nussbaum, Feminist Critique.

45. Catharine A. MacKinnon, Toward a Feminist Theory of the State 190 (1991).

46. Id., at 194.

47. Judith Wagner DeCew, In Pursuit of Privacy: Law, Ethics, and the Rise of Technology 164 (1997).

48. Boyles v. Kerr, 855 S.W.2d 593, 602–603 (Tex., 1993). The plaintiff in the case brought a negligence claim rather than a privacy tort claim, apparently because a negligence claim might have been covered by an insurance policy while an intentional tort would not have been so covered.

8. Academic Administrators and the Challenge of Social-Networking Websites

1. Social-networking websites—such as Facebook and MySpace—are the type of websites featured in this paper because of their widespread popularity among students, not because research indicates that they are more prone to cyber bullying than other websites. Indeed, the primary function of social-networking websites is to help people form positive connections. Facebook, which is repeatedly mentioned in this paper, has taken significant steps toward reducing its capacity to be used for cyber bullying. However, because of their popularity and unique ability to support online communities, social-networking websites continue to be used by students for cyber bullying.

2. Online social-networking sites also present benefits in the form of social capital. See, generally Nicole B. Ellison, Charles Steinfield, and Cliff Lampe, The Benefit of Facebook "Friends": Social Capital and College Students' Use of Online Social Network Sites, 12 *Journal of Computer-Mediated Communication,* Issue 4, 1143 (2007).

3. Facebook, which was started by a Harvard University student in 2004, currently reports having 110 million active users.

4. Facebook tied with drinking beer as the second most popular "in" things on college campuses in 2006. Spring 2006 Lifestyle & Media Study, *Student Monitor.*

5. For example, passing notes, online chatting, and most forms of verbal communication are limited to one-time transactions with limited scope and duration of timing. With Facebook, however, it is feasible for every member of a classroom to have simultaneous access to the same, real-time information.

6. Jeffrey R. Young, The Fight for Classroom Attention: Professor vs. Laptop, *The Chronicle of Higher Education* (June 2, 2006), available at http://chronicle.com/free/v52/i39/39a02701.htm.

7. No studies examining the extent of administrators' awareness of the community aspects of social-networking websites were found. However, "solutions" such as merely disabling Internet use without additional steps indicate that administrators may fail to recognize the unique nature of social-networking websites.

8. Rob Capriccioso, Facebook Face Off, *Inside Higher Ed* (February 14, 2006), available at http://www.insidehighered.com/news/2006/02/14/facebook (relaying specific, vulgar comments, which can be retrieved from this website, and the related .jpg image is available as a link on that web page).

9. Nick Martin, *U of M Probes Cyberbullying on Student Site,* Winnipeg Free Press (March 1, 2008), available at http://winnipegfreepress.com/local/story/3896724p-4506596c.html.

10. Rebecca Camber, "Little Fat Library Man" Ridiculed in Students' Facebook Bullying Campaign, *Mail Online* (July 24, 2007), available at http://www.dailymail.co.uk/news/article-470610/Little-fat-library-man-ridiculed-students-Facebook-bullying-campaign.html.

11. J. S. ex rel. Snyder v. Blue Mountain School Dist., 2008 WL 4279517, *1 (M.D. Pa., 2008).

12. Parents: Cyber Bullying Led to Teen's Suicide, *ABC News* (November 19, 2007), available at http://abcnews.go.com/GMA/Story?id=3882520&page=1; Duncan Gardham, Facebook and Bebo Used to Bully Teachers, Telegraph (June 25, 2008), available at http://www.telegraph.co.uk/digitallife/main.jhtml?xml=/connected/2008/06/25/dlfacebook125.xml. ("Earlier this month Sam Leeson, 13, hanged himself at his parents Gloucestershire home after allegedly being mocked online for being a follower of 'emo' music. And in February it was revealed that a 16-year-old boy from Sussex, who for legal reasons cannot be named, took an overdose of 60 painkillers in a failed suicide bid after being targeted by Bebo bullies.")

13. Tara Parker-Pope, With Bullying, Suicide Risks for Victims and Tormentors, New York Times (July 18, 2008), ("While there is no definitive evidence that bullying makes kids more likely to kill themselves, now that we see there's a likely association, we can act on it and try to prevent it," said lead author Dr. Young-Shin Kim, assistant professor at Yale School of Medicine's Child Study Center).

14. Camber, Library Man ("Mr. Mallaghan has said the bullying had affected his studies and destroyed his confidence").

15. Facebook groups devoted to law school "gunners" (loosely defined as students who talk frequently in class) include: "Law Students against Gunners," "1Ls against Gunners," "2Ls against Gunners," and "Attention All Gunners: Put Your Hand Down and Shut the Fuck Up."

16. Young, Classroom Attention.

17. Katherine Mangan, Cutting the Power, Chronicle for Higher Education (September 2001), available at http://chronicle.com/free/v48/i02/02a04301.htm.

18. Id.

19. Id.

20. Id.

21. Andy Carvin, Facing Up to Facebook, PBS Teachers: Learning Now (December 2006), available at http://www.pbs.org/teachers/learning.now/2006/12/facing_up_to_facebook.html.

22. Id.

23. Id.

24. Stu Woo, The Facebook, Not Just for Students, Brown Daily Herald (November 2005), available at http://media.www.browndailyherald.com/media/storage/paper472/news/2005/11/03/CampusWatch/The-Facebook.Not.Just.For.Students-1044229.shtml.

25. Id.

26. Carvin, Facing Up to Facebook.

27. Id.

28. Woo, The Facebook.

29. Rob Cappriccioso, Facebook Face Off, Inside Higher Ed (February 2006), available at http://www.insidehighered.com/news/2006/02/14/facebook.
30. Id.
31. Id.
32. Id.
33. Louise Brown, Student Faces Facebook Consequences, Thestar.com (March 2008), available at http://www.thestar.com/News/GTA/article/309855.
34. Sameer Hinduja and Justin W. Patchin, Cyberbullying Factsheet: A Brief Review of Relevant Legal and Policy Issues (2009) (available at http://www .cyberbullying.us/01_cyberbullyingfactsheet.pdf.
35. Staff Report, Social Networking Sites Confound Schools, E-School News (November 2006), available at http://www.eschoolnews.com/resources/ minimizing-classroom-disruptions/articlesmcs/index.cfm?i=42038&page=3.

9. Cleaning Cyber-Cesspools

1. Other examples include some of the sites discussed in Danielle Citron's contribution to this volume. Among blogs known to lawyers, the comments section of "Above the Law," http://abovethelaw.com/, is an obvious example of a cyber-cesspool. (The comments are so bad that the proprietors of the site, too lazy to actually moderate them, simply require readers to click on a button, after a warning, in order to read them.)
2. See general, Frederick Schauer, *Free Speech: A Philosophical Enquiry* (Cambridge: Cambridge University Press, 1983).
3. For a useful overview of such proposals, see Bradley A. Areheart, "Regulating Cyberbullies through Notice-Based Liability," http://yalelawjournal.org/ content/view/581/14/
4. See generally Saul Levmore's contribution to this volume.
5. www.leiterreports.typepad.com. At that time, the blog covered professional news and issues in both academic philosophy and academic law.
6. http://volokh.com/archives/archive_2005_03_06–2005_03_12.shtml #1110478573
7. http://volokh.com/posts/1110500300.shtml
8. http://leiterreports.typepad.com/blog/2005/03/penn_law_studen.html
9. Whether I am really a "public figure" for purposes of American libel law is not entirely clear: hence the hedging locution.
10. "Harsh Words Die Hard on the Web," March 7, 2007, http://www.washington post.com/wp-dyn/content/article/2007/03/06/AR2007030602705_pf.html
11. http://blogs.wsj.com/law/2007/05/03/law-firm-rescinds-offer-to-ex-autoadmit -director/
12. Subsequent evidence suggests the individual in question suffers from mental illness, and so there is no point in embarrassing him further in public.
13. After several years, K. eventually deleted his hate blog altogether. I have no idea why.

14. http://www.google.com/corporate/tech.html

15. http://www.juancole.com/2005/03/googlesmear-as-political-tactic-google.html

16. An alternative route to the same conclusion would be to invoke something like Joel Feinberg's "Offense Principle," though for simplicity of presentation I will focus just on the idea of "harm." See generally, Joel Feinberg, *The Moral Limits of the Criminal Law: Offense to Other* (Oxford: Oxford University Press, 1985).

17. See Alexander Meilkeljohn, *Free Speech and Its Relevance to Self-Government* (1948).

18. John Stuart Mill, ON LIBERTY 104 (New Haven, CT: Yale University Press, 2003).

19. The Luddite Sociopath, in other words, wants to eliminate what Daniel Solove aptly calls "the corrective of familiarity." *The Future of Reputation* 37 (2007).

20. Defenders of Section 230, in a discussion of this paper at New York Law School, could point only to various bits of humor (like "rickrolling": see http://en.wikipedia.org/wiki/Rickroll) as "unique" products of cyberspace. Given the harms, tortious and dignitary, that thrive in cyberspace, it seems like a few jokes aren't really enough to justify the lack of legal regulation.

21. Joseph Raz, *The Morality of Freedom* 381 (Oxford University Press, 1986)

22. As Raz, of course, recognizes.

23. Dan Dobbs, *The Law of Torts* 1169–1172 (2000). See also New York Times Co. v. Sullivan, 376 U.S. 254 (1964).

24. Frank Pasquale, Rankings, Reductionism, and Responsibility, 54 *Clev. St. L. Rev.* 115 (206)

25. Dobbs, *Law of Torts,* 1121–1123.

26. Cal. Civ. Code §48.5(1).

27. Copyright infringement is a strict liability tort whereby all parties in the chain of infringement are jointly and severally liable because "all united in infringing, all are responsible for the damages resulting from infringement." Gross v. Van Dyk Gravure Co., 230 F. 412, 414 (2d Cir. 1916). The infringing parties include both the publisher, Abeshouse v. Ultragraphics, Inc., 754 F.2d 467 (2d Cir. 1985), and the distributor, Parfums Givenchy v. C&C Beauty Sales, 832 F. Supp. 1378 (C.D. Cal. 1993). Some commentators think an extension of liability to search engines is not warranted because the lack of an intent requirement "does not preclude the requirement of volitional conduct." William Patry, *Patry on Copyright* §§21.38, 21.39 (Thomson West Publishing, 2009). Some courts have held that there is a volitional requirement for copyright infringement, see Religious Technology Center v. Netcom On-Line Communication Services Inc., 907 F. Supp. 1361 (N.D. Cal. 1995), and that search engines lack the requisite volitional conduct. Parker v. Google, Inc., 422 F. Supp. 2d 492, 497 (E.D. Pa. 2006). However, the issue of whether the strict liability regime of copyright infringement contains a volitional requirement is not decided. See Perfect 10 Inc. v. Cybernet Ventures Inc., 167 F. Supp. 2d 1114, 1121–1122 (C.D. Cal. 2001). See also Steven J. Horowitz,

"Defusing a Google Bomb," 17 *Yale Law Journal Pocket Part* 36 (2007), http://thepocketpart.org/2007/09/08horowitz.html for related discussion.

28. Solove, *Future of Reputation*, 190

29. James Grimmelman, "The Structure of Search Engine Law," 93 *Iowa L. Rev.* 1, 21 (2007)

30. Mark A. Lemley, "Rationalizing ISP Safe Harbors" in *Internet Service Providers: Law and Regulation* (L. Padmavathi ed., 2008)

31. My thanks to Ben Whiting for helpful research assistance and to the participants in the conference at the University of Chicago Law School, November 21–22, 2008. I am also grateful to questions and comments from a workshop audience at New York Law School, and especially to James Grimmelman, my commentator on that occasion. Finally, this essay was much improved by detailed comments from Martha Nussbaum on the penultimate draft.

10. Privacy, the First Amendment, and the Internet

1. David Denby, *Snark: A Polemic in Seven Fits* (New York: Simon & Schuster, 2009), 1, 3, 5, 10–11. Denby, by the way, does not support the enactment of new laws to deal with these issues, because "censorship in any form . . . will choke legitimate critical speech as well as vicious rant" (ibid., 3).

2. New York Times v. Sullivan, 376 U.S. 254, 270 (1964). Note that this principle applies to public discourse. Whether it applies as well to private speech is unclear. But, except for private email exchanges between individuals, most speech on the Internet clearly falls within the broad category of public discourse because it is intended for a general audience. On private speech, see Frederick Schauer, "Private Speech and the Private Forum: Givhan v. Western Line School District," 1979 *Supreme Court Review* 217.

3. Terminiello v. Chicago, 337 U.S. 1, 3 (1949).

4. Ibid., 4.

5. Chaplinsky v. New Hampshire, 315 U.S. 568, 572 (1942).

6. See Ohralik v. Ohio State Bar Ass'n., 436 U.S. 447, 456 (1978) (commercial advertising); *Chaplinsky,* 572 (fighting words); Roth v. United States, 354 U.S. 476 (1957) (obscenity); *Sullivan,* 254 (false statements of fact); Watts v. United States, 394 U.S. 705 (threats); Dennis v. United States, 341 U.S. 494 (1951) (express advocacy of law violation); New York v. Ferber, 458 U.S. 747 (1982) (child pornography).

7. See Hugo Black, "The Bill of Rights," 35 *New York University Law Review* 865, 874–879 (1960).

8. Schenck v. United States, 249 U.S. 47 (1919).

9. Of course, content-neutral balancing is far more complex than suggested by these two examples. See Geoffrey R. Stone, "Content-Neutral Restrictions," 54 *University of Chicago Law Review* 46 (1987).

10. See Geoffrey R. Stone, "Free Speech in the Twenty-First Century: Ten Lessons from the Twentieth Century," 36 *Pepperdine Law Review* 273, 280–283 (2009).

There are a number of "special circumstances" in which this strong presumption against content-based restrictions does not apply. These range from regulations of speech by government employees to regulations of speech on public property; to regulations of speech by students, soldiers, and prisoners; to regulations of the government's own speech; to regulations that compel individuals to disclose information to the government (see ibid., 285–289).

11. On incidental restrictions on free speech, see Michael Dorf, "Incidental Burdens on Fundamental Rights," 109 *Harvard Law Review* 1175 (1996); Jeb Jubenfeld, "The First Amendment's Purpose," 53 *Stanford Law Review* 767, 769 (2001); Elena Kagan, "Private Speech, Public Purpose: The Role of Government Motive in First Amendment Doctrine," 63 *University of Chicago Law Review* 415, 494–508 (1996); Stone, "Content-Neutral Restrictions," 114; Stone, "Free Speech," 297–298.

12. See New York v. Ferber, 458 U.S. 747 (1982); Ashcroft v. Free Speech Coalition, 535 U.S. 234 (2002).

13. Bartnicki v. Vopper, 532 U.S. 514, 534 (2001).

14. See Daniel J. Solove, *Understanding Privacy* (Cambridge, Mass.: Harvard University Press, 2008), 136–140; Neil M. Richards & Daniel J. Solove, "Privacy's Other Path: Recovering the Law of Confidentiality," 96 *Georgetown Law Journal* 123, 157 (2007); Daniel J. Solove, "The Virtues of Knowing Less: Justifying Privacy Protections against Disclosure,"53 *Duke Law Journal* 967, 971–972 (2003); Susan M. Gilles, "Promises Betrayed: Breach of Confidence as a Remedy for Invasions of Privacy," 43 *Buffalo Law Review* 1, 20–25 (1995); Alan B. Vickery, "Breach of Confidence: An Emerging Tort," 82 *Columbia Law Review* 1426 (1982).

15. Cohen v. Cowles Media Co., 501 U.S. 663, 670 (1991). See Erie Telecommunications, Inc. v. City of Erie, 853 F. 2d 1084, 1096 (3d Cir. 1988) ("[c]onstitutional rights, like rights and privileges of lesser importance, may be contractually waived").

16. See *Cohen*, 663 (reporter has no First Amendment right to violate contract not to disclose confidential information); Eugene Volokh, "Freedom of Speech and Information Privacy: The Troubling Implications of a Right to Stop People from Speaking About You," 52 *Stanford Law Review* 1049, 1057–1061 (2000).

17. See, e.g., Snepp v. United States, 444 U.S. 507 (1980) (CIA employees); Anderson v. Strong Memorial Hospital, 151 Misc. 2d 353 (N.Y. Sup. Ct. 1991) (upholding medical confidentiality); Peter A. Winn, "Confidentiality in Cyberspace: The HIPAA Privacy Rules and the Common Law," 33 *Rutgers Law Journal* 617, 679 (2002). For the argument that statutory and common law restrictions requiring confidentiality may violate the First Amendment, see Gilles, "Promises Betrayed," 72–73.

18. See New York Times v. United States, 403 U.S. 713 (1971).

19. For the argument that the law should prohibit the publication of private information derived from breaches of confidential relationships, see Paul

Gewertz, "Privacy and Speech," 2001 *Supreme Court Review* 139 154–155; Solove, "Virtues of Knowing Less," 1017.

20. Samuel Warren and Louis D. Brandeis, "The Right to Privacy," 4 *Harvard Law Review* 193 (1890).

21. Ibid., 196.

22. Ibid., 213.

23. See *Restatement of Torts* 2d §652D; Solove, "Virtues of Knowing Less," 971.

24. Harry Kalven, "Privacy in Tort Law—Were Warren and Brandeis Wrong?" 31 *Law and Contemporary Problems* 326, 336 (1966).

25. The Court has held, however, that an action for invasion of privacy cannot be sustained, consistent with the First Amendment, where the government itself was the source of the private information. See, e.g., Cox Broadcasting Corp. v. Cohn, 420 U.S. 469 (1975) (holding that the First Amendment prohibits an action for damages for invasion of privacy caused by the publication of the name of a deceased rape victim that was publicly revealed in connection with the prosecution of the case); The Florida Star v. BJ.F., 491 U.S. 524 (1989) (same result where the publisher obtained the name of the rape victim from a publicly released police report); Smith v. Daily Mail Publishing Co., 443 U.S. 97 (1979) (same result where the publisher revealed the name of a juvenile offender obtained from police and prosecutors).

26. For example, blasphemy, hate speech, and pornography have all been rejected as candidates for low-value status in part because they are directed at particular points of view. See Burstyn v. Wilson, 343 U.S. 495 (1952) (blasphemy); R.A.V. v. City of St. Paul, 505 U.S. 377 (1992) (hate speech); American Booksellers Association v. Hudnut, 771 F.2d 323 (7th Cir. 1985), aff'd 475 U.S. 1001 (1986) (pornography).

27. I say "usually" because this characteristic is not present for all categories of low-value speech. False statements of fact, for example, do not share this characteristic. Nonetheless, this seems an important if not a necessary factor in low-value analysis, and it is certainly present with respect to some categories, such as fighting words, obscenity, and threats. See Cass R. Sunstein, "Pornography and the First Amendment," 1986 *Duke Law Journal* 589, 603 (stating that speech "that has purely non-cognitive appeal will be entitled to less constitutional protection").

28. See Geoffrey R. Stone, "Sex, Violence and the First Amendment," 74 *University of Chicago Law Review* 1857, 1863–1864 (2007) (identifying these four factors).

29. The noncognitive impact issue is relevant because the First Amendment is designed to promote expression that engages the thought process and attempts to reinforce or alter opinions by rational persuasion. Threats may literally be "speech," but they affect people's behavior by coercion rather than by persuasion. Its primary effect is akin to twisting someone's arm. Similarly, fighting words are analogous to a physical assault. Hurling a personal insult at another person in a face-to-face encounter is more like spitting in his eye than engaging

him in debate. Obscenity is deemed low-value speech in part because it appeals predominantly to the prurient interest in sex. That is, viewing it creates an immediate physiological response of sexual arousal. See Stone, "Sex, Violence," 1864–1865.

30. Thomas I. Emerson, *The System of Freedom of Expression* (New York: Random House, 1970), 326.

31. Cass Sunstein has astutely observed that the low-value theory is essential to "any well-functioning system of free expression" because without it one of two "unacceptable" results would follow: either (1) "the burden of justification imposed on government" when it regulates high-value speech, such as pure political expression, "would have to be lowered"; or (2) "the properly stringent standards applied to efforts to regulate" high-value speech would have to be applied to low-value speech, with the result that government would not be able to regulate speech "that in all probability should be regulated." Cass R. Sunstein, *The Partial Constitution* (Cambridge, Mass.: Harvard University Press, 1993), 233–234.

32. Solove, "Virtues of Knowing Less," 1001. See Note, "The Newsworthiness Defense to the Public Disclosure Tort," 85 *Kentucky Law Journal* 147, 157–164 (1997) (describing judicial interpretations of newsworthiness). Solove makes an admirable effort to define the concept, but the very complexity of his approach ultimately underscores the problem. See Solove, "Virtues of Knowing Less," 1000–1030.

33. Randall P. Bezanson, "The Right to Privacy Revisited: Privacy, News, and Social Change, 1890–1990," 80 *California Law Review* 1133, 1172 (1992). See Diane L. Zimmerman, "Musings on a Famous Law Review Article: The Shadow of Substance," 41 *Case Western Reserve Law Review* 823, 826 (1991) (noting that it "is difficult to achieve stable and serious agreement on the sort of personal information that can readily be foregone"); Emerson, *Free Expression*, 553 (noting that there is no consensus on "what is or what ought to be a matter of public interest").

34. Warren and Brandeis, "Right to Privacy," 215–216.

35. See Jennifer E. Rothman, "Freedom of Speech and True Threats," 25 *Harvard Journal of Law and Public Policy* 283 (2001). For an excellent debate on the definition of threats, see Planned Parenthood v. American Coalition of Life Activists, 290 F. 3d 1085 (9th Cir. 2002). I should note that I agree with the dissenters in this case.

36. See Masses Publishing Co. v. Patten, 244 F. 535 S.D.N.Y. (1917) (Learned Hand); Bernard Schwartz, "Holmes versus Hand: Clear and Present Danger or Advocacy of Unlawful Action?" 1994 *Supreme Court Review* 209, 240–241; Geoffrey R. Stone, *Perilous Times: Free Speech in Wartime from the Sedition Act of 1798 to the War on Terrorism* (New York: W. W. Norton, 2004).

37. For example, if X tried to persuade Y to murder Z in a private conversation, it seems unlikely that the *Brandenburg* test would apply. See Brandenburg v. Ohio, 395 U.S. 444 (1969) (holding that even express advocacy of law violation

in public discourse cannot be punished unless it is likely to cause imminent harm). See Schauer, "Private Speech," (analyzing private speech).

38. Perhaps ironically, Warren and Brandeis understood that private invasions of privacy, illustrated by a conversation between two friends in which one friend reveals private highly offensive and private information about a third person, would not be governed by their proposed tort. This is ironic in the sense that ordinarily we think that private speech is, if anything, entitled to less protection than public speech under the First Amendment. But in this context, Warren and Brandeis reasoned that it was only public dissemination to a large audience that warranted legal restriction. As they observed, the "law would probably not grant any redress for the invasion of privacy by oral publication," because the "injury resulting from such oral communications would ordinarily be so trifling that the law might well, in the interest of free speech, disregard it altogether." Warren and Brandeis, "Right to Privacy," 217.

39. Dun & Bradstreet v. Greenmoss Builders, 472 U.S. 749, 758–759 (1985) (plurality opinion).

40. Connick v. Myers, 461 U.S. 138, 146 (1983). See Rankin v. McPherson, 483 U.S. 378 (1987) (speech involving a matter of public concern).

41. Gertz v. Robert Welch, Inc., 418 U.S. 323, 346 (1974). See also Rosenbloom v. Metromedia, Inc., 403 U.S. 29, 79 (1971) (Marshall, J., concurring).

42. Pickering v. Board of Education, 391 U.S. 563, 568 (1968).

43. See *Restatement (2d) of Torts,* §46.

44. Hustler Magazine v. Falwell, 485 U.S. 46 (1988).

45. Ibid., 53, 55.

46. Howell v. New York Post, 81 N.Y.2d 115, 612 N.E.2d 699 (1993).

47. See *Sullivan,* 254 (chilling effect); Virginia State Board of Pharmacy v. Virginia Citizens Consumer Council, 425 U.S. 748 (1976) (some value); Stone, "Free Speech," 283–285.

48. Warren and Brandeis, "Right to Privacy," 214.

49. Gewertz, "Privacy and Speech," 139.

50. See Solove, "Virtues of Knowing Less," 1053–1063 (arguing that one of the reasons to protect privacy is to facilitate "growth and reformation").

51. Richard A. Posner, "The Right of Privacy," 12 *Georgia Law Review* 393, 419 (1978).

52. See Richard A. Posner, *Economic Analysis of Law* (Boston: Aspen Publishers, 1998), 46; Richard A. Posner, *Overcoming Law* (Cambridge, Mass.: Harvard University Press, 1995), 532; Richard Epstein, "The Legal Regulation of Genetic Discrimination: Old Responses to New Technology," 74 *Boston University Law Review* 1, 12 (1994).

53. Jeffrey Rosen, *The Unwanted Gaze: The Destruction of Privacy in America* (Friday Harbor, Wash.: Turtleback Books, 2006), 8.

54. Solove, "Virtues of Knowing Less," 1039.

55. See *Federal Rules of Evidence,* 404.

56. See Volokh, "Freedom of Speech," 1093 (noting that "in a free speech regime, others' definitions of me should primarily be molded by their own judgments, rather than by my using legal coercion to keep them in the dark").

57. Edward Bloustein, "The First Amendment and Privacy: The Supreme Court Justice and the Philosopher," 28 *Rutgers Law Review* 41, 56–57 (1974).

58. Jacobellis v. Ohio, 378 U.S. 184, 197 (1964) (Stewart, J., concurring) (with reference to obscenity, "I shall not today attempt further to define the kinds of material I understand to be embraced" within that doctrine, but "I know it when I see it").

59. Volokh, "Freedom of Speech," 1092–1093.

60. Diane L. Zimmerman, "Requiem for a Heavyweight: A Farewell to Warren and Brandeis's Privacy Tort," 68 *Cornell Law Review* 291, 332–334 (1983).

61. See Paris Adult Theatre I v. Slayton, 413 U.S. 49 (1973); Miller v. California, 413 U.S. 15 (1973).

62. See, e.g., Young v. American Mini-Theatres, 427 U.S. 50 (1976) (zoning); City of Renton v. Playtime Theatres, 475 U.S. 41 (1986) (zoning); New York v. Ferber, 458 U.S. 747 (1982) (child pornography); Ashcroft v. Free Speech Coalition, 535 U.S. 234 (2002) (child pornography).

11. Foul Language

1. The decisions, e.g., in Texas v. Johnson and R.A.V. v. St. Paul concerning flag burning and cross burning raise separate issues. Flag and cross burning are acts that demonstrate ideas, the violability of the flag and the supremacy of White Christianity, from which the emotions they conventionally express are inseparable. The holding in Cohen v. California, by contrast, applies to words whose conventional emotional expression is separable from the ideas they express.

2. See my review of Douglas Walton, "The Place of Emotion in Argument" in *Informal Logic* 17 (1995): 113–121.

3. Winston Churchill, "Sinews of Peace," speech at Westminster College, March 5, 1946.

4. On this distinction, see J. O. Urmson, *The Emotive Theory of Ethics* (New York: Oxford University Press, 1968), 117–129.

5. Cohen v. California, 403 U.S. 15 (1971).

6. See my "Privacy" in *Contemporary Debates in Social Philosophy*, Laurence Thomas ed. (Oxford: Blackwell Publishing, 2008), 131–145.

7. John Stuart Mill, *On Liberty*, chap. 1., par. 9.

8. Ibid.

9. Ibid., par. 16.

10. See e.g., Frederick Schauer, *Free Speech: A Philosophical Enquiry* (Cambridge: Cambridge University Press, 1982), 11.

11. Mill, *On Liberty*, chap. 1, par. 11.

12. Ibid., chap. 3, par. 1.

13. "But the peculiar evil of silencing the expression of an opinion is, that it is robbing the human race; posterity as well as the existing generation; those who dissent from the opinion still more than those who hold it" (ibid., chap. 2, par. 1).
14. T. M. Scanlon, "A Theory of Freedom of Expression," *Philosophy & Public Affairs* 1 (1972): 204–226. See also Scanlon, "Freedom of Expression and Categories of Expression," *University of Pittsburgh Law Review* 40 (1978–1979): 519–550.
15. Alexander Meiklejohn, *Free Speech and Its Relation to Self-Government* (New York: Harper and Brothers Publishers, 1948).
16. Ibid., 25.
17. I owe this point to Geoffrey Stone.
18. An example of such anger that received extensive coverage in the news and on TV talk shows was the tirade the comedian Michael Richards launched at a Los Angeles comedy club in reaction to being heckled. See "Richards Tries to Explain His Rant at Comedy Club" by Bill Carter, *New York Times* (November 22, 2006).
19. Scanlon, "Freedom of Expression," 224.
20. Plato, *Crito*, 51b3–51b4, 51b9-51c1, 51e4–52a3.
21. See Peter Singer, *Democracy and Disobedience* (Oxford: Oxford University Press, 1973), 65–68.
22. I am grateful to David Rabban for this point.
23. See "Pair Guilty of Homophobic Chants at Footballer Sol Cambell," *Guardian* (May 15, 2009).
24. Ronald Dworkin, "Why Must Speech Be Free?" in *Freedom's Law* (Cambridge, Mass.: Harvard University Press, 1996), 195–213.
25. Ibid., 200.
26. Ibid., 201.
27. Ibid.
28. See Herbert Morris, "Persons and Punishment," *Monist* 52 (1968): 475–501.
29. Indeed, the right would be redundant in any theory that recognized such a general right to liberty. Elsewhere Dworkin denies that there is such a right. See "What Rights Do We Have?" in *Taking Rights Seriously* (Cambridge, Mass.: Harvard University Press, 1977), 266–278.
30. See the chapters in this volume by Brian Leiter, Martha Nussbaum, Daniel Solove, and Danielle Citron.

12. Collective Privacy

1. Daniel Findlay, Tag! Now You're Really It: What Photographs on Social Networking Sites Mean for the Fourth Amendment, 10 *N.C. J. L. & Tech.* 171, at §III.B. (2008).
2. Sarah Lyall, *On Facebook, A Spy Revealed (Pale Legs, Too)*, N.Y. Times, July 6, 2009, at A1.
3. See, e.g., Gill v. Hearst Publishing, 253 P.2d 441, 444–445 (Cal. 1953) (torts); Schneckloth v. Bustamonte, 412 U.S. 218, 228 (1973) (Fourth Amendment).

4. This point is discussed briefly in Lior Jacob Strahilevitz, A Social Networks Theory of Privacy, 72 *U. Chi. L. Rev.* 919, 920 (2005).

5. See, e.g., Anita Allen, Coercing Privacy, 40 *Wm. & Mary L. Rev.* 723, 729 (1999).

6. Lior Jacob Strahilevitz, Reputation Nation: Law in an Era of Ubiquitous Personal Information, 102 *NW. U. L. Rev.* 1667 (2008).

7. Georgia v. Randolph, 547 U.S. 103 (2006).

8. *Id.,* at 120.

9. Rodriguez v. Illinois, 497 U.S. 177 (1990).

10. *Randolph,* at 122.

11. *Randolph,* at 127, 136 (Roberts, C. J., dissenting).

12. *Id.,* at 130.

13. United States Department of Justice v. Reporters Committee for Freedom of the Press, 489 U.S. 749 (1989).

14. 5 U.S.C. §552(b)(6).

15. 5 U.S.C. §552(b)(7)(c).

16. See, e.g., Perkins v. Freedom of Information Commission, 635 A.2d 783, 788–791 (Conn. 1993); Hearst Corporation v. Hoppe, 580 P.2d 246, 252–254 (Wash. 1978).

17. *Reporters Committee,* at 763 n. 13.

18. Terri Villa-McDowell, Privacy and the Rape Victim: The Inconsistent Treatment of Privacy Interests in Two Recent Supreme Court Cases, 2 *S. Cal. Rev. L. & Women's Stud.* 293, 300–301 (1992).

19. New York Times v. Sullivan, 376 U.S. 254, 287 (1964).

20. Santiesteban v. Goodyear Tire & Rubber Co., 306 F.2d 9, 12 (5th Cir. 1962); Ravellette v. Smith, 300 F.2d 854, 857 (7th Cir. 1962); Restatement (Second) of Torts §6521 (1977).

21. *Favish,* 541 U.S. at 170–171.

22. ACLU v. Dept of Defense, 543 F.3d 59, 86 (2d Cir. 2008) (discussing the Supreme Court's *Ray* case in these terms); Jarvis v. Bureau of ATF, available at 2008 WL 2620741, at *12 (N.D. Fla. June 30, 2008).

23. See Associated Press v. U.S. Dep't of Defense, available at 2006 WL 2707395, at *1–3 (S.D.N.Y. Sep. 20, 2006).

24. *Id.,* at *4.

25. *Id.*

26. Associated Press v. U.S. Dep't of Defense, 554 F.3d 274, 287 n. 12 (2d Cir. 2009).

27. See Sadiq Reza, Privacy and the Post-September 11 Immigration Detainees: The Wrong Way to a Right (and Other Wrongs), 34 *Conn. L. Rev.* 1169, 1177–1179, 1183–1184 (2002).

28. *Associated Press,* at 284 n. 8 (citations omitted).

29. Michael A. Heller, The Tragedy of the Anticommons: Property in Transition from Marx to Markets, 111 *Harv. L. Rev.* 621, 633–650 (1998).

30. *Associated Press,* at 287 n. 13.

31. Reza, *Post-September 11 Immigration Detainees,* at 1179–1180.

32. See Boumediene v. Bush, 128 S. Ct. 2229 (2008); Hamdan v. Rumsfeld, 548 U.S. 557 (2006); Rasul v. Bush, 542 U.S. 466 (2005).

33. See, e.g., Michael E. Staten & Fred H. Cate, The Impact of Opt-In Privacy Rules in Credit Markets: A Case Study of MBNA, 52 *Duke L. J.* 745, 748–750 (2003).

34. *Associated Press,* at 293.

35. *Id.,* at 285 n. 10, 289–291.

36. *Id.*

37. William DeJong et al., Requesting Organ Donation: An Interview Study of Donor and Nondonor Families, 7 *Am. J. Critical Care* 13, 20 (1998).

38. Haynes v. Alfred A. Knopf, 8 F.3d 1222 (7th Cir. 1993).

39. *Id.,* at 1233.

40. Doe v. Quiring, 686 N.W.2d 918 (S.D. 2004).

41. The case was discussed briefly in Daniel Solove & Paul Schwartz, *Information Privacy Law* 574–575 (3d ed. 2009). See also Lindsey Weiss, *All in the Family: A Fourth Amendment Analysis of Familial Searching* (Working Paper 2009).

42. See, e.g., State v. Inciarrano, 473 So.2d 1272, 1275–1276 (Fla. 1985).

43. David Greenberg et al., Recidivism of Child Molesters: A Study of Victim Relationship with the Perpetrator, 24 *Child Abuse & Neglect* 1485, 1487–1491 (2000); Karl Hanson & Monique T. Bussiere, Predicting Relapse: A Meta-Analysis of Sexual Offender Recidivism Studies, 66 *J. Consulting & Clinical Psych.* 348, 351 (1998).

44. R. Karl Hanson et al., Sexual Offender Recidivism Risk: What We Know and What We Need to Know, 989 *Ann. N.Y. Acad. Sci.* 154, 155–156 (2003).

45. *Quiring,* at 925 n. 9. The court declared that the plaintiff would have lost because the information at issue was already part of a public record. The law says otherwise. See Kallstrom v. City of Columbus, 136 F.3d 1055, 1063–1065 & n. 3–n. 4 (6th Cir. 1998).

46. *Quiring,* at 918.

47. *Id.,* at 928 (Meierhenry, J., dissenting).

48. Paul Ohm, Broken Promises of Privacy: Responding to the Surprising Failure of Anonymization, 57 *UCLA L. Rev.* (forthcoming 2010).

49. See https://sor.sd.gov/search.aspx (visited June 17, 2009).

13. Privacy on Social Networks

1. *Google/Doubleclick,* FTC File No. 071–0170, at 2–3 (Dec. 20, 2007).

2. Facebook: Statistics, http://www.facebook.com/press/info.php?statistics (accessed June 2008).

3. Catherine Holahan, "MySpace: My Portal?" *Businessweek.com* (June 12, 2008), http://www.businessweek.com/technology/content/jun2008/tc20080612_801233.htm

4. Faultline, "MySpace Music Deal Poses Multiple Threats." *The Register* (September 8, 2006), http://www.theregister.co.uk/2006/09/08/myspace_threatens_record_labels/

5. Facebook: Statistics, http://www.facebook.com/press/info.php?statistics (accessed October, 2008). See, also, Brad Stone, "Is Facebook Growing Up Too Fast?" *New York Times* (Mar. 28, 2009), http://www.nytimes.com/2009/03/29/technology/internet/29face.html?emc=eta1.

6. Facebook: Statistics, http://www.facebook.com/press/info.php?statistics (accessed Nov. 2008 and March 2009).

7. Brian Stelter & Tim Arango, "Losing Popularity Contest, MySpace Tries a Makeover," New York Times (May 3, 2009), http://www.nytimes.com/2009/05/04/technology/companies/04myspace.html?ref=technology.

8. See James Grimmelman, "Facebook and the Social Dynamics of Privacy," New York Law School Legal Studies Research Paper Series 08/09 #7, at 42 (August 2008) (available at http://ssrn.com/abstract=1262822).

9. See Lior Strahilevitz, "A Social Networks Theory of Privacy," University of Chicago Law Review 72 (2005), 919–988.

10. Lotus Dev. Corp. v. Borland Int'l, Inc., 516 U.S. 233 (1996).

11. See Kristen Nicole, "Facebook Blocks Google's Friend Connect. There Goes the Open Web," Mashable, (May 15, 2008), http://mashable.com/2008/05/15/facebook-blocks-friend-connec/.

12. See Erica Naone, "Who Owns Your Friends?" Technology Review (July/August 2008), http://www.technologyreview.com/Infotech/20920/?a=f.

13. See Grimmelman, Facebook and Privacy, at 42.

14. See Michael Arrington, "The Very Curious Microsoft-Facebook Data Relationship," TechCrunch (Nov. 14 2008), http://www.techcrunch.com/2008/11/14/the-very-curious-microsoft-facebook-user-data-relationship/.

15. The Facebook principles can be found at http://www.facebook.com/topic.php?uid=5496447606&topic=7960.

16. The Facebook statement of rights and responsibilities can be found at http://www.facebook.com/topic.php?uid=67758697570&topic=7569.

17. Id.

18. Facebook Principle #3, available at http://www.facebook.com/topic.php?uid=5496447606&topic=7960.

19. Stone, "Facebook Growing Up?"

20. Bobbie Johnson, "Privacy No Longer a Social Norm, Says Facebook Founder" Jan. 11, 2010), http://www.guardian.co.uk/technology/2010/jan/11/facebook-privacy.

Contributors

Karen M. Bradshaw received her J. D. in 2010 from the University of Chicago Law School. She was a comment editor of the *University of Chicago Law Review* and staff member of *The Legal Forum*.

Anupam Chander is a scholar of globalization and digitization. A graduate of Harvard College and Yale Law School, he is professor of law at the University of California, Davis. He clerked for Chief Judge Jon Newman of the Second Circuit Court of Appeals and for Judge William Norris of the Ninth Circuit. He represented sovereigns and corporations at Cleary, Gottlieb, Steen & Hamilton in New York and Hong Kong. In spring 2008, he was visiting professor at Yale Law School, and in 2008–2009, he was visiting professor at the University of Chicago Law School. His recent scholarship has appeared in the *Yale Law Journal,* the *University of Chicago Law Review,* the *NYU Law Review,* the *California Law Review,* and the *American Journal of International Law.* He coedited *Securing Privacy in the Internet Age* (2008). His book, *The Electronic Silk Road,* is forthcoming from Yale University Press.

Danielle Keats Citron is a professor of law at the University of Maryland School of Law, whose work focuses on information privacy law, cyberspace law, and administrative law. Her scholarship has appeared in *California Law Review, Michigan Law Review, Southern California Law Review, Washington University Law Review, Boston University Law Review, George Washington Law Review, U.C. Davis Law Review,* and *University of Chicago Legal Forum.* Danielle is an affiliate fellow at the Yale Information Society Project and blogs at Concurring Opinions. She has presented her work widely, including at Yale Law School, Harvard Law School, University of Chicago Law School, Princeton University, University of Michigan Law School, and New York University School of Law. She received a JD, cum laude, and Order of the

Coif, from Fordham University School of Law and a BA in Comparative Area Studies, cum laude, from Duke University.

John Deigh teaches moral and political philosophy at the University of Texas at Austin. He has a joint appointment in the law school and in the philosophy department. He is the author of *The Sources of Moral Agency* (1996) and *Emotions, Values, and the Law* (2008). He was the editor of *Ethics* from 1997–2008.

Brian Leiter is the John P. Wilson Professor of Law and director of the Center for Law, Philosophy & Human Values at the University of Chicago. He writes primarily on issues in moral, political, and legal philosophy and is the author of more than eighty articles and reviews, as well as two books: *Nietzsche on Morality* (2002) and *Naturalizing Jurisprudence* (2007).

Saul Levmore is the William B. Graham Professor of Law at the University of Chicago. From 2001 to 2009 he was Dean of the Law School. His writing has cut across many fields, and most recently has concentrated on topics in public choice, financial and risk regulation, disaster relief and avoidance, tort law, and corporate law.

Martha C. Nussbaum is Ernst Freund Distinguished Service Professor of Law and Ethics at the University of Chicago, appointed in Law, Philosophy, and Divinity. Her books include *Women and Human Development: The Capabilities Approach* (2000), *Upheavals of Thought: The Intelligence of Emotions* (2001), *Hiding From Humanity: Disgust, Shame, and the Law* (2004), *Frontiers of Justice: Disability, Nationality, Species Membership* (2006), *Liberty of Conscience: In Defense of America's Tradition of Religious Equality* (2008), *From Disgust to Humanity: Sexual Orientation and Constitutional Law* (2010), and *Not for Profit: Why Democracy Needs the Humanities* (2010).

Frank Pasquale is the Loftus Professor of Law at Seton Hall Law School, where he has served as the associate director of the Gibbons Institute for Law, Science & Technology. He is presently associate director of Seton Hall's Center for Health and Pharmaceutical Law and Policy, and editor-in-chief of the blog Health Reform Watch. He has been a visiting professor at Yale and Cardozo Law Schools, and he is presently an affiliate fellow of the Yale Information Society Project. He received his BA degree (summa cum laude) from Harvard, and was a Marshall Scholar at Oxford University. Professor Pasquale clerked on the U.S. Court of Appeals for the First Circuit.

He joined the Seton Hall faculty after practicing at Arnold & Porter LLP. In 2008, he testified before the House Judiciary Committee, along with the general counsels of Microsoft, Google, and Yahoo, presenting "Internet Nondiscrimination Principles for Competition Policy Online."

Ruben Rodrigues graduated with honors from the University of Chicago Law School in 2009. He will be an associate at Foley & Lardner LLP specializing in patent litigation, and is licensed to practice law in Illinois and Massachusetts. He has interned at the Electronic Frontier Foundation and the Massachusetts Governor's Office of Legal Counsel. His areas of research interest include the intersection of intellectual property and antitrust law, privacy law, and patent law. In addition to holding a JD, Ruben has an MPA from Northeastern University focusing on Science & Technology Policy and an SB from Massachusetts Institute of Technology (MIT) in Electrical Engineering and Computer Science, with a minor in Mechanical Engineering.

Souvik Saha is a masters candidate at Columbia University in the School of International and Public Affairs. Prior to attending graduate school, he completed a Fulbright research fellowship to India where he studied foreign direct investment and intellectual property rights, as well as U.S. strategic foreign policy toward India.

Daniel J. Solove is a professor of law at the George Washington University Law School. An internationally known expert in privacy law, Solove is the author of more than thirty articles and essays as well as several books, including *Understanding Privacy* (2008), *The Future of Reputation: Gossip and Rumor in the Information Age* (2007) (winner of the 2007 McGannon Award), and *The Digital Person: Technology and Privacy in the Information Age* (2004). He is also the author of a textbook, *Information Privacy Law* (2005), now in its third edition, with coauthor Paul Schwartz. Professor Solove teaches information privacy law, criminal procedure, criminal law, and law and literature. For more information about Professor Solove, go to http://daniel solove.com.

Geoffrey R. Stone is the Edward H. Levi Distinguished Service Professor of Law at the University of Chicago. After serving as a law clerk to Justice William J. Brennan, Jr., he joined the faculty of the university in 1973. From 1987 to 1994, he served as dean of the University of Chicago Law School and from 1994 to 2002 he served as provost of the University of

Chicago. He has written several books, including most recently, *Perilous Times: Free Speech in Wartime* (2004), *War and Liberty: An American Dilemma* (2007), and *Top Secret: When Our Government Keeps Us in the Dark* (2007). He has served as an editor of the *Supreme Court Review* for the past twenty years, as general editor of a fifteen-volume series, *Inalienable Rights*, that is being published by Oxford University Press between 2006 and 2012, and he is writing a new book, *Sexing the Constitution*, which deals with the intersection of sex, religion, history, and law.

Lior Jacob Strahilevitz is professor of law and the Walter Mander Teaching Scholar at the University of Chicago, and Deputy Dean of the Law School. He teaches and writes about privacy law, property law, and intellectual property law. His recent privacy-related scholarship includes "A Social Networks Theory of Privacy" (2005), " 'How's My Driving?' for Everyone (and Everything?)" (2006), "Reputation Nation: Law in an Era of Ubiquitous Personal Information" (2008), "Privacy versus Antidiscrimination" (2008), "Pseudonymous Litigation" (2010), and *Information and Exclusion* (forthcoming in 2010). He thanks Aziz Huq and Martha Nussbaum for helpful comments on earlier drafts, Katie Heinrichs for outstanding research assistance, and the Morton C. Seeley Fund, Milton and Miriam Handler Foundation, and John M. Olin Foundation for research support.

Cass R. Sunstein is the Felix Frankfurter Professor of Law at Harvard Law School (on leave). Since January 2009, he has been working in the federal government. His essay for this volume was finished before he began federal employment, and nothing said here represents an official position in any way. His many books include *Republic.com* (2002), *Risk and Reason* (2002), *The Laws of Fear* (2005), *Worst-Case Scenarios (2007), Going to Extremes* (2009), and (with Richard H. Thaler) *Nudge* (2008).

Index